The authorized biography of Bob Love

BUTTERBEAN

When Glory's Just a Whisper

Rick Davis

BUTTERBEAN ©
Productions, Ltd.

Editor: Gareth Gardiner

Cover photograph: Michael Billington

Cover and book designer: Curt Neitzke

Publisher's Cataloging-in-Publication Data

Davis, Rick, 1951-
      Butterbean : when glory's just a whisper /
    Rick Davis — 1st ed.
    Chicago, IL : Butterbean Productions, Ltd., ©1994
        p.   cm.
        Includes index.
        ISBN: 0-9642202-5-3

        1. Love, Bob, 1942-   2. Basketball players—Biography
        3. Stuttering—Patients—Biography.
    I. Title.
GV844.L68 1994   796.323'092 dc20   94-66257

Printed in the United States of America

For My Three Suns -
Gloria, Carrie and Kelly

CONTENTS

ACKNOWLEDGEMENTS

It's 5:52 a.m. and daylight is only a rumor. So far, just two of us have answered the bell. And I'm still not sure about Barney, because he's curled up at my feet and his face looks the other way. It's good that he's here because he's been here for the full ride — the mornings, the afternoons, the evenings and the nights. Thanks, ol' buddy.

A bitter winter wind is ripping through the little maple tree in the front yard as I tap three pound signs on my keyboard. There is now a significance to the day which has not yet dawned, for I have completed a two-year Odyssey. The journey is complete. I feel a sense of irony as I write these words of introduction to a work which is now finished. For this section precedes all which have preceded it. No less is the paradox that we reach an end as a new day begins.

This book contains a story of one man's life. It is a story about accomplishment and failure, of towering conquests and the deepest of depressions. It is a true story, written with the cooperation of dozens of people who have endured scores of interviews. This Odyssey has taken two years, but I don't apologize. I'm not slow, just part-time. And now I'm glad it's finished.

I take liberty with these first pages and use them as a thank-you card to some of the people who have influenced my life and my work — my family, my friends, some colleagues. Like Mom and Dad. Any morsel of common sense that I have is hers. Any creativity is his. You know I love you both. Alison and Dirck, too young to be really close, but best friends still. PoPo (Feet up, pat 'em on the PoPo, let's make him laugh!), whose letter to the editor was never published, thank God. Gladys is here, too, aren't you? I loved you a lot. And the ones who pushed and encouraged as I plodded, too many times in frustration, as we bulled our way through this project. Henry, I wish we had become friends sooner, but I think we were good friends, anyway. And Moe, the night we danced and you asked that I take care of her, well, I've tried. Joe Wilkins, who has taught me more than I thought an aging dog could ever learn. For what it's worth, you are a friend. Patricia MacHarg, whose responsibility it was to have me introduced to the subject of this book. Taylor Pensoneau, whose stable I proudly join as I await the break of day. Sheri, who always finds her leader and chief when he needs to be found. Curt Neitzke, whose fine cover design and typography gives the story its final form. Bud Nangle, who pointed the way. You must have known something early that I surely didn't. Herb Jannusch, one of the biggest grouches I've ever loved. Give those angels hell every day in eternity, Herb. Grif and Gleason and Royko, three guys whose work I have admired and attempted to emulate. Bruce Gill, who after nearly a quarter century still admits to being a friend. Love ya, Boo Boo. Chuck Ruch for putting me in a position to win and Benson for playing a foil. Jann and Kate and Buddy, the best hired hands a cowboy could have on his ranch. Sneider Man. I am poorer for not having met you years earlier, but richer nonetheless. J.T. McGraw. So many years ago, you caught me with that cheat sheet and ever since I've not only been repentent, I've tried to make you proud. Inspiration is what you taught. That's good. So many others, like Mikey and Patchew and Meathead. The ones who asked and helped. Nick Bussone, my oldest young friend who is also my youngest old friend. Andrew, don't hang this on the refrigerator. It won't stay. Too many friends to mention, so if I missed, I apologize.

Tom Chapin sings a pretty melody about old friends, about how they mean so much more than the new friends do. They know where you are, and they know where you've been. Sometimes — not often, but just sometimes — new friends have the fit of old friends. My most recent old friend has shared with me some of the agony of this project, and he should share whatever joy comes from it. Thank you, Fred George Lebed, old building and loan pal.

Finally, there are three ladies whose love and friendship earn them the dedication of this book — My Three Suns. They have endured me along the ride as my bride and my daughters, my roommate, my housemates and my soulmates. When I fail to say so, please try to remember that the three of you are my life's true loves: Gloria, Kelly and Carrie (There, Kell. For once you're not last. And Carrie understands, I know.).

This is the first. With luck, it will not be the last.

With really good luck, I'll hit six numbers in Lotto.

Rick Davis
May 1994

LOVE'S MILESTONES

Although he was traded from the Chicago Bulls in 1976, Bob Love still occupies considerable space in the Bulls' record book.

games played
Fourth—592

field goals made
4,948—Second to Michael Jordan

free throws made
2,727—Second to Jordan

career minutes played
22,073—Third to Jordan and Jerry Sloan

field goal attempts
11,497—Second to Jordan

free throw attempts
3,343—Second to Jordan

points
12,623—Second to Jordan

points per game average, season
25.8, 1971-72 (Only Jordan has averaged more)

points, season
2,043, 1970-71, (Only Jordan has scored more)

most consecutive seasons led Bulls in scoring
Seven, 1969-70 through 1975-76 (Mark tied by Jordan in 1992-93)

free throw percentage
.816—Seventh

rebounds
3,998—Fifth

minutes played, season
3,482, 1970-71—First

average minutes per game, season
43, 1970-71—First

most points, game
49—Behind only Jordan and Chet Walker

all star team
1971, 1972, 1973

all defensive team
Second team, 1971-72, 1973-74

all league team
Second, 1970-71, 1971-72, (Only three other Bulls have ever made All-League: Jordan, Norm Van Lier and Scottie Pippen)

PLAYOFFS

field goals made, career
441, Third behind Jordan and Pippen

field goals attempted
1,023, Third behind Jordan, Pippen and Walker

free throws attempted
250, Fifth behind Jordan, Pippen, Walker and Horace Grant

most consecutive free throws made
17-17, First—April 27, 1975 vs. Golden State

rebounds
352, Sixth behind Grant, Pippen, Jordan, Sloan and Bill Cartwright

points
1,076, Third behind Jordan and Pippen

minutes
2,061, Sixth behind Jordan, Pippen, Grant, Cartwright and John Paxson

steals
24, Eighth

C H A P T E R 1

PUDDLES in the RAIN

The smell of fir and balsam was thick against the urban skyline. Perhaps it was the season; more likely, though, the aroma had drifted across Puget Sound, enhanced by the steady, cold drizzle that fell into the night. The large, black man, shielded against the rain and the chill by a beige trench coat, loped down the sidewalk, sidestepping puddles wherever possible. As he made his way down the street of this Seattle shopping district, he couldn't help but notice the reflection of the Christmas lights as they sparkled on the wet pavement in the night. Christmas Eve was an especially difficult time to be shopping, particularly when the pickings were as slim as they were in December of 1984.

For Robert Earl Love, the pickings were slim, indeed. His shopping list was an especially modest one. The gift of employment stood alone atop the wish list of Bob Love. At age forty-two, Bob Love was at the stage of life where many men prepare for their biggest career advancements, when executives carve their signatures into the rich mahogany of corporate board rooms and begin to stitch the golden parachutes that will float them gently and comfortably into retirement in the next decade and a half. A good age to begin to earnestly plan for the nest eggs and vacation homes and grandchildren and ...

Bob Love was born a year and a day after the battleship U.S.S. Arizona was drilled into its grave in the deep, blue waters of Pearl Harbor. There was a time when Bob Love himself was a commodity whose talents and power helped build a few vacation homes, who helped christen a few yachts, who helped a few executives float into wealth and prosperity. From his childhood on the cotton fields of Bastrop, Louisiana, through the glory years that showered his manhood with money and awards and adulation, Bob Love was instilled with the notion that hard work and honesty would sow the seeds of reward. Talent, size, speed and muscle helped, but hard work and honesty were poured at the foundation of Bob Love's life. Ella Hunter had raised up a fine specimen of a man. Ella Hunter, his maternal grandmother, had taught him his lessons of life, lessons that he remembered through the good times and now, the times of desperation and despair. Some men use desperation and despair as an excuse to practice alternative lifestyles and survival. Desperation and despair will drive many men to alcohol, to narcotics. Desperation and despair drive others to crime, toward making a living at the expense of society.

Bob Love can appreciate a cold, wet beer as well as the next man. But not to excess, not even when he was down to his last silver dollar . . .

Memories of Ella Hunter raced through his mind as he walked through the rain that night of December 24. And memories of Kevin, of Pat Williams, of fantasy basketball games and of Denise — they, too, rushed through his consciousness. The frosty drizzle was a sharp contrast to the the warm, muggy nights he spent as a student athlete at Southern University in Baton Rouge. Make that a collegiate superstar who could be counted on for thirty-plus points per game. He remembered Dick Mack and the fatherly advice his college coach bestowed on him. And William Washington — Wash, The Coach. The man who sent him on his way to life. The high school football coach who fed him food for his belly and food for his head. A fine man, perhaps even a great man. The Bulls. The so-close seasons when Bob Love and the Chicago Bulls should have, could have, would have ...

The belch of a car horn snapped his concentration for a moment, just before a Toyota sped past, splashing through a puddle, spraying Bob Love's trench coat and shoes.

"That's me," he thought. "If there's one puddle in the state of Washington that will be emptied tonight, it will be emptied on me." He shook his head sadly and pursed his lips.

The cold water wheezed from his shoes as he stepped ahead. Across the street, he could see the lights of a restaurant as they glistened in the mist. He jaywalked across.

His massive hands were plunged into the pockets of the rain-stained trench coat and he hunched against the gusts of wind that whipped across the street. His six foot, eight inch figure cut a mighty silhouette against the halo of a street lamp. In fact, a woman pedestrian, noticing his change of direction toward her side of the street, did a quick right turn of her own toward what she truly believed was a safer side of the street. Bob Love was oblivious to her approach and he never saw her detour. His attention was fixed on the lights of the restaurant. They blinked: "Nordstrom's."

He strolled toward a canopy that stretched from the doorway of the restaurant to curbside. He peeked inside, shyly trying to escape notice by the patrons within, as if a man his size could hide behind a drizzle. What he saw was typical of the Christmas season. A waiter wrapped a white linen towel around the deep emerald neck of a wine bottle and struggled to pluck out its cork. Two persons at the table — a well-dressed woman and her equally-well dressed escort — smiled as the waiter's lips moved in silence. The woman giggled when the cork finally yielded to the screw. Bob thought — perhaps he imagined, because his imagination was a gift from Ella Hunter — he heard a faint pop. More of a puff than a pop, actually. The waiter, a smile of conquest now creasing his cheeks, gently poured a deep, burgundy liquid from the bottle. Bob's mouth began to water.

He reached into his right pants pocket and felt the only metal coin that was in residence. Pulling it from his pocket, he looked at the 1886 silver dollar and it returned him to Bastrop, 1960.

"Robert Earl, you take this silver dollar," Ella said, a tear swelling in her eye. "This silver dollar was born the same year as your grandfather. It was his lucky silver piece. You carry this with you for the rest of your life and you will never be arrested for vagrancy."

He blinked. As he stared at the coin, he knew that it was the only currency on his person. He reached back his right hand into his pocket but kept the coin clutched in his hand.

His eyes shifted across the dining room and settled on an elderly woman, a stole draped across her shoulders. She was dressed in sequins that sparkled in the candlelight of her table. Alone, she dipped a long, silver spoon into a crystal parfait glass. Clearly, she was at peace with her dessert. At this moment Bob Love could, in the recesses of his mind, taste the dozens of suppers that Dorothy Washington cooked for him as she and her husband-coach battled the malnutrition that preyed on their Morehouse High star quarterback. The Franchise of a state championship football team, Bob Love was.

Her figure blurred as Bob gazed over her head, toward the warm, multi-colored lights that burned from the branches of a festive tree. The lights generated heat that moved the silver strands of tinsel to wave from the branches. Bob's mind jetted back 30 years, to the days of his youth at the South Hall Plantation in Delhi, to the scorching cotton fields near Bastrop. Instantly, the silver tinsel was transformed into the waves of blistering heat as it settled on the late morning land. Across the cotton field, the shiny strings were the "muckies," the heat waves that caused the cotton plants to weave and sway in the sunlight. And in the cutting drizzle, Bob Love, empty of heart and empty of pocket, felt warmth. His dark, brown eyes twinkled sadly, a mixture of mist and emotion as he thought ever-so-briefly of his childhood and his grandmamma, Ella Hunter. He blinked.

From the Christmas tree his eyes shifted their focus to a handwritten sign that was taped to the outside of Nordstrom's Restaurant window. The sign — actually a white gift-box top with the corners torn to make it flat — was half-heartedly covered with Saran Wrap. Written in red marker, which had begun to run from the splatter of raindrops which had leaked under the plastic, was a message: "Wanted. Man or boy to work busing tables/dishwasher. Apply inside."

How many men, he wondered, earn four-year degrees from universities in the United States of America, only to stand before a restaurant window in Seattle, pondering the question whether they should apply for a job as a dishwasher? Make that a busboy/dishwasher. Dishwashers need not have contact with patrons. Dishwashers need only to scrape grease and gravy from plates, need only to plunge plates and knives and forks and spoons into hot water to make them sparkle and shine. Dishwashers need only worry about breaking cups and dishes and fret that spots are removed from crystal.

Busboys are of another cut. Busboys must float and flit among and between tables and waiters. They must pour water into drinking glasses. They must say yes-ma'am and no-sir. Bob Love's brown chin began to tremble. And a tear welled in his eye.

"Spit it out, Robert Earl!" The voice was distant and it echoed in his head. "Spit it out, Robert Earl!"

Bob Love glanced back into the restaurant. The muckies still danced their silvery waltz on the tree branches. The elderly woman took another morsel from her parfait. The man and the woman touched glasses and gazes. Bob Love opened his clenched right hand and stared at the silver dollar. He longed for a steaming hot cup of coffee to warm him from the chill of this Puget Sound night. He put the coin back in his right trousers pocket. He reached his hand toward the window and took the cardboard placard. He pulled it from the glass, folded it in half, thrust it into the pocket of his trench coat and walked through the door of the restaurant.

Inside, several patrons cast inquisitive glances his way. He tried, tried really hard, to pretend he didn't see being seen. The maitre 'd spotted Bob and asked if he wished to be seated. Bob Love shook his head and pulled the cardboard sign from his coat pocket.

"You are inquiring about the busboy job?" asked the host.

Bob Love's eyes flickered nervously and his brow twitched uncontrollably. He nodded that yes, indeed he was.

"Well, you need to speak with Mister Snodgrass. Follow me, please."

The maitre 'd hustled Bob to an office off a hallway adjacent to the lobby. The door was open and Bob could see that Eugene Snodgrass was talking on the telephone. Eugene Snodgrass was a heavy-set, balding white man with two chins and a slight blonde mustache. His eyes twinkled blue and they danced as he chattered into the telephone. He looked much too large for the desk he occupied. When he first spotted Bob's six-foot, eight-inch frame filling the doorway, his first thought was that the restaurant was about to be robbed. He wiped away his smile with his left hand as he hushed the tone of his phone conversation.

Sensing the restaurant manager's discomfort, Bob removed his hands from the pockets of his trench coat and clasped them in front of his waist. Eugene Snodgrass cupped the mouthpiece of the telephone handset with his left hand.

"Can I help you?"

"Mister Snodgrass, this gentleman wishes to talk with you about the position posted on the front window," the maitre 'd said.

"I'll be with you in just a second. Have a seat over there." Snodgrass gestured to a chair just outside the door to his office.

"Mister Snodgrass will be with you shortly," were the host's parting words to Bob Love.

Bob would have removed his trench coat except that he was wearing only a sweatshirt and khaki trousers underneath. He could feel his hands beginning to perspire and becoming clammy as he waited for Mister Eugene Snodgrass to finish his telephone conversation. He needed to introduce himself, he knew, to explain his presence. He needed more than to present a rain-splattered help wanted sign to explain why he was here to see Mister Eugene Snodgrass. Was this to be a job interview? How was he to communicate his circumstances to this restaurant manager, that here he was, just a day before Christmas, seeking a job that teenagers disdain? When Mister Eugene Snodgrass asked him about experience, about references, about whom to notify in case of an emergency, how was he to respond? Would any conversation even reach a point so distant, or would his lock-jaw manner cut the conversation, give Mister Eugene Snodgrass the excuse to terminate the dialogue by receiving a bogus telephone call? Was Mister Eugene Snodgrass annoyed that someone would interrupt his evening routine and barge in, unappointed, looking for a job? Questions swirled through his head. When he played in the National Basketball Association, he never thought about a pivot or a low-arched jump shot or a swat, he simply allowed his marvelous athleticism and muscle memory to take over and accomplish what needed to be done. This was not the NBA. This was scary stuff.

Bob Love felt beads of sweat forming on his brow. Then a click preceded Eugene Snodgrass's voice.

"Come on in and have a seat."

Bob Love rose from the chair in the hall and stepped through Eugene Snodgrass's doorway.

"My name's Eugene Snodgrass," the man said, extending his right hand toward Bob. "I manage this place."

Bob's hand wrapped around that of Eugene Snodgrass to the point where his thumb and middle finger nearly overlapped. This was not an unusual happenstance for Bob Love.

Bob's lips puckered in an attempt to speak. His eyelids flickered. Eugene Snodgrass sensed Bob's uneasiness, which now bordered on abject panic.

"Sorry I took so long on the phone. Some people don't understand that Christmas Day is a holiday, even for a lot of restaurants."

The words spilling from Snodgrass's mouth may have well been Latin or French or Armenian. Bob Love wasn't listening as much as he was trying to bring himself to spill a word or two of his own.

"You know, you look familiar," Snodgrass resumed. "Did you play for the Seahawks?"

"S-s-s," Bob was afraid he was starting to sound like a rattlesnake. "S-s-s-onics," he finally blurted.

"I thought you looked familiar. I'm not that much of a basketball follower, to tell you the truth. They play all those night games when I'm here at the office. But I knew I'd seen you somewhere. Probably saw your picture in the paper."

Now Bob Love was struggling to complete what is to most people the simplest of tasks. His name — just two syllables — fought to escape his tongue: B-B-B-ob L-L-Love.

Eugene Snodgrass was unable to disguise his bewilderment. Perhaps he had misunderstood his maitre' d's explanation that this tall black man, a former professional athlete he now understood, was interested in employment as a busboy. Maybe this guy *sells* dishwashers — the automatic kind — he thought. Why on earth would a former National Basketball Association player walk into Nordstrom's on the night before Christmas to look for a job as a *busboy*? His son, that's it — his kid. That's what he wants. He wants to get his kid on as a busboy, something to get him through the holiday season during semester break. Probably teach the kid some responsibility, give him an appreciation of gritty, hard work for small change. That was the thought that planted itself in Eugene Snodgrass's head when Bob Love's eyes began again to flicker.

"Y-Y-Y—ou, y-y-y-ou need a b-b-b-us a busboy."

"That's right. Does your son need a job?"

Bob felt a cold chill rush up his back. Gooseflesh formed on his neck. He managed a weak smile.

"N-N-N, no. *I-I-I* need the j-j-j-ob."

Snodgrass was taken aback. Thoughts swirled about his head like a nest of honey bees. Drugs. The guy used drugs. He used drugs, spent all his money on grass and coke and God-knows-what-the-hell-else. Bad investments. The guy made bad investments. He got greedy, invested his money — the whole bankroll — on some stupid, greedy venture. Booze. The guy's a boozer. He drank himself out of every job he's had since he retired from the game. The guy's a bum. He can't take care of himself, his family, his financial affairs. A real derelict, to be sure. All that money, all that financial security. All those bonuses and deferred payments and playoff payouts and glory and adulation. This guy used to wear custom-tailored suits, silk ties, Italian loafers. This guy played in the National Basketball Association? This guy dressed in a soiled trench coat and khaki pants and a sweatshirt?

And now he wants to be a busboy.

CHAPTER 2

THE BARON and CLEOPATRA

When her grandson was a small child, Ella Hunter and her husband William moved their family west from Delhi to the seat of government in Morehouse Parish, Bastrop, Louisiana. A town of 14,000, Bastrop is located 15 miles south of the Louisiana-Arkansas border in the heart of bayou country. To the east, the hills fall away into the Mississippi Delta. The rich farmland that surrounds Bastrop is made up of alluvial delta soil and is perfect for raising cotton and rice. In fact, Morehouse Parish typically ranks first or second in Louisiana's cotton crop production each year. The northeast Louisiana soil has a dusty rust look about it which becomes a milk-chocolate brown after a gentle spring rain.

It's been called "a city on a hill," but Bastrop's hill is more of a gradual rise westward from the delta. The backwater bayous which surround Bastrop and dot the entire northeast region of Louisiana are breath-taking. On a sunny spring afternoon, the black bayou waters are still and trees stretch from the murky, ebony waters, some decorated with a moss which drapes from the limbs into the water.

The natives of the area were the Choctaw Indians, who by all accounts received the migrating white man peacefully. The last of the Choctaw left the area for good sometime around 1830.

The town of Bastrop was settled in 1785 on the Bayou Bartholomew by a French Indian trader named Francois Bonaventure. Ten years later, Baron de Carondelet initiated an aggressive colonization policy of the Spanish territory west of the Mississippi River.

The town was named for a man who went by the name of Baron de Bastrop. Depending on whom you believe, de Bastrop was either a Dutch nobleman who fled the French Revolution to settle in America, or a shameless Nineteenth Century hustler who had a tongue as silvery smooth as a Baptist preacher but a business sense like Bart Simpson.

At any rate, the tale most embraced by the locals has the Spanish crown granting de Bastrop 36 square miles of Louisiana soil on June 21, 1796. He agreed to import at least 500 families to create a settlement in the area. A subsequent grant required the Baron to establish either a flour or a grist mill on the parcel. In return for establishing the mill, de Bastrop received exclusive rights to both banks of Bayou Bartholomew from its source to the mouth.

While soliciting potential colonists in Kentucky, the Baron became acquainted with Abram Morehouse, to whom de Bastrop sold large sections of land included in the original grant.

One account says de Bastrop ended up in Mexico where he died. That's probably not true.

Most likely, the true story about Baron de Bastrop, the one to which Bastropians turn an ear, is one of early American wheeling, dealing and failure.

Baron de Bastrop's real name was Philip Hendrick Nering Bogel, born November 23, 1759, in Paramibo, Surinam Dutch Guyana, where his father was a judge. Soon after Philip's birth, the family set sail back to their homeland in The Netherlands. At 19 years of age, Philip joined Holland's cavalry and served his full hitch. After his discharge from the army, he was appointed collector general of ground rents, which is where his troubles began. By 1793, Philip was brought up on charges of embezzling tax funds and he fled to the American colonies, where he assumed his nobleman's title. There is nothing to contradict the business deals that de Bastrop apparently struck with Abram Morehouse. Shortly thereafter, the Baron opened an Indian trader business complete with a warehouse and trading post on his plantation north of Fort Miro.

But by 1804, Philip Hendrick Nering Bogel — or Dutch nobleman Baron de Bastrop, if you wish — had hit the skids and gone bankrupt. The next year he set out for San Antonio, Texas, where he settled into the Spanish territory and became instrumental in opening Texas to peaceful American settlement. In fact, Bastrop, Texas, is included among his settlements and became the second town named in his honor.

When the Baron headed west for Texas in 1805, the racial makeup of northeast Louisiana was comprised of Choctaw and caucasians — French, Spanish and a few Dutch. That makeup would change forever the following year when Abram Morehouse traveled to New Orleans to recruit land speculators for the Ouachita River valley. It was in the Crescent City that Morehouse met Josiah Davenport, a native of Rhode Island. Davenport had salt water coursing through his veins and his life, his love and his lady was the sea. He owned and captained two sailing ships, the *Brunswick* and the *Cleopatra*.

The *Cleopatra* was a vessel used to kidnap African boys and girls and sail them back to the New World. The government declared the capture and enslavement of foreigners to be illegal in 1817, but by then Davenport had sold his kidnapping ship for cash and slaves and was shopping for a market for those he held in bondage. That's when he met Morehouse.

Somehow, Morehouse persuaded Davenport to lend him some cash and the use of his slaves to pull Morehouse's piragua upstream along the Mississippi and Ouachita rivers to the parish which later would bear Morehouse's name. The trip must have been unbelievably grueling for the African men and women who pulled the flat-bottomed, two-masted sailing boat. There were no steam engines at the time, so the slaves were forced to move along the river banks and tow the boat by pulling ropes that were attached to the bow.

Upon arriving in the Ouachita valley in 1806, Davenport became the first white man to make notable use of slaves on a plantation near Mer Rouge, a few miles east of what is now Bastrop.

As plantation owners increased their dependence on slave labor early in the Nineteenth Century, the Louisiana State Legislature enacted statutes that regulated the use of chattel by their masters. Legislation provided for adequate housing, clothing and food. It prescribed care for illness and old age, prohibited mutilation and regulated punishment for those slaves who didn't toe the line. Sunday work was prohibited unless the slaves were compensated with money. No doubt abuse was common, in spite of the prohibitions. After all, where was a slave to lodge a protest? Who would listen? Enforcement of the slave protection laws was dubious, at best.

There were severe penalties, however, for anyone who dared teach a slave to read or to write. By 1857, the average male farm slave laborer was valued at $1,500, the average female at a thousand.

Early in the Twentieth Century, C.C. Davenport, grandson of the man who introduced the black man to Morehouse Parish, authored a series of essays entitled, *Memoirs of the Early Settlement of Morehouse Parish*. In a chapter named *Life on the Plantation When Negroes Were Slaves*, Davenport wrote:

> *When there would be a marriage on the plantation, I always provided a good supper for everybody. I read the marriage ceremony, used the Episcopal Church prayer book. I required the band to escort the bride and groom, followed by every Negro on the plantation. And that night there would be dancing all the night.*

The plantation mentality did not die with the Emancipation Proclamation. To the contrary, it thrived quietly as plantations evolved into cotton farms and straw bosses became foremen. The southern plantation mentality lived at least through Bob Love's childhood, probably longer. Talk to Robert Earl Love, and you might even walk away convinced the southern plantation mentality spread northward as he migrated out of Louisiana to the world of professional sports. And it thrived, he'll suggest, even until after he retired from professional basketball.

AN ENVELOPE for ANDREW McLEOD ■

There's a charcoal gray marble monument on the northwest corner of the Morehouse Parish Courthouse in Bastrop, Louisiana. Encased in glass near the top center of the memorial is a statue which depicts a wounded, helmetless black soldier, his left arm draped for support around the shoulders of a white buddy. On the front of the monument, facing the courthouse, are chiseled the names of the native sons of Morehouse Parish who lost their lives in service to their country in both world wars, the Korean and Vietnam slaughters and the Persian Gulf conflict. On the back of the memorial is inscribed a tribute: *"In memory of those who gave their lives for our country, May their sacrifice not have been in vain."*

Less than 50 yards from this shiny yet drab slab, there once stood a tall, stately oak tree. Old picture postcards show the tree in full bloom and maturity back in the 1930s. The tree was cut down years ago when a new west wing was added to the courthouse, itself originally constructed in 1914 on the Bastrop town square.

On the Monday evening of July 9, 1934, a young man died beneath the branches of that oak tree. We don't know if the setting sun blinded him as his breath was being sucked from his body. We don't even know if the sun shone that summer day in the bayous. Never will. Details are scarce. That sometimes happens when a town tries to hide its shame in the smoky valley of time. What we do know is that a black man was lynched by a mob of white Bastropians. We know the sheriff was present. So was the district attorney. It's debatable whether the dead man's sacrifice was in vain. And it's debatable whether anyone cared.

There's just one recorded account of the lynching of Andrew McLeod, a black man from Jones, Louisiana, who made the fatal mistake of an encounter with a white woman on the Seventh of July, 1934. And that account doesn't provide clear details of the degree of his encounter. We can assume that a rape was alleged, although at least one old timer will dispute that there was a rape at all. The Morehouse Parish Sheriff's Office records reach back only until the late 1970s. Andrew McLeod was brought to a white mob's justice before he could be brought before a judge — much less before a grand jury could consider his plight — so the clerk's office has no docket entry of the case. And while the Morehouse Parish Coroner's Office is the repository of dusty old records which live in the bottom drawer of a file cabinet, and while numerous hand-written papers contain inquest findings, not a word can be found about the death of Andrew McLeod. Dozens of business-sized, plain white envelopes are stashed in file folders in that bottom drawer. There is a handwritten inquest report about the death of a seven-year-old Negro girl who drowned in a Morehouse Parish bayou. There is a handwritten report about the death of a man who collapsed and died while quenching his thirst with ice water after he became overheated in the blistering summer sun. There is a handwritten report of a man who, in his despondence over the loss of his woman, took his own life by firing a bullet into his brain. There are dozens of hand written reports. There are scores of names and hundreds of victims. There are a couple hundred or so envelopes, all of which contain the inquest findings of the coroner's juries which were empaneled by Coroner

R.B. Seawell and his predecessors. Each is a story of a life lost, a story in itself come to an end. A period in the world of punctuation.

But there is no envelope for Andrew McLeod. There is no dusty, handwritten report, first grayed by time, then turned the color of toast by convening years. For Andrew McLeod, there is no story of the end of his life. And the only punctuation is a question mark. For Andrew McLeod there is nothing, not one word.

Some Bastropians, weathered by time and clouded by age, still live to tell their versions of the events of July 9, 1934. Among them is the Reverend E.W. Smith, a retired Baptist minister who in his earlier years was one of Morehouse Parish's most prominent activist black residents. A militant fire still burns in Reverend Smith's heart, and through his eyes you can still see the flames. A survivor of the days when members of the Knights of the Ku Klux Klan, Chapter 34 roamed the bayous, inflicting their personal brand of justice and intimidation on bootleggers and non-caucasians, E.W. Smith, even at 80 years of age, remembers the burning crosses on his front lawn. O.L. Harper, a former Morehouse Parish schools superintendent, knows about the night a lynch mob reached into the parish jail to snatch a life. He wasn't there, but he knows the story. And Harry Howard, retired as chief of the Bastrop Police Department, heard the tales of the lynching from the first days of 1952, when he pinned the police department's badge to his uniform shirt.

"Of course there's no report," offers Howard. "What do you think, that they'd file a report about a lynching? Because that's what it was — it was a lynching, plain and simple."

The only written account of the events of July 9, 1934 appear to be printed on the browned and brittle pages of the Morehouse Enterprise, the weekly forefather of today's Bastrop Daily Enterprise. The front page story, published on Thursday, July 12, 1934 is not encased in a memorial. It has not been reproduced on a plaque, nor has it been restored for display in the Snyder Memorial Museum on Madison Street on the east side of Bastrop's downtown area. Probably the only place where the only recorded history of the lynching of Andrew McLeod exists is in a dusty, black-bound book which contains the Morehouse Enterprise editions for the year 1934. The pages are so brittle that a reader must turn the pages slowly, cradling them with both hands and a forearm lest they tear or crumble into the clouds of memory. It's not easy to make a photocopy of the story, because it was printed in the first column, where the newspapers are bound to the book. But it is there, word for word:

Vigorous Probe of Lynching Now under Way in Bastrop

*Officials Promise to Get to
Bottom of Mob Action
Monday Night*

District Attorney Frank W. Hawthorne and Sheriff J. Fred Carpenter announced Tuesday night after a conference of Parish and city officials that a vigorous investigation is now being pushed to ascertain the leaders and members of the members of the mob who took part in the lynching Monday night of Andrew McLeod, negro, charged with a criminal attack on a 19-year-old Bastrop white girl.

Mayor J.R. Ludlum of Bastrop and C.C. Walton, Bastrop chief of police, joined in the statement with the parish officials announcing the investigation. It was announced that when all information has been obtained and the investigation is completed, it will be placed before the grand jury at its next session in September.

In view of the fact that the District Court recesses within a few days for the summer, it was deemed advisable not to call a special grand jury session, the statement issued by the parish and city officials stated. It was pointed out that to call the grand jury into session now would not allow sufficient time to complete the investigation before the summer recess.

Indications that the International Labor Defense Union may take a part in the investigation were revealed Tuesday by the receipt of a telegram by Sheriff J. Fred Carpenter from the New Orleans District of the

Union protesting against the lynching and urging an immediate investigation.

The telegram read (sic) in part as follows:

"Protest brutal lynching of Andrew McCloud (sic). Hold you and Chief of Police Walton responsible for said lynching. Demand immediate arrests and punishment."

The negro McCloud (sic) was arrested last Sunday morning at his home in Jones, and confessed a short time later, officers said, to an attempted criminal assault on a Bastrop white girl, which occurred near Jones Saturday night about nine o'clock. The girl had been to a dance with a Bastrop white man and were returning when their car went into a ditch. The girl told officers that her escort was too drunk to assist, so she started to walk up the highway to a filling station to tell her story. The sheriff's office was then notified and Sheriff Carpenter and deputies went to Jones to make an investigation. They arrested the negro Sunday morning and after he confessed, placed him in the parish jail.

Late Sunday night Sheriff Carpenter said he was notified that a mob had gathered at the parish jail and he went there and succeeded in persuading the small crowd to leave.

Monday night a crowd began gathering around the courthouse around six o'clock and by seven thirty had reached large numbers, and they started a march to the parish jail. First Sheriff Carpenter and then District Attorney Frank Hawthorne tried to stop them but without success. The mob battered the doors of (t)he jail, took the negro to the courthouse lawn where he was hung (sic) from a branch on the oak tree on the west side of the square beneath the windows of the sheriff's office. Actually, it was estimated about 300 people formed the mob, although spectators including a number of women swelled the crowd to about 1,000 people.

> *So quiet and orderly did the mob do its work that*
> *the people living within two blocks of the courthouse did*
> *not know what had happened until they read it in the*
> *papers the following morning. It was the first lynching in*
> *about 15 years. Sheriff Carpenter estimated damage to*
> *the jail at about $300.*

It's comforting to know that a mob can conduct itself in a "quiet and orderly" fashion, not to mention that damage to the jail was kept to a minimum.

"There was a big, old oak tree on the west side of the courthouse, back before the new addition was built," recalls former police chief Howard. "The story goes that the mob took the poor guy and hung him from the tree. When they took him down, he was probably still kicking. You know, people think that when someone gets hung, the neck snaps, and it causes them to stop breathing and the heart stops. But there are still reflex actions left in the body, and that's probably what was happening. So someone must have panicked because his legs were still kicking, so they slit his throat. The guy who slit his throat — he died a few years ago — he was never the same again."

Former schools superintendent Harper was not a witness to the lynching, but his version of the incident is strikingly similar to that recorded by the Morehouse Enterprise.

"The last hanging occurred, I would say probably in the mid- thirties," he says. "If you go to the courthouse, on the other side there was a tree. Since that time, the courthouse has had additions (constructed) on both sides. It used to be a boxy old thing. Now it's a long thing.

"There was a tree on the other side. And there was a hanging. What had happened is there was an incident of rape. (The Enterprise referred to it as a "criminal attack".) The sheriff picked up the guy and put him in the jail. It was a (situation involving a) black man and a white woman. All of this was alleged.

"I talked to the judge about it. His name was Judge Hawthorne. At the time this (lynching) happened, he was, I guess, assistant district attorney.

"Someone ran to his house at that time and said there was a group of men breaking into the jail. He ran down to the little jail, which was located where the farmer's market is today. That's where the jail was at the time. He ran down there and they had picked up a pole, perhaps a utility pole. And they were bashing on the door. It was a very solidly constructed jail. The reason I know that (is) some of my boys in welding class tore this building down in later years when it was no longer used. Anyway, Judge Hawthorne told me, he said: `I stood up and said, `Men, this is not the way to do it. If you men will disband and just go on about your business, I will bring this before the grand jury. I will expedite it, but this is not the way to do it.' "

Harper continues: "And Hawthorne said that they listened to him for a while and then they told him to get out of the way. And they broke the jail down, they took the black fellow out and they carried him up to this tree on the other side (of the courthouse) and they put him on the hood of a car. They strung him up and they pulled the car out. They backed the car out.

"Whoever tied the knot, it didn't work very well. He fell to the ground and some guy stepped up and slit his throat. I don't think it's even reported in the paper, not to my knowledge. The family of the black people still live here in Bastrop, but they won't want to talk about it. Some of the principals I know, but most of them are dead and those who are living would not want it brought up."

O.L. Harper and Harry Howard are both white and neither lived in Bastrop when Andrew McLeod was strung to the oak tree. But their versions of the lynching are remarkably similar to that of the Reverend Smith, the retired black minister. But there is a key difference in the way E.W. Smith tells the story.

There is a conspicuous irony to the setting in which Ed Smith shares his knowledge of the crime. His backyard is a reserve of peace and tranquility on a warm spring afternoon. Only an occasional barking dog or snorting pig pierces the quiet of the day as Smith sits in a lawn chair beneath a canopy on his patio. From time to time an inquisitive jay or cardinal will flutter into his emerging vegetable garden, curious to find a twig or grass for nesting. Asked if he remembers any public hangings during his life in Bastrop, Reverend Smith replies:

"Oh, yes. It must've been about '34. I had come to school here in '31 and '32. That's when I met my wife. During that time, a white man had accosted a cousin of mine, Birdie Smith. You know where the cemetery is? He met her there, near the woods, and asked her for a date.

"We knew the man very well. But that was usual, see. When a white man asked a black woman for a date, you just hushed about it. You didn't tell. But I remember it very well. The same day he asked her for a date, they lynched a black man by a white woman here in Bastrop."

Ed Smith's eyes evaluate his guest as he speaks. He's looking for a reaction, a twitch of disgust, a spot of guilt perhaps. But he is measured in his words, slow, deliberate and precise. There has been no rehearsal, for Reverend E.W. Smith was not informed ahead of time he would be asked about a lynching.

"I knew the man's brother well. The man's brother was a preacher. What happened was, this black man was dating this white woman. And somebody got wind of it. You know, it's hard to keep a secret, especially in a small town like Bastrop. Well, he met her one night and somebody put the light on him. And of course, in the South ..." his voice trails for a moment. "I can't understand how a black man got by. As I see it now, a lot of black men dated white women even in those treacherous times. They got in the wind of it and, of course, when they're tied to the authorities, you don't have a leg to stand on.

"Well, all they had to do was arrest him. And when the sheriff arrested him and put him in jail — and it was right there where that farmer's market is; you came up that way — that jail was right there.

"They broke that jail open and got that man out and dragged him up to the courthouse square and hanged him in a tree there. On the west side of the courthouse.

"After they took him down, I don't know, he might have still been alive, one of our neighbors allegedly cut his throat. I knew the man well ... his name was Westbrook. That same man, when Jackie

Robinson was in his heyday, he told us there at the (paper mill) plant (where Smith once worked), `I wish I could get a hold of that black S.O.B. I'd cut his head off.'"

It's doubtful anyone will ever know for certain whether it was rape or a simple, consensual relationship that ultimately delivered Andrew McLeod to a makeshift gallows that July evening in 1934. No one will ever know with certainty if he would have been indicted, tried and convicted of his alleged crime. Andrew McLeod, the victim of the last documented lynching in Morehouse Parish, took some of those answers with him to his grave, somewhere in the alluvial soil of northeastern Louisiana. We will probably never know for sure if the men who stole Andrew McLeod from his jail cell that night were an organized bunch, or if they were triggered by spontaneous rage over an allegation that a black man had forced sexual intercourse on a white woman.

But we do know this: At the time Andrew McLeod, negro, was murdered by a white lynch mob, there flourished in Morehouse Parish a group of men who lived by their own brand of justice. They made no attempt to hide their existence, a clear contradiction of their moniker, *The Invisible Empire*. The summer that Andrew McLeod was hanged from an oak tree on the town square in Bastrop, Louisiana, Chapter 34 of the Knights of the Ku Klux Klan celebrated its thirteenth anniversary in Morehouse Parish. And at least one of its members was in attendance and was witness to the lynching of Andrew McLeod. After all, Andrew McLeod left this world by way of the tree branches that spread beneath the man's office windows.

You see, there were times when Sheriff J. Fred Carpenter didn't wear his badge. Especially when he was wearing his hood.

With a heritage like that, who could have blamed Robert Earl Love had he chosen to mistrust his fellow man? The cradle of the Klan is a hard place for a black kid to grow up.

CHAPTER 4

AN INVISIBLE EMPIRE

Sadielee Dade was cast for the part. A gray-haired retiree from Mer Rouge, seven miles up the road from Bastrop, Sadielee spends the spring mornings at the Snyder Memorial Museum on Bastrop's main street. Well cared-for and tidy, the museum is little more than a converted family residence, once owned by a prominent Jewish family, for which the museum is named.

Sadielee Dade will correct you when you mispronounce "Ouachita," an Indian name for the river which cuts through northeast Louisiana. It's pronounced "WASH-ih-taw," she'll tell you. And then she'll lead you to a nest of files in the museum. Tucked away on a shelf in a room off the kitchen is a yellow binder, the cover page of which reads: Some Notes Concerning the Morehouse Ku Klux Klan Number 34; 1921 Through 1924. George Mallory Patton, who helped compile the notes of the Morehouse Klan, writes in his introduction:

It appears that the Morehouse Klan set about to rid the par-

ish of thieves, bootleggers, prostitutes, womanizers, other ha-
bitual lawbreakers or grossly immoral people. The bootleggers of
the Mer Rouge area were organized to a certain extent. They all
distilled their whiskey on the same day. On that day, the bootleg-
gers would build fires in many places and burn old car tires. This
would cause a haze of smoke over a large area. Therefore, the
sheriff could not locate a still by spotting the smoke generated
when a batch of whiskey was distilled.

The white men of Morehouse Parish felt the need to organize a chapter of the Ku Klux Klan sometime during the summer of 1921. On August 26 of that year, an out-of-town Klan organizer named Clapp, first name unknown, took his place at the front of the room. As Exalted Cyclops, Klegle Clapp explained the role of the Klan to the 21 men who had assembled. As he went about his business, seven more trickled into the meeting room bringing to 28 the number of charter members of Morehouse Klan Number 34. The infant Klan chapter went about its organizational business of electing officers and establishing a procedure for paying membership dues. The members took up a collection of $56.25 for Reverend Frank Tripp, pastor of the First Baptist Church of Monroe, Louisiana. According to a footnote penned by Patton, Tripp had been identified in the Morehouse Enterprise as being a supporter of the Klan and its activities.

The minutes of early meetings of Klan Chapter 34 indicate the group was engaged in social activities as much as anything else. There are repeated references to the "enjoyable dinners" which punctuated the "naturalization" ceremonies during which new members were brought into the fold. An entry describing the naturalization of the chapter's charter members describes a veritable feast of "sandwiches, chicken and cakes of deliciousness which would satisfy any hungry man on a cold night ... with beer as a washer." The first mention of any self-appointed vigilance is noted in the minutes of the meeting held early in 1922. There, a story from the Morehouse Enterprise is quoted:

"... the Klan spread leaflets in places around Morehouse Parish. The leaflets warned white bootleggers, whiskey distillers and white men with concubines to repent. Leaflets were signed, 'The Vigilance Committee.'

"About one thirty p.m. on Thursday, December 29, 1921, three automobiles came to Bastrop from the direction of Monroe. Each car contained four Klansmen in black robes and with faces covered. There was also a bootlegger held captive in each car. The three drove through Mer Rouge, Bonita and Jones and to the Arkansas line. (They were) Dropping leaflets similar to those it had been dropping the last few weeks along the way. The three bootleggers were let out at the Arkansas line and told not to return."

By March of 1922 the Klan was at the top of its game, dispensing its sense of justice when and where it wished. If the Empire was Invisible, it could have fooled Clay Osborne. On March 2, 1922, Osborne was standing on the northwest corner of the Bastrop town square near the Morehouse Parish Courthouse in the very heart of the city. It was two thirty in the afternoon — broad daylight — when a car drove up and four men dressed in black robes, their faces covered with black hoods, abducted Osborne and sped away. About an hour later, the car returned and delivered Osborne to the town square. Bloodied, Osborne sported a sign on his back which read, "I was whipped for stealing hogs and cattle, and for bootlegging and distilling whiskey." But the kicker to the red badge of shame which Osborne wore was, "and for being an undesirable in general."

The Klan gave Osborne 48 hours to get out of Morehouse Parish.

But the blackest days in the history of Klan 34 occurred in August of 1922. There was some bad blood boiling between several members of the Morehouse Klan and a handful of Mer Rouge men, all of whom were white. To hear the Reverend E.W. Smith tell it, Filmore "Watt" Daniels and Thomas Fletcher Richards were "fraternizing with black girls." The minutes of the Klan meetings, which include passages from the Morehouse Enterprise, hint that Daniels may have been associated with spirit distillation and bootlegging and had been outright defiant about it, paying no heed to threats from the Klan.

On August 24, 1922, the Mer Rouge and Bastrop baseball teams played a game on the Bastrop diamond. While they were thus engaged, black robed and hooded Klansmen set up a roadblock on the highway between the two towns.

Daniels, Richards, J.L. Daniels, W.C. Andrews and C.C. "Tot" Davenport, great-grandson of the man who introduced African slaves to the parish, were accosted at the roadblock. Andrews and J.L. Daniels were administered beatings with a whip and were released. Davenport was released unharmed. But Watt Daniels and Thomas Fletcher Richards were never again seen alive.

Reverend Smith tells his version of the murders:

"I'm afraid I'm the only living person to tell this," he begins, slowly folding his hands as well as his brow. "My mother and daddy kept me up with history. They met these boys to go whip 'em. But one of those boys, he was an aggressive young man. He wasn't afraid of anybody, not even those men with the hoods on their faces. He reached up," Smith says, raising his right hand above his head, "and pulled the hood off the fellow's face," as he yanks his right hand downward.

"And he said, `Oh, Doctor McKoin. Oh, sonofabitch.'"

Bunnie McEwin McKoin was a prominent physician with a residence in Mer Rouge. According to the Morehouse Enterprise:

"On Wednesday, August second, Nineteen Twenty-Two, Doctor B.M. McKoin made a house call to a patient. About eleven p.m. he received a telephone call and a voice that he could not identify said the man had (sic) got worse. Doctor McKoin drove out to the home and found that the telephone call was not true. He drove back to Mer Rouge and as he entered town and passed the first street light, two loads of buckshot were fired at him and missed his head by inches."

Reverend Smith continues:

"McKoin was a prominent doctor in Mer Rouge. They knew him every day. And when they pulled his hood off, the boy said, `Well, look here. It's Doctor McKoin, the old sonofabitch.' That's when (the Klansmen) said, 'Oh, oh. Now we've got to kill them.'"

Accounts by both Reverend Smith and the Morehouse Enterprise, indicate Watt Daniels and Thomas Fletcher Richards died the most horrifying deaths imaginable. Smith:

"They gave them boys hell. They did those boys just like they did those boys down in Mississippi. They shot 'em. Then they took their bodies to a mill and flattened their bodies out, then they put them in a river. They looked for those boys for weeks. When they found 'em, they had to send the United States militia to Bastrop to keep things from boiling over."

A story in the Enterprise indicates the bodies of Daniels and Richards disappeared for four months.

"Daniels' and Richards' mutilated bodies," reads the story, "were found about dawn of December 22 in Lake Lafourche by John C. Nettles. Autopsies were done by doctors Duvall and Lundford of New Orleans. Autopsies showed evidence of torture, a major loss of blood, broken bones and one was sexually mutilated ... Arrest warrants were made for Klansmen B.M. McKoin and T.J. Burnett ... They were accused of causing the deaths of Daniels and Richards."

E.W. Smith, in part because of his leadership for civil rights in northeast Louisiana, had the occasion to witness the Klan in action throughout the middle portion of the century. For the most part, the Ku Klux Klan was a nuisance. Its members hid behind their hoods by night but went about their business as ordinary citizens by day.

"I can remember the Klan burning their crosses two or three times in the front yard," recalls E.W. Smith. "They'd do that because I wasn't afraid to be out there, fighting for integration."

Melvin Anderson is now principal at South Side Elementary School in Bastrop. Anderson and Reverend Smith's son, Robert, were schoolmates at Morehouse High. Informed that the Smiths' front yard was, from time to time, a repository for burning crosses and hatred, Anderson seems nonplussed.

"Reverend Smith was really vocal in the black community," Anderson offers. "I can remember him well from my days as a youngster. He was a leader in the black community. So I'm not surprised to hear about the crosses. He probably had a few crosses in his yard. As far as burning crosses and death threats, I'm sure he received more than his fair share."

Reverend Smith's memory is sharp, and it can take him back to the days when the Klan burned crosses and more.

"But the first thing I remember about the Klan was when we

used to have an old cattle range down in the swamp. Everybody had cows in the swamp.

"Every two weeks you had to round up all your cows and drive 'em to a big vat to dip 'em. A dippin' vat is a long trench, about from here to that tree (a distance of about 15 feet). Just wide enough for cows to go through. And you'd put a certain amount of chemicals in there to kill all the ticks on the cows. You'd push that cow in there and make 'em swim through it, to the other side. It was a headache.

"But every once in a while, at night, they'd blow the vats up. The Klan blew the vats up. I'd hear it — vvvooooommmm! — a vat went up!"

Oliver Skipwith was a Klokard — the KKK's name for a lecturer — in Klan Chapter 34. Smith's father knew Skipwith and the two had a fairly cordial relationship. E.W. Smith remembers his father telling him about the summer Sunday afternoons when members of the Klan would don their robes and hoods and parade through the streets in an effort to intimidate.

"The Klan would go down into the woods on a Sunday afternoon and dress into their robes and hoods, then parade through the town. The next day Oliver Skipwith would tell my daddy, `I saw you yesterday. You didn't know me, but I knew you.'"

E.W. Smith and his wife Cordie had five children, including Robert, who was a boyhood friend and football teammate of Bob Love's. One reason Cordie would not allow her children to work in the cotton fields was out of her fear, fear of the tales of the Klan and of the lynchings of the past.

"We were afraid," she says, "to let Bob and the rest of our children out to work because of the lynchings that we remembered. That and because of our experience with the Klan."

One evening years ago the Smiths were gathered at the dinner table when Cordell, a son, heard a noise and went to the front door.

"They came out one afternoon while we were having dinner," remembers the retired minister. "It must have been summertime because all the kids were home from school. And Cordell comes back to the dinner table and said, `The Klansmen's out there!'

"They were in a half-ton pickup truck. They used an iron spike to punch a hole so they could drive their cross into the ground. And they set that cross on fire.

"I can remember a time when an FBI agent came out to the house. He said — and I remember it like it was yesterday — he said, `Well, Reverend Smith, they don't burn crosses in Uncle Tom's yard.'"

O.L. Harper, the parish schools superintendent charged with the court-ordered responsibility of integrating Morehouse Parish's schools in 1969, clearly recalls the last gasps of Morehouse Klan Number 34.

"At one time Morehouse Parish and (neighboring) Franklin Parish probably had the strongest Klans in the state. But the final incident of their demise came back in the 1960s.

"I believe it was in 1964 ... the Klan wounded itself so badly that it was not really effective except for causing confusion. But in '64, the Klan had a meeting place in the Second Ward, which is the ward next to Arkansas. I believe they call their meeting place a `Klavern'.

"Anyway, some of their members felt like someone was meddlin' with their little meeting house that they had. Someone was coming in and messin' with their paraphernalia. Anyway, someone set up a pressure bomb under the front stoop of that Klavern.

"What happened is that two young kids — I suspect they were ten or so — and they were hunting near this place. You know how kids will do, well they stepped on that porch. And when they did, the bomb went off. I guess (the Klan) didn't suspect that they'd catch some child.

"It mangled one of their legs pretty bad. The other one, just a little to some extent.

"So after that, I would suggest that most of the decent people dropped out of the Klan, which basically left you with the crazies. And I guess some of the people in the Klan back then would think of themselves as decent people. They were misguided, in my mind, and in other peoples' minds.

"From then on, no one wanted to be associated with the Klan because there were lawsuits filed (on behalf of the injured boys). So the thing piddled out."

CHAPTER 5

THE MUCKIES ■ It was sometime in the summer of 1942 that William and Ella Hunter decided they would pull up stakes and move their family. The question was where. Their 15-year-old daughter Lula was pregnant, unmarried and without support.

The United States was reeling, in a fighter's back-pedal after absorbing a body blow at Pearl Harbor and the loss of the heart of its naval forces. War raged over the oceans to the left and to the right. While much of the rest of the country was immersed in the war effort — scrap drives, rubber drives, War Bond drives — William Hunter set out on a drive of his own. Hitching a mule to a buckboard wagon, William set off across the bayou country of northeast Louisiana. A father of twelve, William Hunter was rolling across Louisiana in search of a home, in search of work, in search of a place where his daughter could give birth to his grandchild.

The Hunters, every able-bodied one of them, were farm workers, uneducated and otherwise unskilled. When the owner of the plantation in Talulla, which was the Hunters' sweat shop, learned that Lula Hunter was with child, he was less than sympathetic.

"I'm sorry, Miss Hunter," he scolded Ella. "But you know my rules. And my rules are very clear and very simple. Everybody in your family has got to work. If you want your family to live in that house, then every one of you has got to work. If she's old enough to get herself pregnant, then she's old enough to chop cotton."

"No, sir," Ella Hunter insisted. "No daughter of mine is gonna be out in that cotton field when she's having a baby."

"Sorry, Miss Hunter. You know the rules."

So it was that William Hunter set out on the buckboard wagon. He headed west out of Tallula, just a stone's toss from the Louisiana-Mississippi border and Vicksburg. After two and a half days, 60 hours during which William Hunter slept under the stars and munched on the sardines and crackers his wife packed in a paper sack for him, he arrived at the South Hall Plantation in Delhi, Louisiana. The South Hall Plantation was larger than the one in Talulla and William Hunter reached an agreement with the owner. His family would work the plantation — everyone but Lula — and the Hunters would receive small compensation and a roof over their heads.

It was that roof that provided the shelter for Lula Hunter to give birth. Her son, Robert Earl Love, entered a world in turmoil on the feast of the Immaculate Conception, December 8, 1942, a year and a day after the Japanese Air Force drilled the U.S.S. Arizona into a salt-water grave in the Pacific Ocean. Thus, Robert Earl Love was the last of the Hunter clan to be born on a plantation. Born helpless into a world in conflict, a world — at least his small corner of the world — dominated by white men who still believed in the policies of their ancestors. Slavery was off the books in 1942. But slavery was still very much on the minds of the cotton farmers of Louisiana.

Robert's natural father, Benjamin Love, was absent when he was born, absent when he grew up. Possibly the only time Benjamin Love was present — with one documented exception — was when Robert was conceived. In later years, Ella told her grandson that his father enlisted in the United States Army just before Lula gave birth. So Robert became another of the already too-many mouths to feed in the Hunter household. The only time Bob Love can recall a child-hood encounter with his father was when he was eight years old. Benjamin Love returned to Ella Hunter's house to visit his son.

"He sat me on his lap," Love now recalls, "and all of us were in my grandmother's bedroom. We didn't have a living room, just two bedrooms and a kitchen. He sat me on his lap and we talked for a while, talked about school, talked about the plantation — we talked about stuff. Then he took out his wallet.

"And I remember what he said, even to this day. There was a lot of money in his wallet. I guess he had just gotten paid. So he took out his wallet and he told me to reach in and to get what I wanted.

"My grandmother later said she was prayin' that I'd reach in and get it all." Bob Love laughs at the recollection. "And I reached in and took me just one dollar. I guess I was too shy or something. Just one dollar.

"I didn't see him again until I was 33 years old."

In fact, Robert Earl Love didn't see his mother, at least that he can remember, until he was four years old. Lula Hunter left Delhi shortly after her baby was born and she moved to Detroit, in search of work. This wasn't a case of abandonment, to be sure. Ella Hunter assured her daughter that Robert Earl Love would be fine with his grandmother.

About the time Robert Earl was four or five, Lula returned to Louisiana with a new husband, Lee Cleveland. But the day Cleveland used the buckle of a belt to beat Ella Hunter's grandson was the last day Robert Earl lived with his mother and step-father.

"If I ever catch you beating my grandson again you're gonna answer to me!" she admonished Cleveland. From that day forward, Bob Love was raised by Ella Hunter.

On a quiet street corner in Bastrop, Louisiana, there once stood a grocery store. The empty lot is located on Dr. Martin Luther King, Jr., Drive. But when Bob Love was a boy, JD's Grocery Store stood on a corner of Haggerty Street, just a block and a half from his shot-gun house on the southwest side of town. The neighborhood has changed little since those early, misty summer mornings of Bob

Love's boyhood. Probably the biggest change is that the Bastrop High School football stadium today takes its space across the street from where J.D. Daniels once ran his grocery store. JD's was the kind of neighborhood grocery store that everyone born before, say, 1965, can still smell in his memory.

Yesterday, the Quaker brand grits are on the third shelf, right above the Cream of Wheat. There is no shortage of McIlhenny's Tabasco, one of Louisiana's proudest of native sons. Synonymous with tabasco, McIlhenny's today has a logo nearly as familiar as any in the business. The pride of New Iberia. Ample also is the supply of Spice Time Cajun Seasoning and a variety of shellfish concoctions which can be boiled into this region's famous, mouth-watering gumbos. The stuff you find on the shelves of JD's, and just about every grocery store in this southern state, is the stuff that causes beads of sweat to form on the back of your neck as you munch a drumstick, a neck bone or a morsel of catfish. The catfish here is not the hybrid fish that have been poured as fry into Midwest farm ponds. This is good, bottom-feeder fish.

Nehi is still the pop of choice at JD's. His patrons have not yet accepted the modern entries to the soft drink market — the diet Cokes, the caffeine-free, sodium-free colas which offer no calories, no jolt, no taste. Crystal Pepsi? Try again a hundred years from now, maybe. Just a fruity, carbonated Nehi, thank you, and we'll be on our way.

As the Twentieth Century made the bend toward the Twenty-First, JD's Grocery was an unlikely point of reference for the field laboring folks of Bastrop here in northwest Louisiana. Remember, this is a sleepy, muggy, quiet corner of the planet. Crime, even today, is much lower than the national average. The people of Louisiana, generally, are hospitable, without a lot of stress and forever willing to make a stranger feel at home with a rib-sticking bowl of gumbo and a rip of cheese-salami bread ...

But JD's is gone. An empty lot occupies JD's space today, with weeds fighting rocks and pebbles for a place on the crusty landscape.

It is on that sleepy, hazy corner that hosted JD's Grocery, that the colored, field laboring folks of Bastrop would assemble each week-day morning from April until August, jockeying for a place in line for the pickup trucks and flatbeds to transport them to the cotton fields. It is nearly a century — a full 90 years to be exact — since Abraham Lincoln decreed that slavery was illegal in the United States of America. And so these workers, these colored, ill-fed, poorly-housed, generally uneducated American people, would gather. Each and every morning, just around four in the morning, they would trickle to the corner, where JD's Grocery stood as a staging area for farm workers.

Bob Love recalls:

"I remember going to work in the cotton fields, man. You talk about a scene. JD's Grocery was the only black grocery in the town. It was a few blocks from my grandmother's house. Can you imagine, every morning at four o'clock, you would see 300 black people, maybe 400, all of them gathered in this one little spot. There were so many people there, all there at four o'clock in the morning.

"All the people — especially the ladies — they'd be wearing their little hats. Some of the women would wear a rag around their heads. We'd be wearing blue jeans and our big, heavy shoes. Everybody would gather at JD's at four o'clock, five days a week."

Four in the morning may sound early even to the most hardened of northern industrial commuters. But this is Louisiana's bayou country, where the Gulf of Mexico seems to crawl beneath the crust of the earth, bringing with it all the steam and gum that the highest humidity can muster. This is a section of the world where moss hangs from trees in the summer because water is forever in the air. If you can't bring up a sweat on a summer day in Louisiana, you'd better call the coroner.

The early morning hours must have been a bonanza for JD's. Latter day business proprietors might have said they'd made their day, that they'd realized their previous year-to-date performance at the till, even before the sun was above the horizon.

As the cotton field workers would begin to arrive at the little corner grocery store, the owner would unlock his doors and flip the sign on his front window from the "closed" to the "open" position.

This, the fourth hour, was as cool as the summer day ever gets in these parts. From here until well after sunset, the Louisiana sun rises into the sky, leaving behind steam and searing heat to cling to the earth millions of miles below. The common, calloused, hard-working colored folk would drift into this corner grocery store and go about their business of preparing for a day under the scorching sun and bayou humidity. As they did, most would purchase food from the store, often using a portion of yesterday's wage to pay for today's lunch.

"JD would open up his store at maybe a quarter to four and people would go in there and buy baloney, bread, sardines and crackers," Bob Love recalls. "This was an important meal for the farm workers. It's what drove the body's engine. You'd take that into the cotton fields with you. You might buy an RC or a Nehi pop. Then they'd give it to you in a bag and you'd write your name on the bag."

By the time he was eight — it was 1951 — Bob Love and his grandmother and his brothers and his sisters and his cousins and an aunt and uncle or two, would arrive at JD's before dawn had a chance to wipe the sleep from the eyes of the Pelican State.

Forty years later, as he describes the early-morning ritual of preparing to work on the plantation, Bob Love's eyes sparkle at the recollection. As he recalls his own boyhood and Ella Hunter and her years of indentured servitude in the cotton fields, his eyes are not sad. They open his soul to what he perceives as a kinder, simpler, more secure time. It was a time that was not bad to a little boy who was growing up in Louisiana. Perhaps because most of us, at age nine, are at peace with the world. In many respects, age nine was Bob Love's happiest of times. It's one thing to take your teammates into the National Basketball Association semi-finals with a 17-foot jumper. It's better to know that your grandmother will never let harm come your way. That your stutter is an inconvenience, not the end of your world. Thrills don't always match security. Inconveniences don't get in the way of happy memories. Ask Bob Love.

In the spring, when the cotton plants are young and supple and not yet approaching maturity, the workers undertake the chore of "chopping" the cotton; that is, weeding the plants, giving the seedlings room to breathe, grow and spread along the seemingly endless rows of cotton; straight, unending rows of cotton that stretch beyond the horizon of a little boy. Beyond his sight and beyond his imagination, no matter that the imagination is every bit as fertile as the Louisiana loam.

"In cotton-chopping season, man, that was hard work. After about a quarter to six you had to take this little walk from the road, you would jump over a fence and you're in the cotton field. Let me tell you, they had some of these rows of cotton and they were two miles long.

"The little cotton plant would be about six inches tall." Love takes his brown hands and extends the index fingers a half foot apart, vertically, to support his measurement of plant and time. "And a lot of times you'd get into some really grassy spots — that was cotton-chopping time."

As Bob explains it, cotton chopping is a lot like weeding your rose garden after you've let the ground harden and the clay to clump. Except that this nine-year-old's rose garden was as broad as the steamy, steel-blue Louisiana sky.

"You try to leave maybe three, four stalks to a row of cotton. The cotton went all the way down the field and we'd cut it into sections. You had to get all the grass out. It was early summer. We had just gotten out of school."

To get to the fields, the workers relied on the white truck drivers to transport them.

"The white guys would bring the trucks down to the grocery store and there might be as many as 40 pickup trucks come to the one little spot, JD's. Nine times out of ten the white guys would know the older black people. My grandmother would have to know the white guy or I wouldn't be able to get on the truck because I was so young. She'd tell the driver, `This is my son, Robert Earl Love. He's a good worker, Mr. Higginbotham. These are my kids. I'm gonna take care of them. Please let 'em come on.'"

More often than not, little Robert Earl would hoist himself onto the pickup bed. From there he'd give Ella Hunter a tug and a boost, and get ready for the ride to the cotton fields. Unattached youngsters who tried to hitch or tag along, or those who became separated from a mama or an uncle or older sibling were left behind.

"You had to have somebody to vouch for you, to assure the white guy that you were a good worker," Love now recalls. "A lot of kids didn't get on the trucks because they didn't have anybody to vouch for them."

By the time the first rays of daylight poke above the horizon to the east, the trucks are rumbling along the nine-mile route from JD's Grocery to the plantation and the cotton fields. Bob and his cousins, like virtually all nine-year-old boys, were usually oblivious to the time of day. After all, boys of any generation are charged with energy even in their sleep, and they would fill their time in the pickup truck with chatter. Ella Hunter made sure her boisterous progenies were at least subdued enough so as not to upset the white man in the cab. No matter that slavery was abolished 90 years before, she was black, and her children were, too. He was white and he owned the truck. And a white man owned the cotton fields. If the boys got too far out of line, she was certain to admonish them with either her strong, forceful voice or, sometimes, with the bleached palm of her weathered, brown right hand.

Arriving at the cotton field, the sun has caused its orange pitcher to pour warmth upon the ground. The truck stops at a shack located on the perimeter of the plantation. There, hundreds of dirt hoes in varying degrees of decay are lined up for yet another day's work. Some are propped against cypress trees, others against the exterior walls of the shack. Yet others are piled like kindling on the ground nearby. The first workers who arrive get the pick of the litter.

"The people would jump off the truck and run to try to get a good hoe. My grandmother really knew how to get those good hoes. She'd run up there and grab a couple of them — however many we needed that day. By the time you got the hoe, it was probably five-thirty. Then most of the people would have to get someone to sharpen the hoe for them.

"They had this guy who'd get down on his hands and knees and sharpen your hoe. He'd charge you ten cents to sharpen that hoe, but for most of the people it was worth it because a dull hoe meant you would get blisters all over your hands. But my grandmother and my uncle would always carry our own files. They'd get the best hoes they could and they'd sharpen those hoes themselves. That way we'd save ten cents a hoe and we wouldn't have to stand in line to get out of the hoe shop. Then, as the day wore on, you could always take a minute to sharpen that hoe again. Nothing like a good, sharp hoe when you're chopping cotton."

Funny how the mind works. Decades after his boyhood experience, Bob Love — a National Basketball Assocation all-star and a man who brought respect and viability to a fledgling, suffering basketball franchise in Chicago, 900 miles north of his birth — talks of his plantation days as if they were his salad days.

"By nine o'clock in the morning you could see the sun getting smaller as it rose in the sky. And, hell, it would just get hotter and hotter and hotter. Man, by ten o'clock you would look down those rows of cotton and all you'd see were those little heat waves, those little mucky heat waves. Nothing but little muckies, those little mucky heat waves across the field. Guys were sweating, peoples' hands were getting blisters on them, man.

"If we were doing a movie, man," now he is laughing, "we could have people dying all over the plantation." He is still smiling as he recalls the labor.

"It might be 100 degrees and you might look up and see nothing but a sea of straw hats and bandannas. We're talking about hundreds of people in the fields. And you had better be doing a good job getting the grass out, make sure you're thinning out grass and not thinning out too many cotton stalks."

Love now chuckles when asked how many white people were in the field.

"No white people, only black people. The white guy was the boss."

There is no bitterness in Bob Love's voice. None at all. Yet in later life, when the straw boss took on a different role ...

Cotton choppers near Delhi were paid between $2.50 and $3.00 a day. Not an hour. A day.

"You had to stay out there from six o'clock in the morning until five o'clock in the afternoon. Now, a lot of kids would get on the truck and get down to the cotton fields. So the straw boss would keep his eyes trained on everybody, but he'd always keep his eyes on the kids to make sure they weren't goofing off, to make sure they were doing a good job. We were just kids so, you know, we were always on the brink of goofing off, just looking for fun. What else do kids have to live for, right?

"If you didn't do a good job, this guy would fire you. Let me tell you, you could always tell when you were going to get fired. If you looked way down the row and the white guy would see you standing in the row too long, he knew you weren't getting the grass. That grass needed to be chopped and those little cotton plants had to be standing by themselves or you got in trouble. You weren't getting the job done. Man, your heart would get to beating really fast and you'd think: `Oh, shit, man, this guy's gonna fire me!'

"Then he'd just come up to you and grab your hoe. He'd say, `*Hey, boy, gimme that hoe!* You know better than that, boy! You should be choppin' cotton!' If he knew your grandmother or he knew your mom, he'd say, `Miss Hunter, you better watch your grandson there. He's not getting this cotton done right. He's not cutting all the grass out.'

"The guys who got fired would all have to walk home together. Remember, that was a nine-mile walk. You couldn't hang around the truck and wait for a ride home. White man would tell you that you couldn't hang around the truck, you couldn't hang around the field. You had to walk home, pal. That was it."

Again, the twinkle sparks in Bob Love's eyes. He's an easy read. Even now, in middle age, that mischievous twinkle finds its way to the surface. Sometimes Bob Love is a still a big, six foot eight inch kid.

"Oh, boy, my grandmother would get pretty upset when I got fired. And I *did* get fired sometimes. There were times when I was glad to get fired, even though we'd have to walk nine, ten miles back to town. Man," and again he chuckles, "sometimes it was worth facing my grandmother just to get out of that heat."

Not at all like basketball practice, something he hadn't had the chance to dream about, not even with his powerful imagination. Basketball practice, though he couldn't yet know it, would be different. It would set him apart from so many other kids, so many other players. Basketball practice, whether he would ever know it or not, would someday set him apart from so many other kids, so many other livelihoods, so many cotton fields.

"But it was all fun. Walking on those dirt roads, the other guys and I would throw rocks at the water, the trains, whatever. Everybody would be laughing, having a ball. We'd try to hitch a ride but most of the time we'd still end up walking. That's basically what you did, but it was really hard times out there.

"You know, in a little town like Bastrop, we did whatever we could to make a little bit of money. We picked cotton, we baled hay, we picked strawberries, we worked in the white peoples' gardens. We'd mow their yards, dig up flower beds, sometimes just to make $2.00 or $2.50. They'd give us a little money. Sometimes they'd give us a little food."

Hard times fortify the soul. Hard times give the strong heart its strength to pump the body's fuel through and to maintain its beat. Hard times nurture a will to survive. Say what you want. Anyone who has been poor and who has also been rich will tell you they'd rather be rich than poor. Rather be a have than have-not. Rather be a swell than a not-so. Anyone who's been through hard times, who's patched the soles of his shoes with cardboard to keep the stones off the soles of his feet, will tell you it's no fun. It's no fun at all. Leave the "hard times" lectures to someone else. When you're in hard times, the best thing to do is to get out. What seems to be fun, or at least what seems to be normal, when you're nine years old, will smack you between the eyes when you're 42. Some people face the crucible later in life than was planned by the crucible itself.

"I didn't realize I was poor when I was little. But when I got to high school I figured it out — I was really, really poor. A lot of my friends — their parents had good jobs, a lot of them went to college and they lived in nicer homes than I did. They'd drive their big cars around.

"Hell, even in Bastrop, everybody had bicycles. Almost everybody. I never had a bicycle. My people never had a car. But we made do. Sometimes I wonder how the hell I made it, how anybody in my house made it. But you know, my grandmother fed us. She fed us with food. Everyone knows you need that. But she fed us with knowledge. She fed us with character. She gave us a foundation for life. It was up to us to make the most of the rest of it."

Ella Hunter's fountain was full of sweet, thirst-quenching nectar. She fortified her grandson with that sweetness and appreciation for life that he carried into his adult life.

"I don't know, really, how I made it. My grandmother had the most to do with it. And you know, when you look back, you realize that you just do it. You make do with whatever it is that you have. I guess that's how I made it."

CHAPTER 6

FANTASY ISLAND ■ Not many kids — at least not many little kids — ever imagine themselves growing up to be certified public accountants. Or industrialists. Or traders on the Mercantile Exchange or real-estate salesmen or divorce lawyers. Not many little kids ever dream in their dreams that they'd be bored to tears in their adulthood, simply making money and mortgage payments and putting the kids through school and braces before setting themselves up for retirement. No, most little kids have enough dream in them to dream about excitement — about flying through the weightlessness of outer space, about riding the open range on a sleek red horse with nothing but the sky for containment. Or about being a war hero, bloodied but never bowed and determined to return home.

These days little kids dream more about being rock and roll stars than anything else. But when Robert Earl Love was a little kid, Francis Albert Sinatra was the closest thing there was to a rock-and-roll star and television hardly existed, so his idols were invisible. Bob

Love may have heard of Captain Video and his Space Rangers and perhaps he had even heard of Jack Armstrong, all-American boy. But not Neil Armstrong, or even Neill Armstrong, for that matter. No one was ever weightless in the searing heat of bayou country. A cowboy? Bob Love didn't see too many horses or cows while he chopped cotton in the fields. And he certainly never had enough money to catch a Saturday matinee double feature starring John Wayne or Gene Autry. Or Dale Evans, as far as that goes. War heroes? Little kids growing up in Louisiana — especially little black kids — had no one to look up to coming back from World War II. The monument at the courthouse in Bastrop, lest we forget, depicts a white and black soldier together. *That* didn't happen before Bob Love's childhood.

No, Bob Love or any other little black kid growing up in the deep south of the 1950s didn't have too many big-as-life idols to emulate.

But the kid had a gift. Call it ignorance or naivete or just plain lack of common sense, Bob Love didn't know he was poor. Bob Love didn't know he was disadvantaged. Heck, for a long, long time, Bob Love didn't even know that he didn't know how to talk the way most people talk. He really didn't understand that he was a stutterer for the longest time.

Perhaps his greatest gift — apart from his grandmother Ella Hunter — was that he felt pressure from no precinct. He loved his grandmamma. He loved his cousins. He loved everything about him — even his poverty, for he didn't understand it. And so, delivered to this little boy from somewhere within the recesses of his mind, was a very creative and enterprising imagination.

"I've been very fortunate," Love now recalls. "I always had a great imagination. I could imagine anything."

And so it was that a little boy growing up in a very big world which would get much, much bigger, could survive. Perhaps, just maybe — perhaps he'd even thrive.

Oh, how the late autumn can enhance and titillate the mind of a very young man. When the leaves turn from green to amber and sunburst and rose, it signals a time of heightened spirit and awareness. It is the season of seasons, a time when love blooms for real, not like in the spring, when infatuation reigns. Funny how true love is born when everything else begins to die in the cycle of life. It is almost as if the cool and frosty air awakens the cells within a brain, awakens them to their imaginative and creative best. Sometimes the moon rises as a silvery white crescent, his head laid back as if he is laughing at the stars. Sometimes it is split evenly in half, like some sort of figure sketched for a geometry problem that most of us cannot solve.

But when he is at his best, when he inspires the poet and the lover in us all, the moon becomes full, a giant ball who has made millions of men wonder and wander since the beginning of time. Only once or twice a year does he truly perform a magic that cannot be duplicated by any magician in this world, and that is during the autumn, during the harvest moon, when he looms above the earth in early dusk like a giant orange head peeking through a window. Try to wave him off and he only slowly rises a bit, then a bit more. He will ultimately take his silver self high enough to illuminate our path so that we might not stumble. But he's still looking at us.

So many nights the moon — in various stages of crescent, half, full and gone — pulled at Robert Earl Love when he would sneak from Ella Hunter's shotgun house to hide in her tool shed. When everyone else in his family was in various stages of relaxation, study, chores and sleep, little Bob Love would steal away to the tool shed, to the friendship of an old Motorola radio. And it was there that reality collided with imagination, where a little boy began to reach for the stars. This was where Bob Love's athletic life truly began.

There were ghosts. At times there were ghosts as real as the muckies that hovered over the boiling cotton fields. As real as the straw bosses who would sometimes send little Bob and his buddies home for goofing off when they were supposed to be chopping cotton. Oh, those ghosts. They were real.

"I used to have a little radio, an old-fashioned radio ..." Bob Love's eyes are alive.

"And they'd have on the North Carolina games. The Kansas games. I would listen to Wilt Chamberlain, listen to Lenny Rosenbloom, all those guys. They were my heroes during that time."

So it was in Ella Hunter's tool shed, just outside Ella Hunter's shotgun house that was too small for her bursting family, that little Bob Love began to meet his heroes, where he began to discover his beliefs, where he began to find himself.

"I didn't know anything about black and white. I just fell in love with basketball. North Carolina basketball. Bob Pettit down at LSU. We'd get the Kentucky games with Cliff Hagan. I would listen to those games at night and then I'd go to bed and I'd dream about them.

"I'd dream about the games that I'd heard on the radio. Then I'd dream about them again. Except in the second dream, somehow I'd be there, right there in the dream. And I'd be playing against Wilt Chamberlain. I'd be playing against Lenny Rosenbloom and Bob Pettit and Cliff Hagan. Man, I still remember those dreams."

Sometimes dreams are all a kid — or an adult, for that matter — ever has. But sometimes things get a little better. For the lucky ones, things sometimes get a lot better.

"As a little kid growin' up ... my grandmother raised me," Bob Love relates. "I was one of thirteen other kids living in this two bedroom house. We only had three beds. Two of the kids and my grandmother and my grandfather slept in one room.

"We had people sleeping on the floor, little pallets on the floor. Man, there were kids sleeping everywhere. On the bed, next to the bed, under the bed. I would dive under the bed because that's where I thought I was safe, where it was quiet, where it was warm."

It didn't take much imagination for Bob Love to figure out that under the bed wasn't the best place to be.

"I just realized at an early age that I didn't want to live like that for the rest of my life. I was going to have to get an education. I didn't have any idea how or where I was going to get it. I just knew I had to ..."

With his imagination in tow, Bob Love began dreaming his dreams in the daylight hours in the backyard of Ella Hunter's home. Nowadays even the poorest of inner-city kids have a basketball — or access to one — and a hardtop basketball court and goal. The black-topped school yards of America produce a constant and rhythmic thump-thump-thump of ball meeting concrete, asphalt meeting ball. Today's NBA stars tell legendary stories of their childhoods, the days when they played pickup basketball games from dawn until well past dark. How many times have you heard Hersey Hawkins or Charles Barkley or Terry Cummings talk about the school yard games, about how they were never the best player in the yard. There was always somebody better. Yet they were the ones who ran the gauntlet, they are the ones who survived and hit the NBA jackpot, because they had something the others didn't have. They had drive. Sure they had the drive to go the basket. But they were also driven.

But for every Kevin Gamble there are a thousand Billy Harrises. For every rags-to-riches story of glory and wealth, there are a million tales of failure, depression and destruction.

Bob Love never owned a basketball during his childhood days in Bastrop, Louisiana. There was no school yard near Ella Hunter's house. But those minor details never stopped Bob Love from playing a game that was slowly beginning to become a part of his persona. In the words of the cliche, where there's a will, there's a way. Bob Love's will took over and he began to teach himself the way to shoot the jump shot and slam the dunk on the dirt floor court of Ella Hunter's backyard.

"I got some of my grandfather's old socks," he remembers. "I'd stuff them with rags and newspapers and try the best I could to make them round. I tied them up with old string. Then I had to build me a basketball goal. I didn't have any money so I just took a coat hanger and nailed it to the side of my grandmother's house."

From the cool darkness of night inside the tool shed, to the blistering sunlight of Ella Hunter's backyard, Bob Love began a long march to the National Basketball Association.

"I always imagined myself playing against Lenny Rosenbloom and Wilt. And I could hear the crowd roaring. Man, I could imagine the crowd cheering every time I touched the ball, every time I took a jumper, every time I grabbed a rebound.

"I could see those guys — Pettit, Hagan — and I'd cut to the basket and I'd dunk. I'd shoot a jump shot over Wilt and the crowd would roar. I would get into my imaginary games so much that I could actually hear the crowds cheering. It would become so damned real to me that sometimes I would get chills. I could really feel it, man.

"I'll bet I played those guys 10,000 times, at least 10,000 games against the best college basketball players in the south. And you know what? I won every time I played against them." Love giggles now. "Course, I was the only one who ever touched the ball."

His dirt floor basketball court was a kingdom and Robert Earl Love was the king, royalty over a court and a host of invisible serfs. Alone he was, and alone he could fly. He was Baryshnikov with a basketball, Doug Henning with a jump shot. Imagine this poor black boy in the dust of bayou country, pretending to be the best the world of basketball could ever offer. Jump shots, slam dunks, pivot left, rebound right. But dribbling socks in the dirt is tough to do, even for a basketball prodigy.

About the same time little Bob Love began his courtship with Dr. Naismith's invention, he began to realize that he was just a little bit different from most of the other kids in Bastrop. He was of average height and average weight. That wasn't the distinction. No, the difference wasn't clear at first glance.

What made Bob Love different wasn't what you could see, it wasn't what you could feel. You had to wait until Bob Love opened his mouth before you knew he was different.

"You know, I never really knew I stuttered until I was about six or seven years old. One holiday ... I had some friends who lived across the street from me. I used to go over to their house all the time. And I just had this thing, this habit where I would say, `I-I-I' all the time. I was just trying to get the words out but there I was, stutter, stutter.

"But I really never knew I stuttered until these guys started laughing at me. They'd laugh and say, `This is how Love sounds: I-I-I. Love can't talk.' And then they'd laugh.

"Before then I never had anything that bothered me. I was never embarrassed by anything. I was just trying to talk. I never considered myself as being different from the other guys."

On his fantasy basketball court, Bob Love shot and jumped and ran. He never had to talk, he never stuttered. On his fantasy court, he never had a coach from whom he would take instruction, no teacher to whom he needed to answer. His fantasy teams had opponents but no teammates. No teammates, no banter. No encouragement to deal out, no cajoling to mete out. Easy stuff, this fantasy basketball. Shoot over Wilt, win 10,000 games, never worry about answering a question from a newspaper reporter, never sweat the television interview, never pay attention to a radio microphone. Just shoot over Wilt. Easy stuff.

"But a lot of times I'd have my little fantasy games and I would run into the house. Man, it would be so hot and I'd be sweating and thirsty and I'd run into the house and my grandmother would be washin' the dishes.

"They had this old wives' tale down in the south that if you hit a person in the mouth with a dirty dish rag, that would stop them from stuttering. That if you put marbles in the person's mouth and if they stuttered, that would stop them.

"I would run in the house and ask my grandmother for some water. And I'd start stammering and stuttering: `Grandmamma, can I have some w-w-w- ...' And before I could get out the word `water,' she'd slap me in the mouth with that dirty old dish rag and she'd say, `Spit it out, Robert Earl. Spit it out.' After a while I learned to stop asking her for water and just went in and got it myself."

During his childhood, Bob Love had no idea, no inkling, no clue about how difficult life would later be because of his stutter. While his handicap did not affect his abilities on the hardwood court, it would have a severe impact on his ability to cash in on his athletic talents. While he would be able to hide his problem from most of the world, he could not hide it from himself. And while very few of his buddies ever let Bob's speech problems get in the way of sports, friendship or hardship, his inability to communicate would haunt him deep into his adult life. His legs were sound. His eyes were clear. His right arm was so strong he could fire a football 70 yards in the air. But he was handicapped. And his handicap was misunderstood and underevaluated. His body was strong and his mind was bright. But Bob Love had a handicap that no wheelchair or seeing-eye dog could assist.

And the day would come when it very nearly ruined his life.

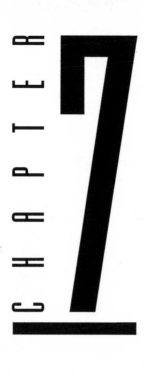

CHAPTER 7

THE AMERICAN WAY

The song of the south, the one that Bob Love learned to sing, was black and white. No gray about it. Black was black, white was white and the two never met. They never met on the bus. They never met in the coffee shop. They never met on the basketball court. And they never met on the football field, the venue where Robert Earl Love, oddly enough, honed the skills that would take him on his circuitous route to the National Basketball Association.

In fact, Bob Love never played against a white athlete in any sport until the very last basketball game of his college career, a National Association of Intercollegiate Athletics tournament game against Ouachita Baptist College. All through his childhood and into young adulthood, Bob Love lived in a segregated world where white people lived in a white universe and treated their black neighbors as aliens. What is truly amazing is that black folks who lived and worked and learned and minded their own business in Bastrop, Louisiana in the 1950s; what is truly amazing is that they did not bitterly resent the segregation of their world from the white world.

That sentiment is echoed time after time by childhood friends, teachers and coaches who grew up with Bob Love in that small northern Louisiana town. Arthur Hamlin is one of those echoes. A childhood pal of Love's, Arthur Hamlin played wide receiver when Bob Love quarterbacked the Morehouse High School football team. A very soft-spoken man with a receding hairline, Hamlin today works as a drug-training counselor in the Bastrop public school system. He also is serving his second term as an alderman on the Bastrop City Council. It shouldn't be this way, but Arthur Hamlin's legacy is what longtime buddy Robert Smith puts this way: "Ask him about the pass he dropped in the end zone. The one that would have won the championship game."

"Oh? That's all they can remember," Hamlin says with a hearty laugh and wide eyes. "But, hey, you know what? You're right. And for two years it hurt me, it hurt me, it hurt me. It took me a long time to get over that."

Hamlin sighs and folds his arms across his chest. Hamlin, along with a half dozen or so childhood friends, was close to Bob Love while they were growing up in Bastrop. They shared the same class in high school, and Hamlin later went on to Southern University with Love, both headed there with football scholarships and dreams of life in the National Football League. But Hamlin and Love — and all their other friends and contemporaries — shared more than just school, athletics and dreams. They shared the experience of living in a white man's world where colored folks were not permitted. Not in the coffee shops. Not on the bus. Not on the football field. Especially not in the classroom.

"To be honest with you, we were poor and we didn't know it," Hamlin says today. "We didn't have much in the way of football equipment. The white schools had all they needed. But with us, we took what we had and what was passed down. What we'd later buy, we took care of it, and kept it because we were taught to take care of whatever it was. I think the only time the segregation thing got to me was when those white guys used to come to our games. You could see them on the sidelines. Don't get me wrong. I didn't have a problem with those guys coming to our games.

"But one night — we were juniors or seniors — there was a car full of us and we drove to one of the white school's football games. We got out and, hey, we just wanted to go to the game. We weren't looking for any trouble or anything like that. But a doggone policeman, as nicely as he could be about it at the time, he suggested that we not go in to the stadium. So we got back in our car and drove around the building to a corner where you could see just a corner of the football field. We sat down and we watched it for a while. But they were gettin' the tar beat out of them so we decided it wasn't worth stickin' around for.

"But we didn't resent the white guys because, well, they weren't winning much back then and we were. We were winning. The four years Love and I played football together, our team lost six games. We lost two our freshman year, two our sophomore year — and one of those was for the state championship. We lost one my junior year, the year we won the championship. The only game we lost that year was to (the) Grambling (high school team) and we always thought we were cheated on that one. And we cried, I'm not ashamed to say, because we wanted to go undefeated that year. And we lost one my senior year. We were undefeated at that point but we won't go into that. That was the only team at Morehouse to have an undefeated regular season."

James Clay is a massive man with thick, strong hands. He looks a man square in the eye when he firmly grips him in handshake. ("When I shake a man's hand, I want to feel that grip. You've shook peoples' hands where you just get a little squeeze, right? I get to know a person right there, you know?") James Clay is a man's man, tough and weathered by time and life. He is wearing a Los Angeles Dodgers cap and a Dodgers T-shirt, but he resembles Hammerin' Hank Aaron, who never played for the Bums. Clay, too, was a classmate of Bob Love's. Like Hamlin, Clay now works as an educator in the Bastrop public school system. As a teenager, Clay was a lineman on the Morehouse High football team. Clay sees some good and some not-so-good in the integration of the school system in his home town.

"I wasn't bitter when I was young because I didn't know any better. You know what I'm talking about? You knew how you were supposed to be, how you were supposed to act and what it took to get along. And you got along. Really, I guess in retrospect, the way the situation was, we got along well here in Bastrop.

"I can remember when we played up at Crossett," a high school just north of the border in Arkansas. "We were playing right up the road and we couldn't play on Friday night because that's when the white kids played. We had to wait to play on Saturday. We couldn't go into the stadium over at Bastrop High, where I'm working right now. We couldn't go in because we were black. Today, I tell my kids the same thing. They can't believe it. We would take a car and park it on the outside of the stadium and sit on top of the car to watch a game when the white kids were playing. The police would come along and make us move. But back then, we wouldn't think anything of it. It is amazing. There were just some things that were the way they were and you knew what you had to do."

O.L. Harper, the white man who was elected to lead the Morehouse Parish public school system during court-ordered integration in 1969, served as the district's superintendent for a decade. He is soft-spoken and casual, a true southern gentlemen. Blacks and whites alike give Harper superior grades for the way he handled the integration of the Morehouse Parish schools in 1969, a decade after Bob Love and his buddies headed off to college. They were tense times indeed.

"I served during the time the school system was integrated by court order," Harper recalls. "Back then, there were no facilities that were integrated as you would think of it today. There just weren't. I mean, we had separate wedding rooms, separate water fountains. You know, all the things that were true of the south back in that time.

"The instant of integration was the court order, which came down in early 1969. And I was elected superintendent early on in that year, sometime around the first of March. I actually started running the schools a month or so later. The court order was finalized around the first week in August. When I think of the time when integration actually occurred in this parish ..." Harper pauses, measuring his words. "It just seems like such a hard word, but I don't know of another word to take its place, really.

"In the late summer, they have what they call a football jamboree. What I mean by that is, two or three different football teams will come together and play a quarter or two against each other, round robin. It's a chance for the coaches to see their boys in action against another school.

"It's not played for scores, particularly. It's not played particularly to win or lose. It's a scrimmage sort of thing. But I remember the evening — and of course in the summertime the sun is still way up at seven o'clock — and just before the scrimmages, the cheerleaders ran across the field. And there you had five black cheerleaders and five white cheerleaders.

"And I think of that, in my mind, as the absolute instant of integration in Bastrop schools. Morehouse Parish was probably unique at the time. According to one of the assistant superintendents at the state department of education, Franklin Parish and Morehouse Parish would probably explode when integration came. You see, these two parishes probably had the strongest Klans in the state."

There's that word again.

Harper remembers the integration process as being a time of nervousness, anxiety and apprehension.

"It was tense, very much so. Everyone was apprehensive. The Klan did do some marching and they burned some crosses and that sort of thing. It was enough to keep up the turmoil in the school, and there was a breakdown in discipline. Some would call it a riot, but I think it was kids just trying to get out of the building more than anything else. Sure, there was confrontation, not unlike what we see on television nowadays in Boston.

"From about 1963 to '69 or '70, you saw a lot of black and white school confrontation on television. Natchez, Bogaloosa, New Orleans. Of course, you had the real bad ones in the voter registration riots in the south. But other than the Klan, there were no marches in Bastrop or Morehouse Parish. There was no arson. Before the Klan got shook up, there were some incidents, incidents in the black community of night riders trying to intimidate people. I guess we call them drive-by shootings now. But I don't think they shot anybody, they just more or less shot up the place, to my knowledge."

Reverend E. W. Smith, ever the militant, even at age 80, paints a different picture of the south. Then again, E.W. Smith was around during an earlier period than were Bob Love's contemporaries.

"It was particularly unfair and hell for black folks," he says, again causing furrows to crease his brow. "It made you spend a lot of frustrated time that you shouldn't have had to spend. To sum it up, the segregation era was hell for black folk. I was fortunate to this extent: My daddy was born and raised in the plantation system. But there was a big difference between the plantation system and the hill system as we knew it a few years back.

"One night years ago I was on the town square and I had on a nice suit of clothes. And right there on the square, well, here's a white man. And I was in a hurry, trying to catch up with somebody. So when I came back, the white men were standing on the street. And they said, `Come here, nigger. If you don't slow down, you better stop trying to walk like a white man. Try to walk like a damned nigger or we will put a pistol to your head.'

"And I slowed down. This was the kind of atmosphere you lived in."

The town square to which Reverend Smith refers, by the way, is the same square which witnessed the lynching of Andrew McLeod. Oh, those ghosts. They are everywhere.

Smith once worked at the paper mill in town, the primary industry in Bastrop. He remembers the days before the civil rights movement, when African Americans began to emerge from their second-class citizenship. And he can fully remember bearing the brunt of the notion that white folks were inherently superior to their black neighbors.

"It was not uncommon to hear white folks callin' black folks `nigger' back then. And I don't mean just among themselves, in the safety of their homes. I mean right to your face, in public. I remember a time down at the paper mill. A black worker, a fine man who worked hard and always did his job, was talking to his white foreman. And the black worker referred to another black man as `Mister' something or other. And the foreman looked right at him and said, in no uncertain terms, `And don't be callin' no nigger a `mister' to me.'"

From time to time, Smith felt the kidney punch himself, up close and personal.

"I was told to fill in one day on a job where I had to watch the paper dryers. And I was told by a white man, `You watch those dryers today, Ed. But don't let it get to your head. That's a white man's job.'

"Or the time I was waiting for someone and I was standing in front of a white barber shop. Back then, there were white barber shops and black barber shops. The man came out and told me, told me right to my face, `I don't let no niggers stand in front of my barber shop, so you better move on.' That's just the way it was."

Melvin Anderson sits in his office at the South Side Elementary School. On a sunny, spring afternoon, the kids are bouncing around the school yard at recess, black and white kids playing together, blind to the differences in their skin color, wide-eyed in their youthful exuberance and friendship. Unlike Hamlin and Clay, Melvin Anderson was not an athlete. In fact, Melvin Anderson was a musician and he played in the Morehouse High band and later in the band at Southern University, where Love starred on the basketball court. Anderson, a thoughtful man who uses his words carefully and with measure, is somewhat puzzled to this day about the social system in which he grew up.

"It's not that we accepted segregation," he recalls, "it's just that when you're born into a segregated high school, you never really come in contact with the other race. As I look back on it, I really can't see that I would be bitter about it — other than the reason we attended Southern."

Northeast Louisiana University is a stone's throw from Bastrop. But Anderson, Hamlin and Love could not attend Northeast because it was a whites-only campus. Instead, they resigned themselves to a four-hour bus ride across the state to Baton Rouge.

"We'd pass by two, three colleges just to get to Southern. As I look back on that, I really can't understand why. I mean, Northeast is just 22 miles away.

"And we had problems with transportation, getting back and forth to school. We could ride the bus, but as far as being able to use the restrooms or go to the lunch counters, all that was closed to us. I remember several times we'd catch the bus to go back to Baton Rouge. A lot of times there'd be so many college students that they'd just put all us black kids on one bus. That way, they wouldn't have to stop here to let the white kids use a restroom, stop there for the black kids to use a restroom. Stop here for the white kids to use a lunch counter, stop there for the black kids to use a lunch counter. They just put all the black kids on one bus to go straight to Baton Rouge."

There is still no trace of bitterness in the eyes of Melvin Anderson. Bewilderment at the nonsense of it all, but still no bitterness.

"It was kind of tough. And as I look back on it, it just seems so stupid. I remember one time — I played in the band at Southern — and we went over to Mobile. It might have been the Jackson State team we were playing. But after we marched into the stadium, we were not allowed to sit on the same side of the field as our football team. They had about 20 white people over there on the Southern side of the field. And they were dressed up in their American Legion hats. And they told us we couldn't sit over there. We had to go over and sit on the same side as Jackson State. There were about 20 whites over there. It was just silly. Just silly.

"Another time I remember coming from Southern to Monroe for a parade. And the bus driver stopped in Natchez. We got off to use the restroom to take care of our restroom needs, when some big policeman comes in, holds the door open and tells us to get out. We weren't even allowed to finish using the restroom.

"Nowadays, the students share. They develop friendships and relationships, and those friendships don't depend on race. When we were in school, we didn't have a chance to build and develop friendships in a segregated society. So things are better today.

"And as you look back on things like that, maybe we should be bitter. But it just seems so stupid, so silly. Use the restrooms? Use the water? That's just a personal need. But there's no bitterness, despite what happened to us."

While the Morehouse High athletic teams were a secret to be guarded within the parish's black community, once in a while a white face poked through the ebony curtain that surrounded their sports. Dick Revels is president and chief executive officer of the Bastrop National Bank, just across the street from the town square and the Morehouse Parish Courthouse. A round-faced man with twinkling eyes, Revels chuckles as he distributes his business card: "A country banker doesn't get to give one of those out very often. I've got a box of them and it will last me forever."

Revels was one of a sprinkling of white Bastropians who had the opportunity to watch Bob Love and his black teammates excel on the athletic fields and courts. Revels is a long and fast friend and comrade of Coach William Washington, a Morehouse Parish legend who looms as large as Eddie Robinson does at Grambling State University. When the schedule did not conflict with the game of the white high school, Revels would take in a football or basketball match involving the Morehouse teams.

"They had such outstanding athletes," Revels remembers, "but no one ever heard much about them because of the segregated situation. Four or five of us white fellas would go to some of their games, although we'd never go as a group. It was probably a little uncomfortable for everybody, because we wouldn't know where to sit. But Henry Adams — a wonderful man and a terrific teacher and coach — would save you a seat. I didn't want any special attention. I just wanted to go and see the games. I would see the basketball games. Not every one, because sometimes they would play at the same time our team would."

What Revels reveals in a conversation about Bastrop and the races is not guilt, but almost a sadness that the two never got together sooner, that segregation was opportunity denied for an entire race of people. A race within which he has many friends.

"This, I guess, is a typical southern community, but we've always gotten along. The two races have gotten along good. We've always had good relations, although not as good as it should have been. We were late getting started, like everybody else, with the education system.

"We got a late start, but we've made a lot of progress. We've never had a march of any kind. I think everybody has tried to do a lot better. I do a lot of things at the bank that nobody knows about ..." Dick Revels realizes that he's said enough about himself. "I don't want to say I'm a liberal, but I love everybody. I have as many friends on that side of town as I do on this side of town.

"You know, we've all got to live together. My kids all went to public schools. The way I feel about it is that everybody's a human being and there's a lot of white people you might not like and there's a lot of black people you might not like. But I have as many friends in the black community as the white."

If segregation didn't cause bitterness en masse among Bob Love's contemporaries, it certainly hits home with Revels, the businessman. He knows how much the system cost gifted black athletes financially, and he's not afraid to say so.

"It's kind of a shame for a guy like Bob Love to have been that good and not get the recognition he deserved. He's got a lot to be proud of, but he missed the boat on the financial end of it. He was ahead of his time, you might say."

The Office of the Mayor of Bastrop is modern. The furniture is new, the carpet is plush and the mayor's desk is smaller than a battleship, but larger than a small bass boat. Behind the desk sits a tall, slender, handsome black man, whose dark skin provides a sharp contrast to his starched white dress shirt. He is sporting a bow tie which he obviously has knotted himself.

Clarence Hawkins entered Bastrop history in 1989, when he was elected as the city's first African American chief executive. When he was first elected mayor, Bastrop had more white voters than black, though admittedly it was a slight majority. Hawkins speaks candidly about his city's race relations.

"We have our racism," Hawkins admits immediately. "Our racism exists because there are people of both races who grew up and developed and were indoctrinated by old philosophies, be they black philosophies or white. We still have some people who want to hang on to an old mentality. But on the whole, the way this country is suffering and the way that small rural towns suffer, folks are beginning to make the realization that we're all in the same bag. And the competition's not between blacks and whites in the south, we're competing internationally. We're competing on a global scale. And none of us will do well until all of us do well.

"We're beginning to realize that it's an interwoven relationship. There are folks who have businesses that need labor and customers and there are customers who need the services provided by providers. Finally, we're getting to that point where it's not the color of a person's skin, but what he or she can do, whether he or she can contribute. Overall, I would say, there's a basic acceptance."

In his first campaign for mayor, Hawkins was the only black candidate in a primary election field of five: Hawkins, a white female and three white males. Under Louisiana law, a general election is not necessary if a primary election candidate wins a simple majority of votes cast among all candidates.

"In that primary, I got 1,840-some odd votes. The closest other candidate received 1,000. There were about 4,000 total votes cast, so I needed about 2,000 plus one to win it outright. So because I fell a little short, there was a runoff between me and a white female.

"Some people said, `Boy, we've got a heckuva choice.' You see, politics in this part of the south has been predominantly white male. So basically, the statement was made among some white people that they didn't have a choice. A lot of white people decided to sit the election out because they felt they didn't have a choice, a familiar choice."

Hawkins is not a native of Bastrop. The son of a Methodist minister, Hawkins was born and raised in Meridian, Mississippi. He says his father instilled in him a philosophy of respect for everyone, be they the community pillars or the homeless and hopeless.

"My campaign was designed and focused: First, I had to convince black people that it was possible to elect a black mayor. They didn't have an image; there wasn't a precedent. This position that I hold — and not because I'm great — but it is the highest elected position that a black holds in this parish. But in the election of '89, some whites were saying, `It's not time yet. Bastrop's not ready for a black mayor yet.'

"And blacks started believing that. I heard some say, `They're not going to let a black man be mayor. They're just not going to let him.'

"So I asked them how a mayor is chosen. How's a mayor chosen? Well, he has to get votes. Well, if you vote for me and I get enough folks who believe in me, to vote for me, then I can be mayor. That's the way the system goes. It's not as if there's some big brother out there. Elections aren't rigged like they supposedly used to be, by stuffing ballot boxes."

A large portion of Hawkins' first electoral base lay with his former students at Morehouse High and later at Bastrop High School, and their parents. When he first arrived in Morehouse Parish in 1965, he was a classroom teacher at Morehouse. This was four years before the courts ordered the public school system to integrate.

"One thing that Bastrop and Morehouse Parish have been sensitive to, is there has never been marching in the streets. There's a pride that exists here. We've never had demonstrations where people march up and down the streets. It hasn't happened.

"Integration of the schools happened smoothly from the perspective that there was no mass boycott on the part of whites. Sure, there were private schools set up. But there was no mass exodus from the public school system.

"We had fights. I'm not going to say we didn't. I was assistant principal at Bastrop High School from 1971 until 1979. So I was assistant principal during those critical years of adjustment. And it was an adjustment not just for the kids, but for faculty members who were there, for parents. For everybody. We were still trying to get accustomed to each other.

"I well remember the time. Black kids didn't want to stand for the National Anthem at football games and basketball games, and they didn't want to say the Pledge of Allegiance in the morning. I had an interesting situation involving a young man who, as a matter of fact, is a minister now.

"He was one of the best French horn players we had in our band, a black kid who played French horn. He wanted to really be militant about things, and he didn't like his home room teacher. So anything he could do to create controversy, he did it. One morning, when they were supposed to stand to pledge allegiance to the flag, he decided he wasn't going to do it. He just sat there. His teacher, who was of the old school ... she was really stern. And she wasn't really a fan of integration. She brings this kid down to the office and says, `He won't stand for the Pledge of Allegiance.'

"So I got him and I said, `Hey, what's going on?'

"He says, `I ain't gonna pledge no allegiance. This country's been unfair to me and the black man and blah, blah, blah. This is not my country, so I'm not going to pledge no allegiance to any flag that supports racism.'

"I said, `Really? Well, tell me this: On Friday night, when the band marches on the field for the football game and plays the National Anthem, are you going to play it?'

"`Yeah, I play it.'

"`But the National Anthem is the song of the country. You know, the USA song: Oh, say can you see?'

"`That's different.'

"`How so?'

"`Well, see, I'm in the band. And that's music.'

"`It's the tune to our country.'

"He started to realize that he didn't have a valid argument and that he was being hypocritical about the whole thing. So I said, `If you're going to be hypocritical about it, then you're going to have to get out of the band. You need to tell Mister Strickland. I need to call Strick and tell him that you can't be in the band anymore.'

"Well, he loved the band. That was the reason for his being. That horn was his life.

"`No, no, no! Don't do that!'

"`Well, if you're going to play the country's song, then it also makes sense for you to not be discriminatory and not say the Pledge.

You know, this country's been good to you. In spite of all the stuff that has happened, we still have more freedom than anyone, anywhere else. You can't go to another country where you're even allowed not to stand up for the Pledge of Allegiance, much less come down here and tell me you're not going to stand for the Pledge of Allegiance.'

"Well, needless to say, I won that debate. He stayed in the band and he played the National Anthem. And he stood for the Pledge of Allegiance."

You see, there's a little bit of Howard Cunningham in all of us.

So Clarence Hawkins, who needed to squeeze every black vote out of every black precinct to stand a chance, also relied on a stable of former students — white as well as black — to put him over the top in his first general election for mayor of Bastrop.

"So when I ran for the first time in 1989, I had a lot of my former students out there, saying, `Yeah, he was assistant principal when I was going to school. And he was always fair to me.'

"I know I got white votes. There's no doubt about it. Even though I carried black precincts and got the majority of black votes — probably 80, 90 percent of the black vote — had I not gotten the white votes, I couldn't have won. And a lot of the white votes I got came from precincts in Bastrop where there were upper middle-class people. And that gave me enough to defeat the other candidate."

Hawkins estimates that while United States Census Bureau figures indicate a 53 to 47 percent black-to-white ratio for the 1989 election, there were 200 more whites registered to vote.

"If it had gone strictly down racial lines, I'm a loser. But I won by 265 votes out of 5,000 cast."

In retrospect, Hawkins is grateful that he didn't receive a majority of the vote in the '89 primary election. While such a feat would have meant his election and spared him the general campaign, it also would have eliminated a crucible he believes he was able to survive. To earn the respect of the entire community — particularly the white community — and to avoid second-guessing among old-line segregationists, Hawkins needed to win his election head-to-head, black against white.

"If I had won the whole thing in the primary, I would have been the candidate elected by black votes. In the primary, I didn't get a lot of white votes, because white people really weren't sure yet. They had to be convinced. And a lot of people didn't want to waste their votes because they weren't sure I had a chance.

"I'm glad I wasn't elected only by black people, because then I would have been looked upon as the black mayor. By my getting enough white votes to get me over the top, I became just the mayor, the Mayor of Bastrop. The mayor of all the people, not just the blacks. So I'm glad I wasn't elected solely by black folks."

Four years later, after his first term as mayor, Clarence Hawkins faced re-election. This time, just one candidate stepped forward to challenge this one-term executive. That's what was needed, right? Solidarity. No splintering the vote, no risk in letting the black mayor win a primary outright and avoid another bitter general election campaign. Well, that may have been a campaign tactic for mayor of Chicago or Boston or New York or Los Angeles. But not in Bastrop, Louisiana.

In the spring of 1993, just one candidate challenged Clarence Hawkins. And he was black. And Hawkins got 95 percent of the vote.

"That was a fantastic vote of confidence and acceptance," beams an otherwise stoic mayor. "I really, really feel humbled by it. It's an indication to me that the people accept what we've been doing, and that they think we're going in the right direction."

Hawkins uses the word "we" instead of "I". Like he said, we're all in the same bag together.

So Bastrop moves ahead. Like the rest of the south, it is growing out of its integration birth pains, trying to leave behind the days of separate drinking fountains, separate lunch counters, separate school systems. Bob Love's old buddy, James Clay, sits at a corner table in a restaurant at the Bastrop Inn. The afternoon sun paints him into a silhouette against the traffic zipping east and west along Madison Street. He lifts his Dodgers cap with his left hand and rubs his forehead with his palm.

"I don't know," waxes Clay. "I'll tell you, I've been in the education field for 24 years and I think we've lost some of our black kids due to integration. In fact, I know we've lost some. Some of them have seen — how can I say this — some of them have seen the other side, the white people in action. And sometimes it rubs off on them that things are going to be the same for them as it's been for those white kids. I try to tell them it ain't gonna be that way.

"Most white kids, their families have something to leave them, you know what I mean? A lot of them have businesses and things to leave them. But these black kids, they don't have anything. You've got to be able to put something down on paper. In order to get a job, you've got to be able to put something down on paper. You've got to be able to fill out an application.

"So, in that regard, it hasn't been good for us. Or maybe it's just a sign of the times. I don't know ..."

James Clay's voice trails away. He's not sad. But he doesn't appear entirely satisfied, either.

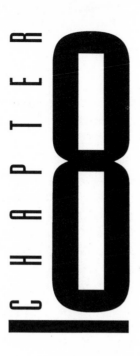

CHAPTER 8

WASH ■ William and Dorothy Washington live in a neat-as-a-pin brick ranch at 506 Haynes Avenue in Bastrop. On their side of the street, the lawns are well-manicured, the boxwoods and holly shrubs trimmed to perfection. It is almost as if the Washingtons represent a rose among the thorns. Across the street, in various stages of decay, sit vacant shotgun houses, their windows boarded up, their foundations giving way to the weight of too many years of neglect and poverty. On the other side of the street, it may as well have been the other side of the planet. Waist-high weeds give way to pristine, delicately landscaped front yards. The shotgun house — the style of home that served as a roof over Bob Love's childhood — is a remnant of southern black poverty from the segregated era. Some shotgun homes in the area, to this day, still do not have indoor plumbing. Just two blocks from William and Dorothy Washington's immaculate residence, dilapidated shotgun houses still provide shelter for impoverished families on Bastrop's west side, the largest pocket of African American families in the town.

William and Dorothy Washington came to Bastrop in 1950, two full decades before the separate and unequal school systems became one, 20 years before black kids got a taste of the perquisites of public education in an integrated society. A grandson of a sharecropper, William Washington was born in 1927 in Vidalia in Concordia Parish. All seven children born to the sharecropper patriarch of the Washington family were college graduates, quite an accomplishment considering that, just six decades earlier, it was illegal in these parts for a white person to teach a black person how to read or write. So the importance of an education was never lost on William Washington.

In the Washington household, putting pen to paper was every bit as consequential for the mind and the soul as putting a spoon to mouth was nourishing for the body.

"Our home place at Vidalia is sitting on an acre of land," Washington says. "In 1918, when the war started, they were building a school for blacks in Concordia Parish. They stopped building the school because of the war, so my grandfather bought that. That's our home place. He had seven kids and all seven kids were college graduates. He sent every one of them away to get an education. So," Washington chuckles, "if I hadn't gotten one, I guess I'd have been killed."

Dorothy Washington laughs at the recollection of the first Washington family reunion she attended.

"In William's family, they had lawyers, doctors, everybody but a preacher. There were seven kids and each one of them had kids, and we didn't have a preacher. Heck, I don't even think they had a deacon!"

But one of what they did have — in William Washington — was an educator. "Wash," as he is affectionately known around Bastrop, for four decades was the role model for young black men in Morehouse Parish. During the 1950s and the early 1960s, there was virtually no athletic event involving young black men that did not carry Coach Wash's imprimatur. By all accounts, perhaps even his own, although modesty does not permit Wash to talk about himself, William Washington is the man who is responsible for the athletic and academic successes of Robert Earl Love.

Dick Revels, the white bank president, counts Washington among his best friends: "Wash. What a fine guy. I still call him 'Coach.' Both of them — both Coach and Dorothy — are just as fine a people as can be."

Revels stops for a moment and calls to a secretary just outside his office at the Bastrop National Bank.

"Do we have any canceled checks from William and Dorothy Washington? You have to see this. This woman has the finest hand-writing of any person I have ever met." Revels is informed that no checks are available, but that Dorothy Washington's signature is on a check cashing card. And Revels indeed is correct. Dorothy Washington's handwriting is as impeccable as the lawn surrounding her home, as tidy as the holly bushes in her yard. It is more calligraphy than it is cursive.

Throughout nearly his first two decades in Bastrop, Wash was a black man who was a black teacher who taught black kids in a black school and a black coach who coached black athletes when they played against other black athletes before nearly unanimously black crowds. But he worked for a school board which was comprised of whites. And they set policy and salaries for white employees as well as black.

"It's in the official minutes of the school board meetings that all white principals would be paid for twelve months, black ones nine. When they decided to put me on a twelve-month scale — their own pay scale — they paid me $9,999.99 for the year. They made sure I didn't get to the $10,000 level. It's there in black and white."

Wash chuckles. He shares no animosity. Frankly, he appears to harbor none, either.

"But I stayed here 40 years, and all 40 weren't as bad as that. I stayed here because I thought I could be of some service."

By 1964, William Washington was working as the principal at Morehouse High School. And by 1969, when the Parish of Morehouse faced the crisis of integrating its school system, O.L. Harper knew exactly who his man was, precisely the fellow who could ride herd over the situation. He never hesitated in naming William Washington, black man and grandson of a sharecropper, to serve as principal of the new, integrated-but-not-yet-proven-as-improved, Bastrop Junior High School.

"Harper didn't take any wooden nickels from anybody," Wash remembers. The Coach's facial expression telegraphs the notion that to this day he still admires his former boss, the white man who was elected Morehouse Parish school superintendent. "White, blue, black or green. A man's color didn't matter with Harper. He was color blind to that sort of thing. And he backed me all the way.

"Oh, yeah, indeed we had problems in 1969. Oh, yes indeed. There were parents who'd come to my office and threaten me. They'd threaten to take me across the bayou and beat me ... almost anything bad that you could imagine. Oh, yes indeed."

Here Dorothy interrupts: "It got so bad that the police had to come out and put a light on that post," pointing to the front of her house, "and one on the other post over there," waving behind her and into the backyard. "It was so bright around here it was like daylight."

Wash picks it up from there.

"I had good support from the police department, and Mister Harper was probably instrumental in that. At one point, a bunch of them wanted to picket in front of the school. And I called (Harper) — and it was hot out there. I guess it must have been about 100 degrees out there on that concrete.

"And I said, `Let them picket. But promise me that you can make them stay so many paces apart. When one of them turns around, then everyone turns around.'"

Whether William Washington knew it or not, he was taking every available precaution to avoid a repeat of Andrew McLeod's demise some 35 years earlier.

"I was hoping that the heat would wear them down, wear down their resolve. Man, it was hot out there. The whole thing lasted just about 30 minutes. Mammas and daddies started dropping their signs and headed for home, taking their kids, too."

That year, some of the tension spilled from the outside in, from the concrete and the blacktopped sidewalks and streets into the hallways and the classrooms. Wash played it like a symphony, but he played it by ear. He played it like a quarterback whose blocking has broken down and who has been forced to scramble out of the pocket. He played it by the seat of his pants. And he never got his uniform dirty, at least not on this play.

"Now, one day we had some racial problems in the school itself. And as I recall, it involved about nine black ones, about nine white ones. So I went and got all of those jokers together in one room. I took the time to talk with some of them ahead of time and found out who the ringleaders were.

"And I got those ringleaders — the black one and the white one — and I told them that the only people who could save us over there, on that campus, were the two of them. We were either going to work together to save ourselves, or we were going to work together to destroy ourselves.

"I told Harper we were going to put them all — the whole student body — in the auditorium, all of them together. And to tell you the truth, old Harper thought I was crazy. And I told him that — and this is true, too — I told him that I didn't have the slightest idea what I was going to tell them.

"He said — and I still remember what he said — `Goddammit. If you mess up, I'm going to fire you!'

"And I said, `If I mess up, you'll have grounds to fire me!'" And Wash begins to shake with laughter.

"So I told the kids — the whole auditorium — that these two boys would be in charge of this assembly. And those kids started talkin' in there, and they told the rest of them that everything I was doing, I was doing to help them, the students. They said that they needed to come together, as a student body, and support me. And they called me by name.

"And from that day until the day I retired, I didn't have any more problems with this kind of thing."

Actually, Wash had just one more problem. And the problem landed right in his family room, right there inside the walls that provided security and sanity for his family. And Wash had to deal with this problem directly. O.L. Harper defines the "instant of integration" of the Morehouse Parish schools as the time the five black cheerleaders took the field with the five white cheerleaders at the football jamboree in the Summer of '69. One of those five black girls — a chocolate drop among marshmallows — was Patricia Washington, William's and Dorothy's older daughter. And Patricia was there not because she wanted to be there. She was a cheerleader because O.L. Harper believed it was critical to send the community a message, a missive that said the hierarchy within the newly-integrated school system was united, that the administration was prepared to do whatever was necessary to smooth the transition. The Washington family, determined O.L. Harper, would serve as a role model for the community. It's one thing for a coach to take up the mantle of being a role model for a young man. It's quite another to place that mantle on the shoulders of a young girl, to force a family member to serve as an extension of his appointive mission.

There was pain. Recalls Dorothy:

"One of the things that really got to us, even though William was principal, is that Mister Harper insisted that our older daughter be a cheerleader. I hated it. She hated it, because it was her senior year in high school. We fought it as long as we could, but at the time there were only two other black girls who were the first to come out for the unit. And at the end of the first six weeks, only our daughter was left. She wasn't just the only black cheerleader in Bastrop, *she was the only black cheerleader in northeast Louisiana.*

"Let me tell you, Mamma and her daughter cried many nights, begging Daddy not to make her go. But he said, 'You gotta go. We've got no choice in the matter.' And I'll have to say this about William: Wherever the kids went — I don't mean just our kids, I'm talkin' about all the kids at school — he was there before they left and he was there when they got back. So we knew that he wasn't asking his daughter to do something that he wouldn't have done himself. He was never like that. He would never ask someone to do something that he wouldn't go out and do himself.

"I used to get so angry because he thought that he was supposed to beat everybody to school every morning. If they got there at seven, he got there at quarter of seven. And he stayed there in that building until everybody was gone home of a night."

Though he was not an athlete and never played for Coach Washington, the importance of Wash as a role model was not lost on South Side Elementary School principal Melvin Anderson:

"Most of the kids at that time — Coach Washington gave them a father figure. Through athletics, he found a way to keep them in school."

And James Clay, Love's Morehouse High School gridiron mate who now teaches physical science at Bastrop High, counts himself among the legions of adults who owe William Washington their career paths and so many of their successes:

"Education was about the only thing that was open to black people back then, back when we were growing up. I was going to go into the Air Force until I got a scholarship offer from Arkansas AM & N (Agriculture, Mechanical and Normal). So in college I lettered in football for three years, graduated on time, got my degree in physical education. But the reason I did all that is because I wanted to be like Coach Washington. All of us did. He was our role model.

"All I had was a father. My mother died when I was passing into the sixth grade. I went to live with my daddy's sister for about two years, and then I came back and stayed with him. My daddy got up every morning and went to work. I had every opportunity to skip school, to play hooky. But everything I had, everything I wanted, was at school. I loved my teachers. I didn't want to be up at the pool hall, although Lord knows I had every opportunity. I wanted to be at school. And I loved my dad. But the man we imitated, who we talked like and walked like — Coach Washington."

Like just about everything else in segregated Bastrop in the 1950s, the black community came by their successes and their achievements the hardscrabble way. William Washington had his work cut out for him and more when he took over the athletic program at Morehouse High School in 1950.

"Well, we had to make everything that we wanted," Wash remembers 43 years later. "When I say `make,' for instance, I mean that during all those years I coached, the Morehouse school board never paid me a penny to coach. If you look at my pay register, even today, you will see that I did not get a penny for all those years I stayed out on that field.

"We got nothing for equipment. We had to raise all of our own money. In those days, it was far from being separate but equal, as some might lead you to believe. Way, way far from being separate but equal. Other parishes may have been a little more fortunate than we were. We didn't even have buses. The kids didn't even have buses to ride to school. And, remember, this was the only high school in the parish for blacks at that time.

"So those parents in Mer Rouge, Bonita, Oak Ridge, if they wanted to see to it that their kids got a high school education, they brought their kids here on Sunday afternoon and paid for a room and board in private homes for those kids to live. Just to get a high school education. Then, a couple of years after we got here, they started running a bus from the parish line east of here and one down from Monroe and one from Collinston, down south of here."

Educators in the rural south of yesterday had obstacles the likes of which their northern brethren would never dream. Like split school sessions — not split days. Split sessions.

"That was rough," he recalls. "We had split sessions. Split session means the black kids went to school in July and August, then they'd close the school for them to go and harvest crops in September and October. So you can imagine how tough it was, how little time we had, to even try to start a football team.

"So we didn't practice in July and August. In October, the kids would come and we would practice. I happened to have two or three buddies who coached at other schools, and they would just hold a date down in October and the first part of November just to play us so we could get in some playing time, get in some games. We'd never play more than four games in a season before playoffs. That's all we could get because we couldn't get any playing time in September and October.

"It was terrible."

As terrible as it was trying to find a *way* to play football, William Washington faced even higher hurdles in finding a *place* to play football.

"We had no place to play football. They wouldn't let us use the stadium. The white school had a stadium. We had no place to play. We played down behind a night club called The Brown Eagle. And they had a big vacant lot back there. It might have been 90 yards long — *might have been*. We played back behind there.

"Then, finally, after years of beggin' and goin' on, they came and they built us a stadium. When I say they 'built' it, what they really did was they came in and they leveled the ground off. No bleachers, no lights. And to cap it off, *they ran that sucker east and west!* You didn't have lights, so you had to play in the afternoon. So now the field runs east and west, so somebody was always looking into the sun."

Wash smiles and sighs.

"But we were winning, we were getting the kids to stay in school and kids were getting diplomas. They were getting their college scholarships and becoming productive citizens."

Dorothy Washington is not afraid to punctuate her husband's interview, adding an exclamation point here, a dash there, an occasional question mark and a comma. It has not been lost on Dorothy that her husband played a critical role in the development of the James Clays, the Arthur Hamlins, the Robert Smiths and the Robert Earl Loves.

Says Dorothy of her man: "William probably won't admit it, but he was an inspiration for a lot of the fellas because he dressed well, and they all wanted to be like the coach."

Even Dick Revels saw the connection, way back when he was one of the few white folks who would bother to sneak in to watch a Morehouse High athletic team play a prep game.

"Those boys were able to see in Coach Washington what they might be able to achieve in athletics," offers Revels. "Wash is a class guy, a good dresser, the kind of guy a young kid could look up to and admire."

"I dressed well?" Wash chuckles. "Well, I don't know if I dressed well or not. But I demanded that *they* dress. And I demanded that they be gentlemen all the time. They went to class to get their lessons and there were no excuses. I expected every child, every football player, every athlete that I had, to be home every night at nine o'clock. And the night before a ball game, I expected them to be in bed by nine o'clock.

"And we called them to see if they were home, if they were in bed. If his mamma said he was asleep, I'd tell her to wake him up. Those who didn't have telephones, we'd go by their house and check. We had our own rules. The kids made the rules, and if anybody broke them, well, the kids decided what they were going to do.

"I had an assistant coach named Fitch. One day Fitch came in and said, `Scobey and Cleon were at the Bobby Blues Land last night at midnight' a couple of nights before a game. So I said to the team, `Okay, fellas, what are we going to do?'"

The initial response from the team was to make Scobey and Cleon crawl through a gauntlet of players, who administered whacks on their fannies as they passed. But, apparently, the gauntlet was deemed insufficient punishment by Lucious Jackson, who later starred in his own right in the National Basketball Association.

"That Lucious Jackson is standing back there — all six-ten of him — and Jackson says, `Leave 'em here. Let's leave 'em here.' I asked the rest of the boys what they thought and they said, `We're with Lucious.'

"I felt like crying," Wash now laughs. "I had one day to get ready to play one of the biggest high schools in Arkansas! But we left 'em. We surely did. And we won the game, believe it or not."

Perhaps it was the coach and the coach's philosophy, his insistence on discipline and respect. Perhaps it was simply a different time. But William Washington claims he never had a problem with an athlete during practice or in the classroom.

"I never had any problems with players coming to practice," Wash explains. "Everybody knew what they were doing at practice all the time. I didn't allow but one whistle on the field at a time, and they knew who was blowing that whistle. They knew the schedule of what we were going to do. If anyone was doing any loafing, then we started that particular cycle all over again. So I didn't have to get on players for loafing. They policed themselves. And I gotta tell you, that's as good preparation for life as there is.

"If you've got your backs and ends over here running pass patterns," he says, pointing to a corner of his family room, "and guards and tackles over there trap blocking," and he points toward the kitchen, "those backs and ends aren't going to put up with loafing by the guards because the backs and ends are running their patterns, doing their work. So they policed themselves, for the most part."

Football practice — any kind of athletic or aerobic workout, for that matter — burns a load of energy in the furnace of a growing teenage machine. Athletes, more so than sedentary folks, need to replenish fuel in a proportionately larger measure. You burn calories, you must replace calories. The muscles need fuel. Strenuous physical activity demands vitamins, it demands proteins, it demands fluids and it demands complex carbohydrates. Sadly, the sort of physical engine that drives a young athlete demands the high octane fuel that a poor family simply cannot provide at their pump.

Ella Hunter did the best she could with the little she had. But when a baker's dozen kids are fighting for food at the breakfast, lunch and dinner tables — that's 39 plates to fill plus your own — well, you can't draw blood from a stone. While the Hunter clan plus Bob was fighting for nourishment, growing it in the yard, buying it on the cheap at JD's Grocery Store, the Washington clan was harboring one of the best-kept secrets in Morehouse Parish.

"I didn't even know this until the last couple of years," Arthur Hamlin confessed recently, "but Mister Washington would take Love home after practice and feed him dinner. I didn't even know that until recently."

Probably because Wash does a particularly lousy job of marketing himself as a role model, provider and a downright good and decent guy.

"Yeah, we did," Wash now concedes. "We did feed him a bit. Well, when I say we did, you see, Love kept complaining of being sick back when he was in high school. And we carried him to every doctor that anybody would recommend to us. After about two or three doctors, they said the boy was just growing so much and that he wasn't getting enough to eat. So we decided — Dorothy and I decided — that we would take him for a week or so at a time for his breakfast and his dinner. And then we paid for his lunch in the school cafeteria."

When Wash and Dorothy discovered it was a hardship for Love to get to and from their home for Dorothy's home-cooked meals, they took the nutrition program to another level.

"When we found out that we were putting a burden on Love getting here — his family didn't have a car so he had a hard time getting here — instead of doing that, we got him set up at a cafe up there on Madison Street. He had the choice to either come here or he could go up there and have his breakfast. And then, after football practice, he could go up there and have his dinner. And we would pay for it. Of course, any time he wanted a meal, even today, he knows he can come here and get it. In fact, some of his clothes are still here."

True enough, in 1992, Bob Love was inducted into the Louisiana sports hall of fame. And who else but Dorothy and Wash were there to break out a spread of food for his belly and a pillow for his head.

"Saturdays and Sundays, if he wanted it, he'd just come here for his meals," the Coach remembers. "His grandmother was still alive, but they were just poor people. They didn't have anything, that's just all there was to it.

"I can remember going down to his place once or twice. The kid might have had a cold or something. Anyway, I went down there and it was embarrassing to him. So I tried to let him know as best I could that when he needed me, I'd be there. I knew his grandmother. She was a real nice person, real compassionate, very religious. She did everything she could for Bob. But they just didn't have much to spread around.

"When he went to Southern, he majored in foods and nutrition. I said, `Love, why did you choose foods and nutrition?' And he was stuttering really bad then. He looked at me and it must have taken him 15 minutes to say that he had been hungry all of his life and he saw those girls coming out of that home economics building, and they all looked like they were full, like they had enough to eat. That's when he said," and now Wash is cracking up with laughter, "`I knew this place was for me.'"

So in addition to their own children, the ones everyone needs to care for within the confines of their own home, the Washingtons took on yet another. He was a young man whose body was exploding with growth, the kind of kid whose parents can never afford — shoes, trousers, shirts, underwear. By the time they're through the rinse cycle of the washing machine, they've already been outgrown.

"I remember one summer, Love went to an aunt's house, I think. We were out of school, I remember that much. And when he came back, I guess that boy had grown six or seven inches. He went BOOM! That was between his sophomore and his junior year. We had given him a jacket, a football letterman's jacket, and I had to buy him another one because the first one looked like a short-sleeved shirt on him, he had grown so much over that summer."

Dorothy, interjects.

"Oh, that football jacket. I can remember him with that football jacket. He came to the gym one day and begged me. He said, `Please, Mrs. Washington, please ask Coach to buy me a jacket.' That jacket that we had given him the year before, this is where it stopped."

Dorothy chops her right hand to the crook of her left elbow.

"It was so embarrassing. But Coach finally gave him another one. See, that was the first time a kid like that ever had a jacket like that. That jacket was very important to the boy. There was a lot of respect for that jacket and what it represented in the school."

James Clay, too, remembers the summer Love's body exploded in growth:

"One summer, Love went to New Orleans to stay with one of his aunties. And he was late coming back from New Orleans. As I remember it, it was summer and we were practicing, but Love hadn't made it back yet from New Orleans. He was just a couple days or so late.

"So while we were practicing one day, I stopped for a minute and I looked up on this hill that was near where we practiced. Love was up there, standing between two trees. And that sonofagun must have grown to six-seven or six-eight. We were really glad to see him, but he must have grown six, seven inches that summer. And that was from, like May to late August. Amazing."

By his senior year at Morehouse, Love was being scouted by

Southern University at Baton Rouge. That's where Wash went to college. But Grambling State was trying to get into the mix. Eddie Robinson, who one day would surpass all other college coaches in the win column, wanted a piece of Bob Love. He knew a quality quarterback and he wanted Love's arm and raw talent. First things first, though. Wash understood that. Before college there were preparations for graduation, for special events and the like. Naturally, Coach was there when Love needed a strong and helpful hand.

"When it came time for his senior year, we got him a job out at the park in the recreation department," Coach says. "And, of course, he wanted a class ring, he wanted to buy invitations for his graduation, all the things a kid wants and should have. So we had us an agreement: He would take so much money and put it aside so that when the time came, he would be able to get some of the things that the other kids had."

And so he did. When it came to a class ring, Bob Love got one. When it came to invitations for his commencement ceremony, Bob Love bought some. When it came to a football jacket that fit him somewhere below his elbows, Bob Love got one of those, too. All of those things, Bob Love got because one man took him under his wing, into his home and into his heart.

Bob Love got a lot out of William Washington. But rings and jackets and paper just don't stack up to what Bob Love got from the wisdom and the strength that Wash laid at Bob Love's feet. For all of his athletic ability and his spiral bullets and his jump shots, Bob Love would have left Bastrop with a hole in his soul, but for William Washington.

You can't buy love. And you can't buy character. But Wash knows the intrinsic value of both of those priceless qualities. And he never hesitated to gift wrap them for the most gifted athlete ever to hear his whistle.

CHAPTER 9

SPICKY-SPICKY-SPEAN He looks just like his dad must have looked 30 years ago. He sounds like Lou Rawls, which is interesting, considering Rawls is a native of the west side of Chicago, and Robert Smith is a product of the west side of Bastrop, Louisiana, some 900 miles to the south. Robert Smith, today better known as Doctor Robert Smith, serves as chancellor of Southern University's campus in Shreveport, Louisiana. He is the shepherd over an institution of some 3,000 undergraduate students. He is articulate and he is polished, this son of E.W. and Cordie Smith. And his eyes have a twinkle about them, the sort of giveaway that warns you to watch your flank, else someone might stick a wad of chewing gum in your hair.

But Doctor Robert Smith gets a chapter in this book for one very important reason. You see, Smitty — Doctor Robert Smith — is the person responsible for creating Bob Love's trademark nickname. More importantly, he's a good guy, but Robert Smith is the fellow who coined a name that would stick with Robert Earl Love throughout the rest of his life.

"He was a con man, but a con man in the best sense of the word," says Smitty's former football coach, William Washington. "He was very, very likeable. Here's a man who can do almost anything that he's given the task to do. When he was here, he kept everybody in good spirits. Somebody would be down, he'd pat him on the head and say, 'Come on, brother, we can do it.'

"I guess back in that day we called them spiritual leaders. So I guess if we had a spiritual leader back then, he was it. He kept Love pumped up all of the time. Even after they got down to Southern. During the basketball games, he'd get under the basket where Southern was shooting and they would, well, they had signals they'd give each other — on the kneecaps. He's just the kind of guy that everyone likes — easy to get along with."

Arthur Hamlin, who played wide receiver to Love's quarterback, chuckles when asked about Robert Smith.

"Smitty gave everybody a nickname," he remembers as he checks off the roster of his football teammates. "You know James Clay. Well, one day James washed his practice uniform, and it was white. But he must have had something red in the wash. And whatever it was, it turned his practice uniform pink. Ouch! So Robert Smith started calling James Clay 'The Pink Elephant.'

"I guess he named me 'Ham,' which is pretty tame compared to The Pink Elephant."

In a restaurant in Baton Rouge, Doctor Robert Smith is brimming with giggles as he shares a late night dinner with his boyhood pal, Bob Love.

"I'm probably credited with a lot of eccentric things," smiles Chancellor Smith, who tells you he's far more comfortable if you call him "Smitty." "And I'm probably the kingfish of nicknames. We used to travel as a football team to our games and most of the games were pretty far off, and I was pretty locquacious. I was always into jokes. I'd joke about how Love enjoyed butterbeans and that his eyes were pretty large, too. I was getting off one of those rhythmic jokes that rhymed."

Love, who is seated across the table from his boyhood buddy, is cackling at the reminiscence.

"Smitty was always the team clown," Love remembers. "He was the guy who was always talking, always telling you jokes. This was the guy who kept everybody laughing all the time. And Smitty was the guy who gave everybody their nicknames. Everything was spicky- spicky this, spicky- spicky that. Hey, man, spicky- spicky spize, look at Love's two big eyes."

"That's right," Smitty confirms. "I said one day, `Spicky-spicky-speans, old Love's got eyes like butterbeans.' At this point — and I can still remember this to this day — the bus is moving and everybody on the team just cracked up. Our coach would never laugh at anything, but even Coach Washington cracked up laughing, too."

Says Love, giggling, "Yeah, with me liking butterbeans, all of a sudden everybody started calling me `Butterbean Eyes' and `Butterbean Love' and anything else with a butterbean in it."

"And the thing is, it never left him," says Smith. "It stuck with him from high school. As I remember, the `Butterbean' thing got lost in the shuffle for a while when we were Southern, except for the home boys and girls. Then, when he went out for the Olympic team in 1964, that's when I started to hear the `Butterbean' thing outside of Bastrop circles. I can remember reading a sports magazine, when he was playing for Cincinnati, about him and a big bowl of brown beans." Smitty is chuckling at the recollection: "And I said, `There it is. They got his name back again.'"

Love's first roommate in the professional ranks, Hall of Famer Oscar Robertson, knew a good thing when he heard it.

"Yeah, you know, Oscar Robertson, he was kind of like my mentor back then," Love explains. "And he liked the name `Butterbean.' He liked it a lot. I guess that's one reason the name stuck with me once I made it in the pros. It never hurts to have someone like Oscar Robertson out there, pushing your name."

Nor does it ever hurt to have a loyal buddy like Robert Smith. Loyal buddies are hard to come by and they can help you survive when times are tough. Like when it dawns on you, that even though you might be an athletic prodigy, for some reason, glory is just a whisper.

		Form K-102 50M 5-34-21			

MEMBERSHIP AND DUES RECORD

Name .. *Higginbotham, Willie* ....

Res. Adr's ..... *Mer Rouge* ....

Bus. " ....

Occupation .... *Farmer* ....

Mail to .*Res.*. Address. Phone ....

Klan No.	Invisible Empire, Knights of the Ku Klux Klan	Realm of .... Located at .... State	Transferred from Klan No...... Realm of ....19.....	19....	19....	
				JAN.	JAN.	1st Qr.
				FEB.	FEB.	
			Naturalized ....19.....	MCH.	MCH.	
				APR.	APR.	
			Age ....Yrs.	MAY	MAY	2nd Qr.
				JUNE	JUNE	
			Color Hair	JULY	JULY	3rd Qr.
			Eyes	AUG.	AUG.	
			Height ..ft. ....in.	SEPT.	SEPT.	
			Weight ....lbs.	OCT.	OCT.	4th Qr.
			Single Married Widower	NOV.	NOV.	
				DEC.	DEC.	

Suspended	Exiled	Banished	Transferred	Died
19	19	19	19	19 ....

NOTE: Write ALL REMARKS on other side.

		Form K-102 50M 5-34-21			

MEMBERSHIP AND DUES RECORD

Name *Carpenter, J.F.* ....

Res. Adr's .... *Bastrop, La.* ....

Bus. " *Sheriff* ....

Occupation ....

Mail to *-----*.Address. Phone ....

Klan No. 34	Invisible Empire, Knights of the Ku Klux Klan	Morehouse Realm of ...... Located at .. *Bastrop* State *La.*	Transferred from Klan No...... Realm of ....19.....	19....	19....	
				JAN.	JAN.	1st Qr.
				FEB.	FEB.	
			Naturalized ....19.....	MCH.	MCH.	
				APR.	APR.	
			Age ....Yrs.	MAY	MAY	2nd Qr.
				JUNE	JUNE	
			Color Hair	JULY	JULY	3rd Qr.
			Eyes	AUG.	AUG.	
			Height ..ft. ....in.	SEPT.	SEPT.	
			Weight ....lbs.	OCT.	OCT.	4th Qr.
			Single Married Widower	NOV.	NOV.	
				DEC.	DEC.	

Suspended	Exiled	Banished	Transferred	Died
19	19	19	19	19 ....

NOTE: Write ALL REMARKS on other side.

Above, left and right—These are copies of receipts for membership dues recorded for the Knights of the Ku Klux Klan, Chapter 34, in Morehouse Parish. At left is a receipt for Willie Higginbotham, who owned a farm in Mer Rouge. Years later, Bob Love may have picked cotton on the same farm. At right is a receipt for J.F. Carpenter, sheriff of Morehouse Parish when Andrew McLeod was lynched by an angry mob.

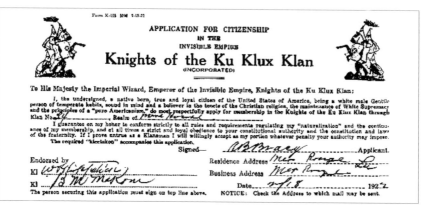

Form K-115 50M 7-15-21

APPLICATION FOR CITIZENSHIP IN THE INVISIBLE EMPIRE

Knights of the Ku Klux Klan
(INCORPORATED)

To His Majesty the Imperial Wizard, Emperor of the Invisible Empire, Knights of the Ku Klux Klan;

I, the undersigned, a native born, true and loyal citizen of the United States of America, being a white male Gentile person of temperate habits, sound in mind and a believer in the tenets of the Christian religion, the maintenance of White Supremacy and the principles of a "pure Americanism," do most respectfully apply for membership in the Knights of the Ku Klux Klan through Klan No. *34*, Realm of .*Morehouse*...

I guarantee on my honor to conform strictly to all rules and requirements regulating my "naturalization" and the continuance of my membership, and at all times a strict and loyal obedience to your constitutional authority and the constitution and laws of the fraternity. If I prove untrue as a Klansman I will willingly accept as my portion whatever penalty your authority may impose.

The required "klecktoken" accompanies this application.

Signed— *A.B. Macy*.................Applicant.

Residence Address *Mer Rouge, La.*

Business Address *Mer Rouge, La.*

Endorsed by

Kl *W.F. McKoin*

Kl *B.W. McKoin*

Date *7/8* 1922

The person securing this application must sign on top line above.   NOTICE: Check the Address to which mail may be sent.

Bottom—Here is a copy of an application form for membership in Chapter 34 of the Knights of the Ku Klux Klan, dated 1922. One of the men endorsing the applicant is B.M. McKoin, a Mer Rouge physician at the time.

Left—During his career as an All-America forward at Southern University in Baton Rouge, Bob Love scored a school record 2,323 points. His college coach, Dick Mack, contends the total would have been much higher had the three-point field goal existed when Love played for the Jaguars.

Below—Drafted in the fourth round by the Cincinnati Royals, Bob Love was the thirteenth player on a twelve-man roster his rookie year out of Southern. He was the last player cut before the NBA season began and was sent to Trenton of the Eastern League for a year of seasoning.

Opposite page—As a Trenton Colonial, Bob Love put points on the board and spectators in the seats for a franchise that was near death. His coach at Trenton, Chick Craig, said Love was one of the most talented players ever to play in the EBL. As expected, the Colonial Love affair lasted just one season before Love was back in Cincinnati.

Above—With the Chicago Bulls, Love was voted to the NBA All-Star team three times, primarily for his scoring prowess. However, his coaches at every level of play noted that his defense was well above average. Here he slaps away a shot against Philadelphia.

Opposite page—Until Michael Jordan eclipsed his mark, Bob Love was the Bulls' career leading scorer and led the team in that category seven straight seasons. He was noted for his flat, low-arched jump shot which at least one college coach tried to fix to no avail. Here, Butterbean sets for two against the Knicks.

Above—Today, Butterbean serves as the formal goodwill ambassador for his old team, the Chicago Bulls. As the team's director of community relations, Love concentrates on motivating school kids and alerting them to the dangers of drugs and gangs.

Above—Two of the major influences in Bob Love's life were on hand January 14, 1994 when the Chicago Bulls retired his uniform number 10. Here, Love readies an embrace for William Washington, his high school coach. Between Love and Washington is Dick Mack, his coach at Southern University. *(Photo: Fred G. Lebed/The Prairie Group)*

Left—Former Bull's star Jerry Sloan embraces Bob Love as former Bulls' coach Johnny "Red" Kerr looks on. Sloan's and Love's uniform numbers are the only two ever retired by the Chicago franchise. Sloan was on hand the night the Bulls honored Love. *(Photo: Patricia MacHarg/Butterbean Productions Ltd.)*

Bob Love gazes toward the rafters of the Chicago Stadium as his retired uniform number 10 is displayed for the first time during ceremonies in his honor. The retirement of his Bulls' jersey was a climax to his All-Star NBA career. *(Photo: Fred G. Lebed / Little Eddies)*

CHAPTER 10

THE SINGING QUARTERBACK

The tulip and crocus bloom in the spring. Sometimes their spiked green leaves, which give way to colored plumage of reds and whites and yellows and purples, poke their noses through a late spring dusting of snow, letting the world know that winter's raw edge is again giving way to rebirth and regeneration, to sweetness and light. The marigold, the hardy mum and the zinnia are more partial to the warmth of late summer and the nip of early fall. Their luscious red, chocolate brown and soft amber colors flow across the landscape like an autumn quilt, as they remind the world that the cycle is continuing, that rebirth and warmth and regeneration will give way to death and chill and hibernation. That is the way of this earth. The seasons have their own features, their own superstars.

Michael Jordan, perhaps the greatest player in National Basketball Association history, was once cut from his high school basketball team. If the tulip and the crocus, the marigold and the zinnia, if they are superstars among their respective kingdom, then Michael Jordan was a super nova in the kingdom of professional basketball. Yet, obviously, Michael Jordan was not a crocus; he was not a tulip. Before his flower blossomed, the spring had to give way to summer. Michael Jordan was a marigold, and Everett McKinley Dirksen would have absolutely loved him.

Bob Love, like his friend Mister Jordan, was a marigold. Perhaps because of his size as a child, perhaps because of his lack of access to quality nutrition, perhaps because he was denied the equipment and the guidance that he most certainly would have received had Bob Love been a young white man, he bloomed a little late in the season of life.

"I don't know," Robert Smith ventures, "if Bob ever told you about how he became a varsity basketball player in high school. Outside the varsity basketball team, our school had a very profound intramural league. And as it turned out, we had several very good basketball players playing in the intramural program. Obviously, the varsity players weren't allowed to participate in the intramural games. Love and I ended up playing on opposing teams in intramurals. I was a junior and 'Bean was a sophomore. My team won the championship, but Love and I were the stars of the intramural league.

"After the intramural season was over, the coach asked Love and me to join the varsity team. The varsity team only had maybe five or six more games left in the season. So when the season was over, well, I wasn't a basketball player. I didn't want to be a basketball player. In fact, I didn't even go out for the team my senior year. But Love, they brought him back. Even so, when you think about it, here's a guy who played all those quality years in pro basketball, but he didn't really even start playing basketball until his junior year in high school."

That is, he didn't play basketball with a real ball until then.

No, Love's athletic reputation was not crafted with a round leather ball, it was built around an oblong one constructed of a hog's backside.

"When I was a kid," Love says as he transports himself back to

Ella Hunter's yard behind her shotgun house, "I could imagine myself as Johnny Unitas. We had an old Chinaberry tree in my grandmother's yard. I would tie a rope to a tire, and I would spin that tire as hard and as fast as I could. I had an old rubber football and I got so good that I could throw that football through that tire, even while it was spinning. That tire would spin, and I could throw that sucker through there and it wouldn't touch nothin'."

William Washington, the Bastrop coaching icon, was Love's gridiron drill sergeant, as well as his role model. Washington says it didn't take him long to understand that what he had in Bob Love, his Morehouse High School quarterback, was his own, young, black Johnny Unitas.

"Love was an exceptional football player," remembers Wash. "He knew the game. He knew everybody's assignment, what they were supposed to do on a given play. And he had a good arm. He had an exceptional arm. That boy could throw. I mean, he could lay it in there, with a good touch and everything. He was an excellent football player.

"Now, he didn't have any football speed, so we didn't expect him to do something he wasn't capable of doing. So, basically, he didn't run the ball. And the kids took pride in not letting him get his uniform dirty.

"We ran a passing offense — a drop-back offense, because he just didn't have any speed to get outside. And I didn't want him trying to get outside anyway." The Coach laughs. "I wanted to keep him as healthy as possible."

James Clay — never mind what Smitty called him — was one of the work horses whose job it was to protect his thoroughbred quarterback, to keep Butterbean's arm sound and his butt clean.

"We didn't want anything to happen to Bob," says Clay. "We used to pride ourselves as a team. Bob used to come out on the field, in a muddy game, with his uniform clean. And when he walked off that muddy field at the end of the game, he walked off the field with his uniform clean. We took pride in that. And we took care of him because of his speech problem. We did it in a way that, well, even our opponents had respect for him."

One must wonder, however, how a quarterback can call a play in the huddle, and bark a signal at the line, when his speech is riddled by a stutter.

"You know," says Butterbean sincerely, "I never got called for too much time in the huddle. You see, when I got on the football field, I was in my own world. My cousin played center. His name is Claude Lee. There might have been a couple of times during a game when I would get in the huddle and I would try to get the number out. Basically, our plays were numbers, like split-26 or swinging-30. So you didn't really have to call out a lot of complicated formations. But sometimes I would get hung up a little and my cousin, Claude Lee, would hit me in the head and say, `Spit it out, Robert Earl, spit it out.'"

At least Claude Lee didn't have a dirty wash rag in his hand.

"So they'd hit me on the helmet or hit me on the back, and all the guys would crack up. We'd get to the line of scrimmage and I'd say, `Hut one, hut two,' and we'd get the play off, somehow."

Wash had heard said his star QB had a truly fine singing voice, that he could sing without stuttering, without losing his concentration. Mel Tillis in shoulder pads was headed for the National Football League.

"The stuttering caused us some problems at first," Wash recalls, "but one day we found out that Love could sing, and as long as he sang, he never stuttered. And from that day, as long as he was in high school calling plays, he would sing those plays. The first thing he would say in the huddle was, `Now, gentlemen ...' and he would go into his plays, singing all the while. With his count at the line of scrimmage, he never broke it. He was just as smooth as he could be. Of course, when he was off the field and he'd start talking, it would be 15 minutes before he could get out a word.

"If he had been enrolled at an integrated school back then — if there had been such a thing back then — he would have gotten help. Help was being given at Bastrop High School during the time he was in school. We didn't know anything about special education, not a thing in the world. Our kids were never tested for anything.

"Let me give you an example: We never would have known if he was dyslexic because we'd never heard of such a thing back then.

Those people on the school board, the ones who did the administration, you'd see them maybe twice a year. The superintendent came to the opening session to make greetings, welcome the students, whatever. And we saw him again at the end of the year for commencement when he came back to give diplomas. And that was it. Nothing in between."

Receiver Arthur Hamlin, he of the ignominy of dropping the championship game-winning pass in the end zone, remembers his singing quarterback.

"Mister Washington came up with the idea of having him sing the signals. It worked. I guess I even noticed it in singing class back in high school. I never heard him stutter while he was singing. Then again, did you ever hear anyone sing and stutter? I don't believe I have.

"Love didn't stutter that much around us in a normal conversation. Love stuttered most when he was with people he wasn't familiar with or close to, as he was with his friends. When he'd go into a stutter, we'd give him time, maybe pat him on the back.

"Mister Washington used to tell us, when we were in the huddle, that when he'd start to stutter, just pat him on the back. That was kind of my job. But most of the times we knew the series of plays we were going to run. A lot of times, if he was stuttering, I'd just call the plays. But we basically knew what the next play was because we'd have a series of three or four plays we knew we were going to run."

Melvin Anderson, today's grade school principal, believes Love's demons would have been driven from his soul early in life had he been born into an integrated society.

"We didn't know anything about speech therapy when we were kids," offers Anderson. "It was just something they put up with. The only help he could have gotten back then was from the classroom teacher. In most cases, they were not trained to help a student like that. Back in the '50s, a speech therapist? We never heard of them.

"Nowadays we have special programs. The way it's done today is a classroom teacher who identifies a problem like Love had will recommend the child see a therapist here at the school. That child is then tested and, if he needs help, then we'll get it for him.

"But back then, you almost accepted his speech problem. At the time, they were not able to help him because they were not trained in that area. The only help he probably got was, 'Okay, Love, slow down and talk. Slow down, take your time and think about what you're going to say before you say it.' That's about the only help he got because the teachers were not trained to help that type of a student."

James Clay shares Anderson's assessment.

"When we were growing up," recalls Clay, "we had a lot of different problems, different handicaps. But we didn't have any place where they could get help. Nowadays, they've got places where they can go for therapy, for whatever handicap a child may have. In the old days, no one ever thought of that. We just figured that was the way it was, that we'd have to make do with what we had.

"There were kids who had seizures. Everybody knew they had seizures, but when they'd have a seizure, we just looked after them. If he'd been in an integrated school system, I'm sure he would have been able to have something done. He'd have probably had some special education. But back then, we had no idea about that sort of thing. We had no special education teachers or tutors. We never gave it any thought. In Bob's case, it was just common. It was something we never thought about. And it didn't bother him, either."

Arthur Hamlin should never have been required to endure the pain of dropping that last-second end zone pass. His demeanor is too quiet, his voice is too soft. And, frankly, one senses the hurt is still there. But Hamlin perks up immediately when asked how good his famous teammate was as quarterback and team leader.

"He," slowly, "was," measuredly, *"great,"* emphatically. "He didn't run it. He didn't want to run it. But Love had those big hands, so he could fake it. He was so smooth. He could work the drop back to pass, and he never had any trouble seeing us receivers because of his height. And if you think about it, heck, at that time, you didn't have too many six-foot quarterbacks in high school back in the '50s.

"No, he didn't want to run it. So when you went out for a pass, you knew that he was going to deliver the ball, that someone was going to catch a pass. He did not want to be caught with that football."

Clay continues:

"Sometimes he'd have trouble getting his signal out. Claude Lee Hunter — he was our center — and he was about the only guy who would mess with Bob. He'd tap him on the top of the head, from time to time. But he was the only guy who would mess with him. But we ran our plays in sequence anyway, so we knew just about every time what we were supposed to do next."

Coach Washington, reflecting on the proficiency of his quarterback disciple, believes Love had the ability to play in the NFL.

"I believe he would have been good enough to play in the NFL, sure I do. You didn't have any black quarterbacks in the pros then, but I can compare him to other black quarterbacks from the area. James Harris, the one they called `Shack,' he was from Monroe and I had the chance to see him play." Harris spent several years in the NFL as a quarterback with, among other teams, the Los Angeles Rams. "Love had a much better touch and a stronger throwing arm than Shack did. Love was a much better quarterback than anyone else I've ever seen."

Smitty agrees and makes a stab at putting it in current perspective: "He could throw a football as far as Randall Cunningham. Love could throw a football in normal action — without exaggeration, mind you — 70 yards. He could do it. I don't think he ever took athletics seriously until probably his senior year in high school."

And even then, even when his own coach, his own teammates, his own people, even when half the town of Bastrop, a goodly slice of Morehouse Parish and more than a few college recruiters knew how good Bob Love was on the gridiron and the hardcourt, there was an entire society that didn't have a clue.

Dick Revels, one of the few white men to see Butterbean perform in his own home town, thinks Love was probably under-appreciated in his own community. Even today, there are legions of white people who do not know they had a local hero in the NBA. But Butterbean Love was black, and black athletes in Bastrop weren't touted for heroism either off or on the athletic fields.

"I'm sure he was the greatest athlete we ever had in this part of the country," challenges Revels, "but he didn't have any opportunities. As I remember, he just kind of came up ... and I wasn't really around him nearly as much as the later players, after segregation. But he was such an outstanding player. Coach had himself a football dynasty out there. They won everything. And Love excelled at both football and basketball.

"But like I said, he didn't have many opportunities."

Former Superintendent Harper agrees.

"The whites pretty much had their athletes and the blacks did, too," remembers Harper. "And the communities were somewhat left unto themselves. Consequently, very few people around here were fully cognizant of Bob Love. That was also true, maybe not *quite* as true, as far as that fellow from Collinston, Lou Brock. I guess that name rings a bell, doesn't it? He lived seven some miles down the road from here."

But at least two colleges — both black institutions — made a bid for Bob Love. Both Grambling State's Eddie Robinson and Southern University's A.W. Mumford recruited The Singing Quarterback. In the end, Love chose to sing in Mumford's choir at the same school that graduated his role model, William Washington.

"I probably would have played football if I had gone to Grambling," 'Bean says today. "I was a helluva quarterback. A lot of people don't believe this. Hey, I might have been before my time. Maybe they wouldn't have let me play because of my speech problems. But once I got out there on that football field, I was an entirely different person. I was an athlete. That was my domain out there. When I was in high school, man, I could throw footballs, I could throw baseballs, I could throw anything. I remember, beginning in probably the eleventh grade, I could throw that football from end line to end line — the end zone line to the end zone line. People do not believe that, but I could throw the ball so far. I could do it 80, 90, almost 100 yards, all of the time.

"Coach was amazed. I was a skinny kind, too, but that's all I did was throw. I used to carry a little rubber ball around. I didn't have any idea about wrist power, but I used to read about Hank Aaron all of the time, how strong his wrists were. I said, `Shoot, I'm gonna make my wrists strong, too.' We didn't have any weights or weight training then, so I would push myself up against the wall. Nowadays they call that isometrics.

"By the eleventh grade I began to see what a good athlete I really was. I used to float around the basket like Michael Jordan. A lot of people don't believe that. I was doing 360s when I was just a little kid. My last year in high school, I could stand under the basket and spin around underneath the basketball goal and dunk. I didn't really know what that was. I didn't really appreciate what I was doing.

"But I could throw that football. Oh, I loved football. It's all I ever dreamed about for a while. I loved all sports, but I wanted to be a football player. I really wanted to be a football player.

"And don't forget, I used to have my little fantasy games. All my friends would go out on dates and almost all through high school I never had a date. I had my first date when I went to the junior-senior prom. I spent all my time on the basketball court, the ball field, whatever. I was ashamed to go around girls because I didn't want them to know how I talked."

Ah, but the singing quarterback would not have been able to carry a tune, much less a championship football team, if he'd never taken a music class.

"I guess I realized just how good I was when one of my music teachers — we were in music class and we were talking about great artists — she was talking about what makes a great artist. The teacher said, 'You know, we really have a great artist right here in this classroom. Robert Love is a great artist. You watch how smooth he is on the football field, how he throws the ball. You watch how smooth he is on the basketball court and how he can float from one side of the basket to the other.' I was unbelievably ahead of my time. And I always had that great imagination. When I started to think that I really was an artist, I would imagine myself throwing a football or going to the basket with music."

Those days at Morehouse High must have been something. Here's Bob Love and Arthur Hamlin, working in the fields, picking cotton when most assuredly Arthur wanted to be picking off passes and 'Bean wanted to be spinning them. But ...

"We used to take the buses to our away games and I always kept my quarterbacks sitting with me," says Wash. "We were always in the front seat, so if I needed to go over anything with the quarterback, we could concentrate a bit. I can remember riding on that bus, and we'd pass the cotton fields. I'd look over toward Love and he'd be looking out the window. And Robert Smith — we always called him 'Baby Brother' — old Baby Brother would stop everyone cold and say something like, 'Hey, look at old Butter, checkin' out the fields. Tomorrow he's gonna be out there pickin' that stuff.'"

The boys on the bus would get their jollies from whatever flew past their windows, it seems. But not at the expense of someone's pride. James Clay, whose father delivered groceries for J.D. Daniels for some 40 years, never worked in the cotton fields like Arthur Hamlin and Bob Love. Yet Clay had a great deal of respect for those who did.

"Sometimes those guys would have to take off and they wouldn't be at football practice for three days out of a week. But the coaches understood it. They knew those guys had to work to help out their families. We used to tease them when we'd get on the bus and go to a game. Oh, we'd be going to Jonesboro or Grambling and we'd pass by a cotton field. We say, 'Love, you should be out there gettin' you some.' And he'd start to grin and then he'd say, 'Yeah, man, tomorrow I'll be out there gettin' me some.'

"And you know, he had those big hands, so we'd tease him: 'Hey, man, with those hands you must get about ten pounds every time you go to the sack,'" Clay laughs.

So Love was the object of his fellow jesters, but no one ever put a cruel spin on the jokes hurled toward Butterbean Love.

"No, no. Never," says Wash. "Nobody ever made fun of him. I can't recall a kid making fun of Love and his speech impediment."

Dorothy Washington agrees: "He was never ridiculed here, not that I knew of. It was just something we accepted. We knew Love had this problem. In fact, the kids were almost sad for him and they sensed what he was trying to say when he got tied up."

Still, the demons persisted to torment the soul of Robert Earl Love. Athletics held the hope of his future, just as it holds the hope of too many young black kids today in Brooklyn, Watts, Detroit and on the west side of Chicago, where the Chicago Bulls play half their games each and every season. Had it not been for sports, for basketball and football, Bob Love's tale might have been one of rags to rags forever instead of rags to riches squared. Those fantasy basketball games and the spinning tire dangling from Ella Hunter's Chinaberry tree could have marked a pinnacle, rather than starting blocks, in the life of a cotton picking boy from Morehouse Parish.

Anderson says today he can appreciate the struggles that faced his college roommate virtually every day of his life.

"It says a lot for Love to have even gone to college. So many other people would have given up, would have just said they were too poor, that there was no use to even try to go to college. But he went, and he made it. I think that says a lot about Bob Love."

CHAPTER 11

IT ENDED WITH a GUNSHOT

If you can somehow reach down, reach way down into the depths of his soul, you might be able to withdraw from Arthur Hamlin's heart the real reason he couldn't stay at Southern University past his freshman year. If you can somehow psychoanalyze this quiet drug counselor, who spends his days devising ways to keep poison out of the hands, lungs, veins and brains of the kids who go to school in Bastrop, Louisiana, you might learn the truth. You might even learn it if you ask him outright. But that pass from The Singing Quarterback, the one that ended Arthur Hamlin's high school football career with a thump and a splat, that pass may have been the reason Arthur Hamlin just couldn't stay at Southern. It hurt too much.

"After two years, it still hurt me. It hurt, it hurt me bad," Hamlin still remembers. He sighs as he explains. "It took me a long time to get over that. That game was played not far from Baton Rouge, and we stayed at Southern and we practiced there before the game. That whole year I spent at Southern as a freshman, I used to think about that game. A couple guys that we played against that day, they were at Southern, too. So it was nearly impossible to forget. That championship game meant so much to us. It took me a long time to get over that. I had to put it behind me. So finally I said to myself, `Hey, I did as much for Morehouse as Morehouse did for me.'"

The next year, Arthur Hamlin packed his bags and moved across the state to Eddie Robinson and his Grambling State Tigers. He managed to snag a football scholarship, which he managed to cling to, even though he never realized what it meant until he aged a bit.

"You know," he now wistfully reminisces, "I was never outstanding. I got my attitude wrong. Back then, I was playing just to keep my scholarship. But I'll never forget what Coach Robinson said. He told us that a degree is worth $100,000. Damn! I need to get a degree, I thought. That really stuck with me. You think back now and between '61 and '65, me coming back to Bastrop and making $100,000. That was a lot of money back then."

Well, Arthur Hamlin, mild-mannered drug counselor, does not make $100,000 a year working in the public school system in Bastrop, Louisiana. But he makes a difference, even if he tells you that he never encountered the challenge of drug abuse in his younger years.

"The biggest thing that a guy had down at Southern at that time was a bottle of wine. We didn't know what grass was," he giggles. "At that time, I don't think anyone ever even sold grass in Morehouse Parish. Drugs were no problem back then. The first time — you ready? — the first time I saw someone with marijuana, it was a buddy and he had dropped out of school to go to the army. We were all home for something and that was the first time I ever saw or even heard of marijuana."

Okay, okay. The Pass. The Dropped Pass. The Dropped Pass Which Lives Yet Today in Infamy.

Bob Love has just one more chance to pull this one out for Morehouse. He breaks his teammates out of the huddle. Folks, you should see this. All of these boys have been involved in a gargantuan struggle this afternoon. The rain has absolutely soaked the field and mud is caked on the uniforms of every Morehouse player — except for Bob Love, their quarterback and their leader. His blockers have managed to keep the tacklers away from the quarterback. They walk to the line of scrimmage. There is probably time for just one more play. A touchdown wins this thing for Morehouse. Even if a field goal would help — and it won't — I don't think Coach Washington would risk it. The field is too slippery.

Love crouches down under center Claude Hunter. He begins his cadence — he sounds almost as if he's chanting his cadence. There's the snap, Love drops back to pass. He looks left and fakes left. He rolls just a little to the right and he fires a tight spiral toward the right side of the end zone. The ball is floating toward a Morehouse receiver ... his jersey is covered with mud ... it looks like ... **Bob Love has Arthur Hamlin alone in the corner of the end zone!**

"Man, I can still see it," Hamlin sighs. "When the gun went off, the ball was in the air. I know all the basics: Catch the ball in your hands! Don't trap it.

"It was wet. It was muddy. I was wet and as the ball came my way, I tried to jump. But I was so heavy with mud that I just couldn't jump high enough. And it hit my shoulder pad or something. It never touched my hands. I broke all the rules of receiving on that one. I know how you catch a football. Oh, what the heck."

The ball floats toward Arthur Hamlin ... he jumps ... oh, no, the ball bounced off Hamlin's pads ... it's incomplete ... and there's the gun ... the game is over ...

The puff and crackle of the official's pistol ended the high school football careers of a few Morehouse High School players on that wet November afternoon. Those times have faded into the mist of a late fall memory.

The high school gridiron careers of Arthur Hamlin and Robert Earl Love ended with a gunshot. But it could have been much, much worse. A gunshot ended Arthur Hamlin's football career. But today, he's working to make sure such a thing never ends something much, much more precious to a child in his Bastrop public schools.

CHAPTER 12

RED STICK and TEAR GAS

The main campus at Southern University in Baton Bouge, Louisiana, rolls along the banks of the Mississippi River, high above the water. Some day, perhaps not too distant in the future, the Mississippi will move on, like so many of Southern's former students, as time and the river's own muscle change the waterway's course away from Baton Rouge as it snakes its way to the Gulf of Mexico. But today, at least, the Mississippi rolls by, just as it did centuries ago when the Red Stick Indian tribes chose Scott's Bluff as their settlement. And it is a good place to build a settlement, this highest point of elevation in Baton Rouge.

Today, a red steel sculpture juts out of the ground and stretches itself skyward atop Scott's Bluff, overlooking the churning river below. The steel artwork has been placed there as a monument to the Red Stick Indians, who moved westward when the Spanish and French, and ultimately the African American, displaced them. How ironic that one persecuted minority, the Native American, would find itself supplanted by yet another persecuted minority, the African American. Southern University and its very impressive campus atop this rolling bluff today is comprised of some 11,000 students, all but 700 of whom are African American. Today's Southern University boasts an enrollment that includes students from each of the 50 states in the Union. Some 20 yards from the Red Stick monument, planted in the earth of Scott's Bluff, is the body of Felton Gradison Clark, who served the university as its president from 1938 until a year before his death on July 6, 1970. It is Felton Gradison Clark who is generally credited with fashioning Southern University into a credible institution of higher learning. Two days after his death, President Clark was eulogized by the Baton Rouge *Morning Advocate:*

> *... Doctor Clark's contributions to the advancement of Louisiana and all its citizens were remarkable. Many of them went unpublished, for in the delicate area of racial relations in this area for the last quarter of a century, he was a whiz at solutions acceptable to both black and white — decisions which were sometimes best executed without fanfare. He moved without apology or timidity for the advancement of the black people of this state; he acted without rancor and with understanding of the feelings of both black and white.*

Your guide during a tour of the Baton Rouge campus this late winter's day is Doctor Henry Wiggins, a professor in the College of Education here at Southern University. Now in his late 60s, Doctor Wiggins is a product of the segregated south and served in the U.S. Army during the mid-1940s. For that, Bob Love affectionately calls Professor Wiggins "Major". Though you may be 30 years his junior, Professor Henry Wiggins addresses you as "sir," mostly because he is a true gentleman, partly becaused he remembers the drill from his days in military service.

As you tour the Southern University campus, it is in the midst of an impressive and aggressive construction and renovation program. Today, a modern, 10,000-seat basketball arena lies adjacent to the 30,000-seat A.W. Mumford Football Stadium, a monument to the legendary gridiron mentor who coaxed Bob Love into attending Southern University. Across a parking lot or two sits a much more diminutive building, eroded by time and nearby construction, but still proud in its struggle against age and progress. Carved into the facade of the facility are two simple but definitive words: The Gymnasium. The Gymnasium, before progress plucked its heart from its chest and moved it across a parking lot or two, was the home of the Jaguars. Known lovingly as "The Matchbox," The Gymnasium served as the garden of Robert Earl Love's blooming years, the time when he blossomed into an NBA prospect. But take away the heart and the soul remains.

Ghosts. Still there are ghosts. On a vacant, manicured field near Mumford Stadium, if you close your eyes and concentrate, you can feel the ghost of Lou Brock, pride of Collinston, as he streaks for second base. A cloud of dirt causes you to blink as Brock slides in ahead of the catcher's throw; another stolen base. The ghost of Butterbean Love is here, too, somewhere at The Matchstick. Difference is, Brock can articulate his base running acumen when talking to the spirits of reporters. When Bob Love pops another 17-foot jumper, his ghost remains silent.

It is ironic that both Brock and Love, star products of the Pelican State and of Scott's Bluff above the Mississippi River, were later in their lives the subjects of lopsided player trades after they turned professional. Brock, of course, was a young outfielder of promise whom the Chicago Cubs swapped to the St. Louis Cardinals for an aging veteran pitcher named Ernie Broglio. And Love, young, talented but filled with National Basketball Association question marks, was shipped along with guard Bobby Weiss by the Milwaukee Bucks to the Chicago Bulls for forward Flynn Robinson. The Cubs traded Brock because some thought he couldn't hit. He proceeded to lead the Redbirds to the World Series and to set a major league season and career record for stolen bases. (Both records have since been eclipsed by Rickey Henderson. But Brock's feats were not diminished.) The Bucks, says Love, traded him, "Because they thought I couldn't talk." And he later led the Bulls ...

Southern University was founded in 1881 and was first established in New Orleans. In 1914, the Louisiana legislature appropriated $10,000 to relocate the campus up the Mississippi to a landfill at Scott's Bluff in Baton Rouge.

Today, where there once stood a landfill, John Brown talks about life, about football, about coaching and recruiting. And he talks about Butterbean Bob Love. John Brown is a large, garrulous black man with a thick chest and broad shoulders. He is a product of the Great Depression and Roosevelt High School in Gary, Indiana, a rustbelt steel-producing town about as different from Baton Rouge as an elephant is to an apple. Over lunch in a faculty cafeteria on campus, John Brown talks proudly of the work ethic:

"My mother was making ten dollars a week during the Depression, and my grandfather worked for Fruit Growers Express, up near East Chicago, filling boxcars. He never allowed us to go on welfare, although I suppose we qualified. He just wouldn't let us go on it."

John Brown earned his masters degree in physical education from Northwestern University and a doctoral degree in highway traffic safety from Michigan State. After his collegiate and military experiences, and before he landed at Southern in 1957, Big John Brown was a professional football player both stateside and in the Canadian Football League. Back home, he was a lineman for the long-defunct Los Angeles Dons. North of the border, he played in Vancouver and for the Winnipeg Blue Bombers in the CFL. Among his teammates in Canada were Bud Grant, who later coached the Minnesota Vikings to the Super Bowl, and Neill Armstrong, who worked his way up as a Grant assistant before becoming head coach of the Chicago Bears.

Big John whistles a familiar tune when he speaks of his experiences in the professional football ranks at the time when Jackie Robinson was crashing through major league baseball's color barrier in Brooklyn.

"When I played football my first year, we used to go to Baltimore," muses Brown. "And, of course, we couldn't stay in the same hotel as the white players on the team. Lenny Ford was on the team, and his family lived in Washington, which of course is just down the road. We used to go over to Washington from Baltimore and stay with Ford's family. There were three of us. No team had more than three black players at once back then. Shit, we loved the fact that we couldn't stay with the rest of the the team because it gave us freedom of movement and action, you understand?

"But in terms of the conditions under which we had to do it, well, it was despicable, really. I mean, we had more fun than anyone else because we were on our own. We had no curfew, no one to check up on us. But the circumstances under which we had to have the fun were really poor."

The eyes of Big John Brown, the windows to his soul, have seen more than most men. For a black man born during the first quarter of this century, he has traveled as a soldier, as a professional football player and as a basketball coach and recruiter. Throughout his travels he has felt the sting of racism, perhaps in every precinct. As a soldier he witnessed it. Obviously, as a professional football player he lived in its wake. And as a college recruiter of student-athletes, he felt its sting, just as Bob Love felt the sting of the Puget Sound drizzle that lonely December night in Seattle.

"Racism is fascinating," says Brown. "I used to think about racism against blacks because I'm black. But you know, I grew up in the middle of the Serbs and Croatians in Gary, Indiana. And we — the blacks — we ended up in the middle because they couldn't stand each other," he chuckles just for a moment, then quickly wipes the smile from his face. "See, some things never change. But, anyway, my best buddy was Joey Mahalovic. Whenever I went home to see my parents, I'd always go to see Missus Mahalovic. And she'd treat me like I was a long-lost relative, like I was one of her own. But the point is, it didn't matter that I was black because between the Croatians and the Serbs, they didn't like each other, and they're all white.

"You know, when I played football I lived in Winnipeg, which is really a polyglot. They've got almost everything in Winnipeg that you can find. But the people who controlled it were the Germans and the Scots. But they got along, people got along." John Brown pauses for just a second. "Maybe it's the cold weather, huh?"

During his decades of coaching in the college ranks, chiefly as a coach for an all-black university in an all-black athletic conference, Brown and the rest of the Southern University athletic staff has had to compete for players with white coaches, white systems and white money. To attract a superstar black athlete is a task, he argues.

"Ballplayers make coaches. Coaches don't make ballplayers. I learned that a long time ago. There's just a handful of coaches who truly make players. Bobby Knight, for example. I might not like Bobby Knight, but he's a helluva coach. He graduates his players and they leave school worshipping him. But in most cases, if you've got some horses, if you've got some good ballplayers, then you're going to be a pretty good coach.

"But the key down here is getting the horses. When you're recruiting students — players — to an all-black school, you have got your work cut out for you, brother. What amazes me is the high school coaches are so reluctant to send the best kids to you. They think all white coaches are smarter," he laughs, "but I know better.

"We haven't gotten out of the stage in the south — at least in Louisiana and maybe Mississippi — where you accept the status quo, but you accept it with reservations. It's difficult. I'm telling you, it's difficult. We've got a white kid here and he's a pitcher. It's the first white kid we've ever been able to influence to come here. We have a good baseball team, but we can't compare to LSU, we can't compete with them. And the main reason we can't is that we can't get pitchers. We can get fielders and hitters, but we can't get any pitchers. The white schools eat 'em up. They can offer them more, even if they're black."

Brown's analysis is not that blacks cannot pitch as well as whites, just as he will be the first to tell you that a black quarterback can be every bit as good or better than a white one. But pitching, at every level, from the time a kid gets out of tee ball until he steps into Comiskey Park, is the premium position in baseball. And those who have, get; those who have not, want.

"It's economics, really. We can't give them what the white schools will give their family. No matter what you think, no matter what you read.

"Let me give you an example. I tried to recruit Elvin Hayes. Love was in school at the time. We brought Elvin down here and kept him a week. He didn't want to go back after he came here. He got to know Love and some of the other guys and they told him how things were here and how he could expect to be treated. And, you know, the kids you've got are really the best recruiting tool available to you.

"But the coach from Houston went to meet the family. And soon after that, there was a new roof on their house. His sister was president of the Southern Alumni Association, he had another sister graduating from here who was an honor student in math, and a brother who was a junior and an honor student. His high school coach graduated from here.

"Well, they took him over to Houston and they gave him a job making $600 a month, which was a lot of dough then. And all he did was play basketball all day.

"Let me tell you about Don Cheney. Don Cheney went to school in Baton Rouge. His mother used to work in the credit union here. And I almost married his mother trying to recruit Don Cheney." Big John Brown is laughing heartily at the reminiscence. "But he ended up at Houston, too. You don't have a chance. You just don't have a chance."

John Brown claims responsibility for Dick Mack. Nothing wrong with that. Dick Mack, today a man who looks 20 years younger than the 75 he's seen, is a quality gentlemen with a mellifluous voice and a quiet but confident demeanor. Dick Mack was head basketball coach of the Southern University Jaguars when Robert Earl Love enrolled as a top quarterback prospect for A.W. Mumford's Southern University Jaguars football team.

"I was responsible for Mack being here," Brown will tell you. "The football coach asked me — and remember, I was the assistant basketball coach — and he said, `John, do you know anybody you think you can get to coach basketball that you might be able to get along with?' I said, `Yeah, Big Mack.' And that's how we got the ball rolling with Coach Mack."

Some head coaches see a microphone and flit to it the way a bug chases your porch light. Others do the same job the concrete company did when they poured the foundation for your house. They measure, they level, they make sure the temperature is right and then they pour the concrete. When the concrete hardens, they'll know, because they know their trade. And once they are satisfied their work will support the weight of your house, they move on to the next project, confident they have done their workmanlike best, that no water will ever seep through your foundation and into the basement. Dick Mack was the kind of guy who poured basements when he coached at Southern. He mostly leaves the talking to those who want to talk. Dick Mack — he'd rather bask in the successes of his most prized player. But he does offer a few words about the best player he ever coached, the nicest house ever to sit upon one of his foundations.

"I just want to tell you how we got Bob Love," Coach Mack says, his clear, chocolate-brown eyes dancing with pride. "Bob Love was an all-state basketball and football player. He was a quarterback in Bastrop, Louisiana. And he was recruited by the football team.

"When I came here to coach the basketball team, Coach Mumford told me: `Mack, football is first here. Baseball is second here. And track is third. Basketball is fourth and all I can say is, you're going to have to do your best.'

"So they brought Bob here as a football player. But I had the pleasure of seeing him play a pickup game in the gymnasium. All the students would come up to me and say, `Bob Love is coming. Bob Love is going to be in the gym.' So I figured I'd let me go and see this Bob Love play basketball, see what he could do.

"So I went to the gym and I sat up high. I saw Bob Love down there playing. And I said, `My God. That boy is good. That boy is incredibly good.' So I went to Brown and I said, `I want you to come over and see this fellow play. I asked Brown what he thought and he never hesitated. He said Love was a winner. It was then that I made up my mind that I was going to over to see Coach Mumford and ask if it would be possible that Bob Love could switch from football to basketball."

"That's exactly what happened," chimes Brown. "We went down and we saw him in a pickup game. "Coach Mack saw him first and he asked me, `You think he's good enough to come out for the varsity?' And I had only seen him play that one time, just that one time in the pickup game. And I looked at Coach Mack and I said, `You damned right. You damned right he's good enough, and I sure as hell hope you can do something about it.'"

Back to Mack: "So I went right up to Coach Mumford — we called him 'The Old Man' — and asked if Bob could switch, and he said he'd first have to see how the rest of his quarterbacks looked.

"Right about that time I looked out the window and I saw Bob Love throwing a football to a tight end, a big old boy who was about six-ten, 250 pounds. But there they were, throwing the football back and forth to one another. I watched him for just a few moments. I said to myself, 'Let me go down there and stop this right now!' So I went down to the equipment room and I got two basketballs."

Dick Mack is smiling as wide as his mouth will stretch.

"I got down to him and I threw one of those basketballs at him. And Bob Love went like this." Coach Mack thrusts his right hand out and level to his right shoulder and mimes a one-handed catch. "And I threw the other ball toward his other hand and he went like this." Same way, just do it in the mirror.

"Then I said, 'Now, give me that football.' And I took the football and I said, 'You, son, are going to play basketball. Don't get it mixed up.'

"A few days later I went back to see The Old Man, and I asked him if he had a chance to check out his crop of quarterbacks. And that's when he said the words that made me a very happy man. He said, 'Mack, if he wants to go, I'll let him go.'"

Love himself laughs when he recalls his transition from college football recruit to college basketball player.

"Man, that was scary. I remember going down on that football field and seeing those guys with their pads on. They were soooo big, man. They scared me to death. I saw those guys and I thought to myself, 'I don't want to go out there, those guys are gonna kill me.' And I never played a down. Coach Mack and Coach Brown saw me playing pickup basketball games in the gym. Thank God."

Like William and Dorothy Washington, Dick Mack and his wife Arlee learned their prodigy had as ravenous an appetite for food as he had for basketball. Mack laughs at the recollection:

"I was just telling my wife a while ago. I was eating a ham sandwich and it reminded me of the time when Love came over with a big old center that we had back then. They'd come by on a Sunday afternoon and when they did, we knew exactly why they'd come by. And I always told my wife to take out whatever it was that you want them to eat.

"So, once we had this big, old picnic ham in the refrigerator. It was a big old thing. So Love and this other boy came over to the house and my wife knew what they wanted. So she just put that big old ham out there for them to eat. Well, later that night I went back for a midnight snack and I opened the refrigerator. I looked inside and all that was left of that big, old picnic ham was two bones. I asked my wife what happened to all that ham and she just said, `I just wanted to make sure they had enough.'

"I guess it was okay. I needed to go on a diet then, anyway. I weighed 260 pounds."

Dick Mack in summary: "So Bob Love started here as a football player, and he became one of the greatest basketball players — I say one because I don't want to get into an argument — he became one of the greatest basketball players ever to play here at Southern. I can say that he is one of the greatest basketball players that I've ever seen, and that Coach Brown and I have ever coached."

His eyes tell the story. One look tells you of the immense pride Dick Mack has in his star pupil, even though that star passed through Baton Rouge nearly 30 years ago. In Dick Mack's mind, in Dick Mack's heart, that star burns as bright today as it did in The Matchstick so many years ago. And he clarifies himself.

"He was the best I ever coached. He could pick it up easy. I happened to go through the gym one night and I saw him practicing on his own. And he'd take the ball behind him and I'm thinking, `Okay, now he's gonna try some of that Globetrotter stuff on me.' So I watched him, and he just got smoother and smoother. I wondered if he was ever going to try that behind-the-back move in a game, because I knew he wouldn't ever think of using the move until he had it down to perfection. But I never said anything to him. I didn't want it to affect him either way. I just wanted to see how things would develop. Sure enough, one night we were in a game — I don't remember the situation, if we were ahead or behind, that doesn't matter — and he put on that move. And when he did, the place just went wild. From then on, it just became part of his act, part of his game.

"In fact, I think one reason no one ever made fun of the way he talked was because of his play. His playing always overshadowed it. I know I had a little bit of a problem with his stutter when he first came to Southern. But after a while I learned how to handle it all right. Whenever he got ready to talk, I would just stop and I wouldn't try to rush him. I'd take my time with him. All in all, he had a pretty good time speaking to me, talking with me. In fact, even with his stuttering, he grew into being a leader. Eventually he even got along all right with the girls." Mack laughs. "After he got used to them, he had no problem there."

Perhaps Butterbean found that comfort zone with his old coach, the same comfort zone he shared in the huddle and at the line of scrimmage with Arthur Hamlin and James Clay and Claude Lee Hunter.

But Arlee Mack can remember trying to talk with Love and having a difficult time getting a word to spill from his mouth.

"He never had a problem talking with my husband," she says. "But every time he tried to talk to me he couldn't get a word out. He'd call on the phone and if I answered, I always knew who it was because no one was talking. No one was talking because he couldn't get a word out."

Butterbean was so easy-going and such a raw talent that his coaches rarely had a problem with him. As good a practice player as he was a gamer, coaches were able to concentrate on other players, other aspects of the game when Love was going through his paces on the practice court.

"One thing about Love," says Brown, "is that he wasn't difficult to coach. The most interesting thing about him, really, was his dedication to getting better. He was always outstanding. I never saw people work as hard in practice as he did. He was out there when he had to be and, more importantly, he was out there after that, when he didn't have to be. He worked hard at whatever he and the other guys had to do. It just didn't happen. He worked for it. If it took two hours to do it, then he gave it two hours. If it took three hours, then it got three. He did it by himself when it had to get done, by himself in the gym.

"And he didn't just work on shooting. He worked on footwork, he worked on defense. You know, he was a great defensive player. And he had great speed. For a big guy, he had great speed for a basketball player. He could always shoot. He had a flat shot and I used to try to get him to arch it, but I gave up trying because he kept on making it. You don't argue about success, you know."

Big John Brown demonstrates a genuine affection for the man whom he helped guide when the man was little more than a boy. While he admits he admired — in fact was awed by — Butterbean Love's basketball skills, muscle and drive, he will tell you that his true admiration is reserved for the muscle that pumps life's blood through Bob Love's veins. And Big John wanted to see his best player get more out of life than simply a degree in physical education.

"He's always been a good kid. He's still a good kid," Brown says, forgetting for a moment that people who live five-plus decades probably aren't kids anymore. "I'm the one who started him in foods and nutrition. I figured that we already had too many athletes who were majoring in physical education because they wanted to be coaches and stay involved in athletics. Nothing wrong with coaching, mind you." And John Brown winks and grins. "But I just thought he'd be better off later in life if he took a different course, a different angle.

"There was a lady in home economics named Pinky Thrift. And she loved him. She just loved him because he was a good student. He was a never a poor student. Even with his speaking difficulties, he was never a poor student. He just couldn't talk. And as I told you before, I never realized until later years that it bothered him as much as it did. Maybe I didn't realize it because his speaking problems never bothered him on the court, never bothered him on the floor. And when he sings? He sings very well. He has a beautiful singing voice and he never stuttered when he sang. They tell me up in Chicago he used to stutter in the huddle. But as I was saying, he never stuttered when he was out there on the floor or when he got into the huddle. Here, I guess he just felt more at ease."

So Robert Earl Love, The Singing Quarterback of Morehouse High School in Bastrop, Louisiana, could have become The Singing Power Forward of the Southern University Jaguars. Or better yet, The Singing Gourmet?

Buddy Arthur Hamlin, who roomed with Love their freshman year at Southern before moving on to Grambling, still remembers the night his roomie broke the news about Butterbean's intended major.

"One night we were sitting around in our dormitory and Love looks at me and says, `I think I'm gonna major in foods and nutrition, you know, so I can be around it.'" The soft-spoken Hamlin erupts into spontaneous laughter. "I thought he was kidding. At that time I don't know if there were any other guys majoring in foods and nutrition at Southern. So he says, `Yeah, Ham, I think I'm gonna do it. I think I'm gonna major in foods and nutrition.'"

Hamlin's eyes grow wide and his voice changes to a high-pitched falsetto.

"`You what? Foods and nutrition? What's wrong with you, Love? Boys don't major in foods and nutrition!'"

"`Yeah, man. That way I won't have to worry about havin' somethin' to eat.'"

"I still thought he was kidding, just pulling my leg, because like I said, I don't know if any other men were studying it at the time. It didn't seem proper for boys back then."

Big John Brown believes Love's willingness to study in a field that was off-limits to men in his time is just another element that set Butterbean apart from his contemporaries.

"I've always loved him, and that's the truth, and not just because of his athletic skill. You know, he could throw a goddammed football 75 yards, and I'm not sure he wasn't a better football player than he was a basketball player. He could play. He was an athlete.

"But I've had other athletes. We had a kid from Gary on the same team who had as many skills, and that's the truth, too. He could play. He could do everything you could do back then. He could broad jump 24 feet. He could run the 100 in nine-eight. Anything he shot up was gonna go in the hole and if you were going to have a free throw, you knew damned well he was the one who wasn't going to miss it. And he could have played football, too, if he'd been interested in school.

"But he wasn't interested in school. He wasn't interested in paying the price to be successful. I think that's probably what set Bob Love apart from a lot of the other guys who were around at the same time he was. He was willing to pay the price to be successful. Whether it was in the classroom or on the practice floor, Bob Love was willing to pay the price of success."

But if you are led to believe that circle above Bob Love's head is a halo, look behind his neck and you'll see the coat hanger which supports it. He's human as the next guy, and his humanity contains its share of mischief. And John Brown was witness to the mischief that is inherent in virtually all college boys, no matter the generation.

"We used to go on road trips to basketball games," goes the story according to Big John. "And we would tell the guys they had a certain time they had to be in. Almost everywhere we went, there was someone in the area that I knew. So I'd always be out at night, all the time.

"One night we were in Atlanta. I think we were in a pre-season tournament. And I was coming in, oh, it must have been about two-thirty in the morning. I see Love and a boy named Jasper Wilson, who later played with the New Orleans Jazz when they were still in town. So I drive up in the parking lot and here they are, just coming in. And they see me. And when they see me, I saw them. So I walked up to them and said, `Hey, where you guys been?'

"`Coach, we've been over to the dormitory, visiting our buddies. And the time just got away from us.' Now, we were staying at the Inter-Denominational College in Atlanta, a school which produces Methodist ministers. And I know damn well they don't know anybody who was studying to be a Methodist minister," says Brown laughing.

"But you know how coaches are, and in my years I liked to intimidate the kids whenever they pulled a stunt like that. So I said, `All right, that's fine. But you two boys are not going to play tomorrow night.' They were down-trodden and, of course, I was lying because

I wasn't the head coach and it wasn't my decision to make.

"They might have been dragging in at two-thirty in the morning, Lord knows doing what. They'd been out somewhere. Who knows where they'd been. But they didn't drink. We just didn't have the same problems then that we have now with kids. Oh, I guess there might have been one or two players on the team who did drink, but they didn't drink around the other basketball players. They didn't smoke, either, and if they did smoke you never saw them.

"I used to see kids smoking and when I did, I would catch it in their hands like this," he says as he extends his left hand and squeezes your right. "And while the cigarette was in their palm, I'd look them straight in the eye and I'd say, `How are you?'

"I was kind of a tough guy. I never took excuses and I never gave excuses, either. The kids respected me and they liked me because I used to tell a lot of lies and tell a lot of jokes. That way I could demand more. If you can add humor to their suffering, you can help them get through it."

Nineteen Sixty-One, the year John Fitzgerald Kennedy ascended to Camelot's throne as the nation's 35th president, might as well be a million years ago. Television sets, for the most part, beamed forth but two colors: black and white. Old Glory was still getting accustomed to the two new stars that had been stitched into her national fabric just two years earlier. Roger Maris spent the summer swatting 61 baseballs into the laps of paying customers who sat in the outfield between two mustard yellow poles. For that he got a * next to his name in the record book. At least he got one of those. Today all they seem to care about is the almighty dollar sign: $$$$.

Nineteen Sixty-One was one of the last years of innocence. Ozzie and Harriet and Donna and Alex Stone may still have been around, but their days were numbered, whether we knew it or not. In the wings loomed the likes of Archie and Edith and Rowan and Martin and those brothers Smothers, the symbols of change. While most northerners continued to exist in the world of Eisenhower and the 1950s, the south was becoming increasingly restless. The likes of Kennedy and a young preacher named Martin Luther King were beginning to help black people in Alabama and Mississippi and, yes, Louisiana, believe that their future had a brighter filiment than did their past. The freedom marches were beginning in earnest. College campuses — at least in the south — were beginning to awaken to a new vision of the future. It would take white students nearly another decade to take to the streets in protest against their own enemy, the Vietnam War. But in 1961, Bob Love's freshman year at Southern University in Baton Rouge, Louisiana, black students were ready to raise their voices, if not their fists, to protest what they believed to be second-class treatment by the white man's establishment.

"I was in college," remembers Love. "Let me tell you about my freshman year in college. It was 1961, and the civil rights movement had just started. We were fighting for what we thought was ours, for what we believed in. That was the year we marched on the city of Baton Rouge. I'll never forget it, man. It was a rainy day — either a Thursday or a Friday. And we marched five, maybe six miles from the campus to downtown Baton Rouge."

The target of their march was a tall, obelisk-shaped building in the downtown area. The building very nearly resembles the Empire State Building in miniature. Compared to other structures of its ilk, the Louisiana State Capitol, the building in which Huey Long was assassinated, is odd. Most state capitols are pattered after the nation's Capitol in Washington. As such, they have wings and a dome and they spread across the landscape not unlike a big spider. The Louisiana State Capitol is a tall stick.

"I was in class with — you ever heard of this guy, H. Rap Brown? — well, we were real good friends in school. We took a few classes together. Anyway, he helped organize a march to the Capitol in downtown Baton Rouge."

Melvin Anderson, now principal at South Side Elementary in Bastrop, was with Love the day they marched on the Capitol. In those days, star athletes didn't live in exclusive jock dormitories with other carefully-sculpted athletes who concentrated more on their play books than their text books. Anderson, the musician, was one of several young men who shared a room with Butterbean Love during Love's stay at Southern University. And while many — perhaps a majority of — college students are broke more often than flush, Anderson, Love and their Southern student body brethren were especially so. After all, many came from poor, rural homes where there was little or no promise of upward mobility.

"You know," recalls Anderson, "everybody helped each other. Everybody had the same thing because we all shared. To give you an example, Love was poorer than we were, but at the same time, we didn't have that much more. But we shared. Like food. Bob and myself and another friend left here together to Baton Rouge when we finished high school. Our parents didn't have enough money to send us to college, so we left Bastrop on our own, so to speak. And we left with very little money. Whatever money we had, we had to share with each other. When we'd get money from home — sometimes my parents would send me a little money — it was all of our money. We shared it all. If I had $5, Love and the rest of us spent that $5. I remember one summer we stayed together down there, and we'd go out to buy food. We lived off campus at the time, and whatever money we had, we just pooled it together and we helped each other.

"Of course," says Anderson with a broad smile, "we never shared clothes. Love was much taller than the rest of us."

So Melvin Anderson was accustomed to sharing whatever he had with someone who didn't have it. And he was more than a little puzzled that other people, an entire race, for that matter, did not share such a basic tenet of life. If he was willing to share half of his ham sandwich with you — when he was hungry enough to eat two of them — why would you not see the way in your heart to share a toilet? Or a bus seat? Or a lunch counter?

"As far as the demonstrations are concerned, I participated in the demonstrations. I just felt that it was time for a change. We had a right to go into those lunch counters, just like other people, just like anyone else. I can remember it just as good as if it happened yesterday. We marched from Southern to Baton Rouge, about a five mile walk. Once we got downtown, around eleven or twelve o'clock, there must have been hundreds of people, hundreds of us marching.

"The leaders of the march told us it was getting close to twelve o'clock and we were getting hungry. It was time for us to go to lunch.

We were hungry and we were determined we would go to the lunch counters and be served.

"Well, we went in, but they didn't serve us. Me and Bob and the rest of us went in. And like I say, it was five miles down there and we had walked every inch of it. And we were growing young men, so we were hungry. But they didn't serve us."

By that time, however, the Baton Rouge police were moving in to dismiss the protest march with the idea they would send the Southern University students scampering back to campus.

Love's butterbean eyes grow wide with the recollection:

"Man, there were cops with their damned sticks and these big fucking dogs. Man, big fucking dogs on a leash. And it was raining, kind of a misty rain, a lot like wintertime is in Baton Rouge. And we were down there near the Capitol and all of a sudden a guy came on the loud speaker and said, `You've got five minutes to clear out, to go back to campus and disperse.'

"Well, nobody moved, so soon enough the man says, `You've got two minutes.' All of a sudden, everybody stopped moving. We had these people who came down, I guess, from New York, to organize it. Hell, they told everybody to stand still. The fucking cops, man, they brought the fucking dogs up and one cop says, `All right, you've had your chance.' And all of a sudden they turned the fucking dogs loose, those big German shepherds. It was a madhouse. They were hitting people with sticks, they were spraying tear gas. I think I might have got hit upside the face with some Mace just before I fell and rolled down a hill."

"That's right," agrees Anderson. "We had tried to get served at the lunch counter when the next thing we heard was a loud noise. It turned out to be tear gas. They gassed us and then they put the dogs on us."

Love, the athlete, says he ran all the way back to campus.

"They had all these paddy wagons and the whole fucking town was full of smoke from the tear gas. I ran all the way back to campus. Maybe 1,000 or more kids, we ran all the way back to campus, maybe five miles. But I made it back to campus safely."

Anderson, the musician, recalls his trip back to the Southern campus a little differently.

"And if I remember, but I'm not sure, but we had a lot of white people who were in favor of the demonstrations, in favor of blacks being able to go into a lunch counter to be served. Because as some of us tried to get back to campus, some white people stopped to give us a ride back to Southern.

"That was something, though. I can remember just as clearly as if it happened yesterday. We had that tear gas smell in our clothes and it bothered the people who gave us rides back. They were shedding tears just like we were."

Anderson said the board governing Southern at the time decided enough was enough. The administration closed the school so that no more demonstrations would disrupt the state capital.

"Once we got back to campus from that first march, they dismissed school," Anderson says. "They told us that, as of five o'clock that afternoon, everybody who lived in the dorms had to be out. So they sent us all home. They closed the school down and they told us not to come back until we got a letter from the administration. If you didn't get a letter to come back, well, let me put it this way: Some of the students didn't get letters. The so-called leaders didn't ever come back."

John Brown and Dick Mack probably had as much to protest as the students they coached. The two-tiered economic system of southern higher education meant the black coaches at the black colleges were paid less than the white coaches at the white colleges. Public institutions of higher learning in Louisiana were separate and they were unequal. Remembers John Brown:

"Back in 1960, I was making $6,000 a year — $500 a month for twelve months out of the year. A white assistant at a white school was making between $15,000 and $20,000 a year. I remember when Mack didn't have soles in his shoes. You know those goddamned cardboards you get out of laundered shirts? Shit, those used to be his shoe soles.

"I can remember when the kids down here were protesting. And they had a lot to protest about. Since then, black people have made progress. They can eat in the restaurants of their choice and no one tells them what rest room they can or can't use.

"But," he sighs wistfully, "I really think we're retrogressing. I think we've advanced, in terms of relationships. But I think we've retrogressed in terms of accountability and responsibility. I feel saddened for black young men. I don't know what's going to become of them. I don't have the least idea. You have options. You have the option of going to school. It's always been our exit. It's been every group's exit out of poverty. And then there are prospects, but you never know what your prospects are going to be. If you get out of school, just because you majored in a certain area of study doesn't mean that's what you're going to spend your life doing.

"There is a way out. But you, the individual, are responsible for coming out of poverty and despair if you want to come out. No one is going to do it for you. No one else is responsible. You've got to do it yourself. In that sense, the conservatives are right. You are responsible for your own fucking self. No one else is responsible for you except yourself. No one owes you anything; the government doesn't owe you a thing. You owe yourself. And if you can't overcome that, if you can't understand that, then you won't overcome anything. And if people don't instill that in their kids, then the kids are just going to be lost. That's all there is to it."

John Brown's prized former student-athlete talks today as if he has learned John Brown's lessons of life.

"I think going to an all-black school really helped me," offers Bob Love. "You're not disillusioned about a lot of things, by a lot of pretense. I'm not so sure these black kids coming out of major colleges get the same guidance and common sense drilled into their heads as I did. Those teachers in college really gave you a background in what to expect from life. They give you a realistic idea of what the real world is and what you have to do to blend in.

"Now, look at these black kids today who are going to the major white colleges. They come out of college and half of them don't even have an education. And they become disillusioned by the world. They come out angry and they don't really know why they are angry. I went to college to get an education.

"I didn't have any idea about pro basketball when I was going to school at Southern. I just wanted to be good enough at basketball so that I could stay in school on my scholarship. After I accomplished that, I wanted to be the best player on the team. Then, when I found out I was the best player on the team, I wanted to be the best player in the conference. And when I found out I was the best player in the conference, hell, I wanted to be the best player in the whole damned country. That was all I had on my mind back in those days. I didn't date girls. I didn't have a girlfriend because I was afraid to try and talk around them, afraid to be embarrassed. So I did my best to try to express myself on the athletic field or on the basketball court.

"In a lot of ways, I really think that having the speech problem helped me in some ways. No matter how people might have laughed at me, no matter how bad I wanted to talk, I could always channel that frustration onto the basketball court. So, sometimes I'd see a girl and wanted to talk to her, but it wouldn't come out. When that happened, I took the frustration with me to the basketball court and made it work."

Tears can shed for a million reasons. Be they caused by poverty or pain or tear gas, they are tears just the same. If you were schooled in life by the likes of John Brown, then you understand your responsibilities to yourself. Channeling frustration into a positive manner helps. But just channeling and struggling and trying and working won't necessarily stop the tears from flowing. Sometimes it helps if you can talk about things. So it's a lot tougher on people who can't talk.

CHAPTER 13

THE SPICE of GLORY

A hundred times and 25 more did Robert Earl Love pull on and peel off his pale blue and gold Southern University Jaguars game jersey. A hundred or more times the sweat that soaked jersey number 41 helped drench the Jaguars' opponents as Love poured points into the picture the way a bartender pours beer from a tapper. During his years as a starting forward for Dick Mack's Southwestern Athletic Conference basketball squad, six foot eight Butterbean Love was, as a guy named Reggie Jackson once said, the straw who stirred the cocktail of victory in Baton Rouge, Louisiana. Had the three-point line been established for 19-foot jumpers during his hitch as a Jaguar, Bob Love most assuredly would have ended his collegiate basketball career with a run at 2,500 points points.

His outside shot was as deadly as a bayou cottonmouth's bite.

"Love was a guy," recalls Dick Mack, "if we ever got short at the guard position, I could play him at guard. He could take care of the guard on defense and he could shoot from out there, too. Heck, if we'd have had the three-point shot back in those days, his average would have been way up there."

As it was, Butterbean Love's offensive output was in a region where an oxygen mask would have helped. Through three years of regular season games at Southern, Bob Love scored 2,323 points, an 18.6 points per game average. Dick Mack's best-ever basketball player had become the first Southern University squad member to eclipse the lofty 2,000-point career scoring plateau. And when it really mattered, when the Jaguars were fighting their way through sudden-death valley in the National Association of Intercollegiate Athletics post-season tournament, Dick Mack gave the ball to Bob Love. His star senior forward ripped the net for 130 more points in post-season play before his collegiate career ended that final evening in 1965. A 26 point average in the games that mattered more than the rest is what Robert Earl Love paraded before the scouts who bothered to attend those games in Kansas City.

The Jags had breezed their way through the SWAC schedule in the 1965 campaign, running and gunning their way to an average of more than 100 points a game in conference play. And while it may take more than a couple of horses to carry a team to the century mark in scoring every night, it was Bob Love who clearly was the swiftest and most valuable thoroughbred in Dick Mack's stable. Naturally, Love earned all-conference honors on the SWAC first team honor roll for the third straight year. But he also earned the attention of national writers, ringing up a spot on the All-South first team, sharing the spotlight with the likes of Miami University's Rick Barry and Billy Cunningham of North Carolina.

And when the last grains of sand trickled from the hourglass that clocked Bob Love's college basketball career, he had been named to the United Press International Little All-America's list as a first-team forward.

As the Jags marched their way through the early NAIA tournament games, Butterbean Love reached down, sucked it up and offered his broad shoulders to Dick Mack and Company. Against Indiana Tech, Love carried Southern to an early first round win by pumping in 34 points. Against Eastern Montana State, the senior forward led the charge to victory with 27.

By the time the Jaguars rolled into the Show-Me State of Missouri, they were the third seed and could smell the aroma of a national tournament championship just as clearly as they could sense the fragrance of a Kansas City barbecue pit. Back home, in the building where old Huey Long met his Maker, the success of the Southern Jaguars had not gone unnoticed. Indeed, the Louisiana legislature was making preparations in the event the hometown boys advanced to the semi-final round against the University of Southwest Louisiana. But the buzz around the Capitol was not one of excited anticipation about an intra-state rivalry. As John Brown remembers it:

"USL was a basketball power back then, and they were also at the NAIA tournament. And if we had beaten Ouachita Baptist, we were supposed to play USL."

Imagine, the exhilaration felt in California at the prospect of a UCLA-USC game to help decide a national championship. Or the thrill of the Wolverines playing in Lansing with a national title hanging in the balance. DeKalb would explode in a riot if the hometown Huskies ever had the opportunity to knock off the University of Illinois in a game to crown a national champion. (It is a fact. Sometimes truth is stranger than fiction.)

But for the folks in Lousiana, the prospect of a Southern-Southwestern Louisiana showdown in Kansas City meant agitation, not excitement. Instead of feeling delirium at the prospect of the two homestate schools squaring off in the semi-final round of the NAIA tournament, the folks in the state Capitol were irritated. Rather than enthusiasm, the folks who wrote the laws for the Pelican State were immersed in a furor.

"I can remember it like it was yesterday," continues Big John Brown, "the legislature had already said that if we had to play each other, they were going to bring USL home. They weren't going to let them play against the black school from Southern. I can laugh about it now, but it didn't seem funny back then."

Two gentlemen — one named Albert Tucker, the other David Kossover — saw to it that peace prevailed in Baton Rouge. Neither Tucker nor Kossover were legislators, nor were they law enforcement officers. They were Baptists. Albert Tucker scored 35 points as Oklahoma Baptist College hustled past Southwest Louisiana, 95-82 in a quarterfinal matchup. So, in that regard, Albert Tucker did to USL what the German shepherds and the tear gas did to Bob Love nearly four years earlier.

The next night — March 11, 1965 — the Jaguars came within three seconds of advancing to the NAIA's version of the Final Four. Dick Mack brought his scoring machine into the arena that night, and Butterbean purred like the powerful engine he was. Show them he did. But Ouachita Baptist didn't run and they didn't gun, a trademark offense that to this day dominates the all-black Southwestern Athletic Conference. With a minute left, Aaron Regan hit a 17-foot jumper to drag the Jaguars to a 62-61 lead over Ouachita Baptist. Thirty-two seconds later, Southern forward Bob Love was fouled, and with just 28 ticks left on the clock, Butterbean went to the line for a one-and-one.

"This is what I had been playing for all my life," Love remembers. "I was a little nervous, sure, but I knew what I had to do and I knew what I could do."

What Love did do was hit both ends of the one-and-one to put Southern on top by three with less than a half minute left. The Baptists took eleven more seconds to bring the ball up court and dish it to Leon Clements, who drilled a field goal to bring Ouachita to within one. And with just three seconds separating Dick Mack from a Final Four appearance in the NAIA Tournament, Southern's Samuel Butler fouled David Kossover. And just like Bob Love, David Kossover knew what he had to do. And he did it. At the buzzer, the scoreboard flashed the story: Ouachita Baptist 65, Southern University 64. Bob Love led all scorers with 25 points on nine field goals; he was seven for nine from the free throw line. On this March evening, the better team lost the game. Ouachita Baptist wasn't even seeded in the tournament.

Naturally, the loss eliminated the Jaguars from the tournament and David Kossover placed a period at the end of Butterbean Love's collegiate basketball career. But there were six men who sat through most of the tournament games with their attention turned to that six-foot, eight-inch forward from Bastrop, Louisiana, by way of Baton Rouge. They were Red Holzman of the New York Knickerbockers; Marty Blake of the St. Louis Hawks; Earl Lloyd of the Detroit Pistons; George Lee of the San Francisco Warriors, and a portly young gent named Jerry Krause, who was picking up his paychecks courtesy of the Baltimore Bullets. The last in the contingent of National Basketball Association scouts on hand for the tournament was Pepper Wilson of the Cincinnati Royals. And, as most everybody knows, butterbeans served Cajun-style are always dashed with pepper.

CHAPTER 14

THE CINCINNATI KID

That Butterbean Love was scouted at all as a collegiate basketball player was due to Southern University's surprising performance in the NAIA playoffs during the spring of 1965. Had the Jaguars been eliminated from the tournament before they rode the train to Kansas City, this book most likely never would have been written. For all of their adeptness at caring for and nurturing their players, neither Dick Mack nor John Brown had a pipeline to the National Basketball Association's inner sanctum when Bob Love was about to emerge from his collegiate cocoon to spread his wings as a professional. In fact, Brown claims it was a player, not a scout or a coach or general manager who provided the conduit Bob Love needed to be seen and evaluated before the NBA conducted its draft following his graduation in the spring of 1965.

"The way Cincinnati drafted him," remembers Big John Brown, "is that we had told Wayne Embry about him when Wayne was still playing for the Royals. Wayne was the only player in the NBA at the time that we knew. We weren't the best of friends, but we knew each other.

"Well, Coach Mack called Wayne up and told him we had Love down here, and they sent Pepper Wilson down to the NAIA when we were playing in Kansas City. I guess Pepper must have liked what he saw — at least a little bit, anyway — because they drafted him. Of course, the draft wasn't as big then as it is now, nothing like it is now. And the fourth round wasn't high at all."

Fourth round draft picks in the '90s might just as well dust up a resume and prepare for life in the Real World, life where leather attaches take the place of leather balls, where the only height advantage you have is your office location and your place in the corporate food chain. Today, because of the opulence of professional basketball, where millions of dollars are spilled upon a first round draft pick weeks, even months, before he pulls on his first NBA jock strap, a first-rounder is virtually assured of a place on the roster. Management cannot afford shelling out that kind of money to a player who proves he can't cut it in the world of professional basketball, in a world where the streets are paved with gold and shoe companies spread wealth like so many arch supports. Nor can management afford to endure the humiliation that comes with an admission that their scouting reports were wrong, that their judgement was oblique, that the promise on the horizon was really nothing more than a mirage, a mucky hovering over a Louisiana cotton field.

But for a fourth round NBA draft pick in 1965, there was a glimmer of hope. On the eve of the 1965-66 basketball season, there were nine franchises in the National Basketball Association, four in the Eastern Division and five in the West. The Hawks called St. Louis their home, the Bullets played in Baltimore, the Warriors battled across the bay in San Francisco and the Royals, of course, were still two moving van hauls and one name change to the east of Sacramento. Today there are 27 teams banging around the NBA, scuffling in such venues as Charlotte, North Carolina, Phoenix, Arizona, and East Rutherford, New Jersey. In 1965, the year before the Chicago Bulls were born, neither Mickey Mouse nor the Magic were the king of Orlando, Florida. Today it's a tossup whether the Mouse or Shaq rules Central Florida, though it's certain that both are much hotter than the team that plays in Miami.

The year Robert Earl Love left Southern University with his bachelor's degree in foods and nutrition, 108 players did the work of what 324 must accomplish in today's National Basketball Association. Yet among those 108 basketball players were some of the brightest stars ever to burn in the NBA's heavens. By the spring of 1965, Wilt Chamberlain had left Kansas and the old Motorola in Ella Hunter's shed to emerge as the premier Dipper in the NBA, leading all scorers with nearly 35 points per game. In his vapor trail were Jerry West of the Lakers, Sam Jones of the Celtics and Elgin Baylor, West's teammate in Los Angeles. Boston's Bill Russell, the Dipper's perennial nemesis, led all rebounders with 24 boards per game.

And emerging in the Queen City and Cincinnati Gardens, hard by the banks of the Ohio River, was a six foot five, 205 pound guard who had also played his collegiate ball in Cincinnati, for the hometown Bearcats. In 1965, Oscar Robertson, in his fifth season in the NBA for the Cincinnati Royals, had developed into one of basketball's true superstars. As the 1965-66 season closed its books, The Big O finished third in scoring behind Chamberlain and West with a 30.4 points- per-game average. He led the league in assists that season with nearly twelve a game, four more on the average than his closest pursuer, little Guy Rodgers of the San Francisco Warriors. That year the Royals finished with a 48-32 record, good for second in the East behind Boston, which devoured the league with a 62-18 record. Robertson and the Royals were eliminated in the first round of the playoffs, three games to one by the Philadelphia Seventy-Sixers, whose 40-40 record was as much a mirage as the muckies of Bastrop. Midway through the season, the Sixers acquired center Wilt Chamberlain and his 35 points per game from the Warriors. With The Stilt filling the middle for Philly, the Sixers brushed past the Royals, three games out of four, and extended the defending champion Celtics to the full seven games in the Eastern Division playoff final round. In fact, Chamberlain came within just five seconds of carrying the Sixers into the championship round against the Lakers, when the Celtics' John Havlicek intercepted an in-bounds pass under the Philadelphia basket to preserve a 110-109 Boston victory. The Seventy-Sixers arguably would have assumed the NBA crown had they knocked off the reigning champs; after scrambling to dispose of Philadelphia, Boston cruised past Los Angeles, four games to one.

In the spring of 1965, out of LSU and Bob Love's radio days, the Hawks' Bob Pettit became the most prolific scorer in NBA history, passing the 20,000 point plateau. That spring Pettit pulled a Michael Jordan and bowed out of professional basketball with his skills and his 26.4 points-per-game average still intact.

Just a few months after Pettit announced his retirement from professional basketball, Robert Earl Love reported to coach Jack McMahon's camp as a fourth round draft pick by the Cincinnati Royals. For the first time in his two decades on the planet, Bob Love was dispatched to play basketball for a team that called somewhere besides Louisiana its home. For only the second time in his life, Bob Love walked into a locker room to find teammates whose skin was a different color than his own. And for the first time ever in Bob Love's 22 years, the man who sat behind the desk, the man who blew the whistle, the man who choreographed the offensive and defensive schemes, was white.

"I was scared, no other way to describe it, man," Love remembers today. "I was away from home — really away from home — for the first time in my life. All of a sudden, I was in a northern city, playing basketball for white folks. I'm not sure I was prepared for any of that. I'm not even sure I was able to appreciate the odds I had overcome to even be drafted by the fourth round.

"I came from a small school, plus there were only nine teams in the entire league at the time. The scouting system was not as thorough or as complicated as it is today. The money wasn't nearly as much as it is today. A lot of guys got overlooked because the scouting systems couldn't possibly cover the entire country and no one had access to television or film or tape back then. When I think back to the draft, I guess I was pretty lucky to have ever had a chance to play professional basketball."

Butterbean Love, confused, frightened, yet seldom overmatched, did what he could under Jack McMahon's tryout camp system. Because he was scouted only in the most rudimentary sense, there was no way that general manager Pepper Wilson or Jack McMahon or anyone else in Cincinnati could have known that Robert Earl Love, a fourth round draft pick out of Southern University in Baton Rouge, Louisiana, couldn't talk. So when he reported to the Royals camp in the fall of 1965, Jack McMahon and the Cincinnati Royals could only assume one thing. When asked a question about an offensive play or a defensive alignment, Bob Love remained silent. When cajoled to hustle or when whistled for an infraction, Bob Love remained silent. Off the court, his timidity was misinterpreted, his reticence misunderstood. And Bob Love remained silent. The Royals assumed what to them was the obvious: Bob Love was stupid.

"It was the first time in my life that my stuttering really became a problem," Love recalls. "All during my high school and college days, my coaches would take extra time to make sure I was comfortable, to see to it that I could relax and perform. But at Cincinnati, no one cared. It was a big business and no one wanted to take the time to figure out that I had a problem with my speech."

So on the final cutdown day, the day the Cincinnati Royals trimmed their roster to twelve in order to engage in the battle of the oncoming championship season, Bob Love got his pink slip and was sent packing to the Trenton Colonials of the Eastern Basketball League.

But before he left, Butterbean left a lasting impression on one of the greatest players of his time. In fact, you can pick a fight — or at least precipitate a serious debate — with Oscar Robertson very easily. Mention the name of Michael Jordan and suggest that, in his time, The Big O *might* have been Michael's equivalent. Suggest that, were he playing today instead of thirty years ago, Oscar Robertson could *perhaps* perform at a level in the same stratosphere as Air Jordan, and Robertson will not snap. He will not growl. But he will, under no uncertain circumstances, leave you to understand that his career speaks for itself and that Mr. Jordan's statistics among all his hype do not intimidate Oscar Robertson. Want to be dressed down?

Just insinuate that Oscar Robertson's skills, determination and fire were of another era and of another level than those of Michael Jordan.

"You think I might be *equivalent* to Michael Jordan?" he inquires menacingly. "You're saying it like you have some doubts. If you want to talk about Bob Love, then let's talk about Bob Love. If you want to talk about who the greatest player was, just look at my record. We'll talk about Bob Love, if you don't mind."

Look at the record, indeed.

As a rookie in 1960, Oscar Robertson exploded into the National Basketball Association with a 30.5 points-per-game average and nearly ten assists an outing. He was the runaway rookie of the year and heads turned throughout the league.

Over the course of fourteen years as a player for the Cincinnati Royals and the Milwaukee Bucks, Oscar Robertson averaged 25.7 points per game, with 9.5 assists and 7.5 rebounds. Today, the formula for granting an assist on a given play is much more liberal than when Oscar was in the league. Yet it can be effectively argued that The Big O was the Father of the Triple Double: two digits each per game for points, assists and rebounds.

The Official NBA Guide is liberally sprinkled with the name Oscar Robertson. His career numbers, indeed, argue his case that The Big O was one of the true greats of the game: Seventh all-time in most field goals attempted (19,620); sixth in most field goals made (9,508); fifth in minutes played (43,886); fourth in free throws attempted (9,185); second in free throws made (7,694); second in assists (9,887); eighth in scoring average (25.7), and fourth in total points (26,710).

In an interview in 1990 with Robbie Andreu of the Fort Lauderdale *News and Sun-Sentinel*, Robertson vented some of his disdain on people who today are consumed with statistics:

"People are so stat-conscious today. They try to make a big thing out of someone who gets a triple-double. I had those all the time, but no one ever made anything of it. With all the television exposure, it is a media-type game today.

"Sometimes it gets out of hand. You read all the time now

where a guy had 20 assists or more in a game, and that's ridicu-
lous. When I played, you had to earn assists. Today, they hand
them out if you make a pass to a guy who then dribbles and
shoots a 20-footer. I wish someone would go back and look at a
play-by-play of one of my games and record assists the way they
do today. I'd probably have 25 a game. That would look good in
the record book."

Even Bob Love, who watched in awe the acrobatics of Michael Jordan, will pit his mentor against Sir Air, one on one:

"They can talk about Michael all they want to," says Butterbean. "Oscar was the same player. I mean, Oscar would dominate Michael Jordan because Oscar was bigger. Bigger, stronger. Now, Michael would be able to score against Oscar, all things being equal. But Oscar had the same mind-set that Michael has. That iron mind, that fierce competitiveness. I mean to tell you, Oscar Robertson would just eat you alive."

When Love returned for his second crack at making the Royals' roster, the crack that opened the view to a glimmer of hope for his NBA career, Oscar Robertson, National Basketball Association superstar, was there. In fact, upon Butterbean's return to Cincinnati in the fall of 1966, Love was paired as Robertson's roommate for the team's road trips. They roomed together the full two seasons that Love played for the Royals. And even today, both men speak of one another with the sincerest of admiration, mutual respect not only for athletic skills but also as human beings.

Robertson still resides in his adopted home of Cincinnati, though he is native to the little town of Charlotte, just outside Nashville, Tennessee. Today Oscar Robertson, The Big O, directs a corporate team rather than an NBA one. He serves as owner and president of ORCHEM (Oscar Robertson Chemicals), a firm that blends specialty chemicals to be used in food processing plants throughout the United States. ORCHEM has been in business eleven years now and Robertson is pleased with the direction his corporate life has taken: "It's like everything else in the economy today. We are dependent on economic factors beyond our control, but overall I'd have to say that business is good."

Life, in general, has been good to Oscar Robertson. His basketball portfolio would certainly be stuffed with mountains more cash had he been born in 1968 rather than 1938. Yet life has still been good to Oscar Robertson. He snagged his biggest professional basketball contract after moving on to the Milwaukee Bucks in the early '70s, after ten years of working for the Royals. ("It was three hundred some thousand," he says matter-of-factly.) As any working stiff knows, three hundred some thousand is a stash, the kind of money spilling out of Lotto pots all over America, the kind of dough most people work a decade or more to earn. But compared to today's NBA standards, a three hundred some thousand dollar payday is peanuts. So you ask The Big O what he would be worth in today's inflated market, minus even a shoe contract.

"Oh, I don't know. Who cares? I've been asked that several times but I say it doesn't matter because the game right now is getting to the point where it's ridiculous."

In Oscar Robertson's voice there is not a trace of bitterness that he was born too soon to reap in the harvest of professional basketball's abundance. No, but there is, undoubtedly, resentment within Oscar Robertson, chemical executive. His resentment, understand, is with the direction of the sport he loved to engage, with the dependence on agents and what might be perceived as a lack of appreciation by today's megabucks players. One gets the impression that Oscar Robertson, basketball Hall of Famer and chemical executive, believes there aren't too many working stiffs in today's glamour world of the National Basketball Association.

"You know, Larry Johnson is making $84,000,000. And then you have a situation down in Houston where a football player (Oilers lineman David Williams) wants to see his baby born so he misses a game. Then an agent gets involved in it? It's getting to the point where we might as well just let the agents go ahead and play football and basketball."

Play basketball is what both The Big O and Butterbean Love wanted to do. But as so many players will testify, professional sports is every bit as political as any elective office in the land. And perception in professional sports is every bit as real as perception in the world of politics. In fact, Robertson today believes that a fourth round selection in his day had a better chance of making a team than a higher pick might have in today's inflated market.

"Back then, a fourth-rounder would have a chance to play. Now, it's a lot different because you come out of school and you're making so much money. You give a kid out of college two million bucks and a no-cut contract, and whether he's any good or not, he's gonna be on the team. And that happens a lot. During those days, very few guys had a no-cut contract. That was a very, very difficult thing to get back then. No one had guaranteed contracts. You had to make the team and you had to make it every year. A lot of things have changed since then."

One thing that has not changed is Oscar Robertson's opinion — socially and professionally — about his friend.

"Bob's a very nice person, really," says Robertson. "And he was a very good basketball player that the Royals didn't quite appreciate. But that's neither here nor there. They thought that because Bob had a speech impediment, that he didn't have the intelligence to play ball, that he wasn't as intelligent as other ballplayers. But during the '60s, you had a lot of people, especially when it came to a black person, who were set in their thinking. Whites had very little tolerence for people like that."

Robertson is a member of a club that subscribes to the idea the Royals had no idea Love stuttered when they made him their fourth round choice in 1965.

"Probably not. They really didn't go into any detail or check anyone at all back then. I'm sure they didn't."

Would it have mattered? Would the Royals have taken a pass if Pepper Wilson had filed a scouting report that read, "Lovely jump shot; below-average speed overall but above-average quickness; well-coached; better-than-average defense. This guy can shoot the lights out if left alone in the corner. But he can't talk."

"Could have. Eventually, they got rid of him and you saw what he did after he left here, after he left Cincinnati as a basketball player. He really started to improve and grow as a professional athlete."

Robertson shares the view that most athletes are perceived as just another side of beef on a hook, available to any bidder who can barter something in return. In that regard, the Royals never saw any value in providing speech therapy for Bob Love.

"Of course not. Why should they do that?" The Big O now has a sense of cynicism in his voice. "They couldn't see his merits of being a great basketball player, so naturally they wouldn't try to improve his speech."

In fact, Robertson suspects that if Bob Love were a professional basketball commodity today, 20-some years after the fact, it would be a corporate sponsor and not a basketball franchise that would spring for the therapy he needed to become communicative.

"I think what you have today, with the marketing aspects that are involved with gifted athletes — plus the fact that Bob Love was a star — that a product that needed his endorsement would probably have to take a chance. Someone who would have wanted his endorsement today would probably get him the therapy he needed to get the job done. Look what happened at Nordstrom's, when he started to work out there. They saw the qualities inside Bob. They saw his character and they took the initiative.

"I'd like to think that a shoe company or a T-shirt company or a card company would have taken a Bob Love today and made sure that he could have gone out in public and communicate — as he's doing right now, because of what Nordstrom had done for him."

By the time Bob Love had earned an NBA uniform for keeps, Oscar Robertson was an accomplished superstar. The Big O was recognized throughout the league as a premier scorer and all-around offensive menace. He was secure. He was smooth. He was The Franchise in Cincinnati. Yet it was simply coincidence, Robertson believes, that the rookie from Bastrop out of Southern University, was paired as Oscar's roommate. The two, born four years apart, had enough in common to bind them as teammates and later as friends for a lifetime.

"He's from the South and I'm from the South. When we roomed together, we talked about situations in the South. I'm sure he's from a religious background, which is where I was from myself. So we had a lot in common."

In retrospect, Oscar Robertson was the left shoe to Bob Love's right, the silk necktie perfectly matched to a three-piece suit. The Kid needed a Big Brother and The Big O was it.

"Probably so. I never try to impose my will on any other people, especially when I was an athlete. But Bob was new on the team and he had a lot of concerns about the team, about making the team and about making himself a better life. So we just talked about life.

"We talked about the pitfalls in pro ball and what owners and managers try to do to you. We worked on shots and shot situations. I showed him some things and explained to him what he should try to accomplish as a basketball player. Bob could always play, but when you first come into the league, you really don't know what to do. You really don't know about pro ball when you're coming out of college. It's all new to you."

Oscar Robertson was, in fact, an inspiration and a comfort for Robert Earl Love. The proof was in Butterbean's speech patterns whenever he was around his friend.

"Actually, when he was around me he didn't really stutter that much," Robertson remembers. "We'd have conversations and, sure, he'd stutter a few times. He'd stutter once in a while. But he was just so comfortable with me that I don't remember him stuttering that much at all, to be honest. But I know he did stutter when he got into situations where he wasn't confident."

Like around journalists. So many journalism schools around the country today teach their students to yield little to the makers of news, to the government officials and the politicians and, yes, even to the athletes that reporters cover during the course of their jobs. Tell-it-like-it-is was Howard Cosell's style years before it was Woodward's and Bernstein's. Lord knows, during Watergate's aftermath more cynicism developed among the Fourth Estate than during most any other time during the Twentieth Century. Yet some journalists have enough common sense to carry with them a grain of humanity to the press box and the television and radio booth. The '60s were a less complicated time and reporters generally shielded someone like Bob Love, someone who had a handicap that may have been painful, but that really had no effect on his performance on the basketball floor.

Such was the case with Cincinnati's Ed Kennedy, the Radio Voice of Royals Basketball during the 1960s and '70s.

"I recall a situation with Ed Kennedy," says Robertson. "And it's one reason I will always have a high regard for Ed Kennedy. He wanted to do an interview with Bob Love. He knew Bob from the days when Bob played here because he did the games on radio. And after Bob went up to Chicago, Ed did something for Bob which I thought was tremendous. He did an interview with Bob Love and Chet Walker together. Bob Love had an outstanding game against us, and Ed Kennedy was so sensitive to Bob's situation — he knew about Bob's problem — that he brought both Bob and Chet Walker in for the interview. When he asked Bob questions, he asked questions that he knew wouldn't call for long answers. Then he'd let Chet talk a little bit longer and then he'd ask Bob a question where Bob could answer `yes' or `no' and go on with it. Answers like that. I thought that was tremendous."

Ask Oscar Robertson if Bob Love got a fair deal in Cincinnati and he'll tell you he probably didn't. The NBA was a different animal in The Big O's era. Just two decades old when Bob Love carried his bags into Cincinnati, the National Basketball Association was just beginning to allow the black player to assume the mantle of The Franchise. As The Dipper and The Rabbit and The Big O introduced black dominance to the league, there was resistance. Black players were clearly becoming a force in professional basketball, yet rosters were frozen with white players. Not until the 1970s did they open to allow blacks to assume a majority status among most teams. And Bob Love's first attempt at securing a roster spot with the Royals fell victim to white dominance at the time, in Oscar Robertson's opinion.

"If he was white when he was a rookie," offers Robertson, "I think he would have stuck. Let me tell you this: A lot of things happened in those days, where black athletes were never given a chance. If you were not a star — and I mean a real star — you were simply not given a real opportunity of making a lot of the teams. They played a lot of favorites and there was a lot of favoritism on the part of coaches, and the favoritism did not include a lot of black athletes.

"If you bummed around with a coach, if you went out drinking beers with him or something, that helped your situation."

Oscar Robertson wasn't one to drink beers or bum around with a coach. With his talent and established worth, he didn't need to. But he was witness to the prevailing white attitude of the era. He wasn't blind; he could see it.

"Of course I could. But I could get around a lot of it because of my status. A lot of players could not. Of course there was racism then. When I first started playing, if you had over three blacks on a team, that was a lot. Some teams had just two. And that stigma stuck around for a long time.

"The same situation exists today in football with black quarterbacks. Still, the press — and I'm including the print media, the television and the radio — will never come to grips with that. They try to avoid it because they know there's so much blatant racism regarding quarterbacks that it's unbelievable. Not even the black athlete on the field will say anything about it."

Through it all, The Big O reached out and pulled Butterbean up when the kid was down. They talked about life, for sure. But they also talked about basketball, and Bob Love learned from Oscar Robertson the same lessons he learned from Ella Hunter: Hard work will overcome most odds.

"I owe a lot to Oscar Robertson," Love tells anyone who will listen. "When I was first in Cincinnati, when I was just trying out for the team, I hung around with Oscar a lot. Oscar would invite me over to his house and he really, really made me feel good, made me feel at home. You know, both of us were from the south so he knew what I was going to be up against, being a kid out of a small black college and playing for the first time in the NBA. He knew about what I was up against, trying to get over the things that were really bothering me.

"I got to be friends with Jerry Lucas and Connie Dierking. The white guys all really took to me. They liked the fact that I was from the south and they found it interesting, I guess, that I stuttered. I kept everybody laughing because I stuttered, I guess." Bob Love now laughs at that notion.

During the Royals camp, Oscar Robertson stressed that Love needed to develop an outside shot that would set him apart from the other big men who were struggling to stick in the NBA. Something that he could turn to in a crunch. Bob Love needed a signature shot.

"I told him to develop a shot," says Robertson today. "Develop a shot where he could always get a shot to the basket. Work on something like that. Because no matter what you do as a basketball player, you've got to be able to shoot the ball. If you can shoot the ball, it bails you out of trouble. And he developed a pretty good turn-around shot and he had a nice little hook shot right in-close."

And he had a nickname. Don't forget the nickname. The Big O did not discourage the nickname.

"I guess it was pretty cool, the Butterbean name. I had a nickname, The Big O. And Wilt was The Dipper and Elgin, they called him The Rabbit. A few white guys had nicknames, but not many. It was mostly the black guys. That's kind of odd, isn't it?"

Perhaps. But it was more than nicknames that set the black players apart as Bob Love sprouted in the National Basketball Association. White guys were growing their hair longer and their sideburns thicker. Black guys were letting their kinky hair puff out until they looked like streaking ebony mushroom caps. And basketball was undergoing an evolution.

"How would he compare if he were playing today?" Robertson repeats the question. "He'd be like Bob Love. I don't think any player today plays like Bob Love played. Bob Love played sort of a forward-low pivot sometimes. He was very adept off the pivot, a very smart player inside with the basketball. He didn't make a lot of mistakes and he could really fill it up. He could score. Who plays like that anymore?

"These guys today, you know, they dunk a ball once or twice and they make $2,000,000. None of the players that I see today, the ones I see inside, are as prolific as Bob Love was with the basketball. What's a player like Bob Love worth today? Oh, $3,000,000 or $4,000,000. A year, of course. Times have changed a lot."

You sense the pride Robertson has in the rookie he once took under his wing. The kid who once could hardly speak today serves as director of community relations for the Chicago Bulls, the team whose canvas he once painted, the team whose streets he helped pave for Michael Jordan, Scottie Pippen and three consecutive NBA championships. And while Robertson shares his protege's joy in his new position for the Chicago NBA franchise, he is nonetheless critical of the Bulls, who he believes took advantage of someone else's insight and compassion.

"Yeah, he's doing a great job for the Bulls now. But the Bulls got him back after all the therapy. They did not take Bob Love when he really needed the help, when he was really in a desperate situation. Here again, everybody uses you for their own needs. And I'm glad that Bob was in a position where he could be used like that. But don't think the Bulls did this when he was in Seattle, when he had no job and when he was struggling through a divorce. They didn't do that."

CHAPTER 15

COLONIAL SHUDDERS

As the leaves on the trees turned from green and soft to red and orange and yellow, then again to a crunchy brown and gray, the Cincinnati Royals went about the business of trimming their roster in anticipation of the 1965-66 season. The leaves lost their death grip on the limbs that held them through summer, sometimes one by one, sometimes in clumps and bunches. So, too, were NBA hopefuls sent home without much hope of ever playing a regulation minute in a Royals' uniform. Bob Love was the last leaf to fall from the Royals' family tree that autumn, the thirteenth man on a twelve-man roster. He had performed unexpectedly well in pre-season — he exceeded the club's expectations — yet for whatever reason, he was the guy without a seat in the final round of musical chairs. The music had stopped, temporarily at least, and Bob Love was asked to look for a different shirt.

Today, nearly three decades later, Love disagrees with the decision to keep him off the team his first year out of Southern.

"I should have made the team," he says without contrition. "When they brought me to rookie camp, they had about 1,000 guys in camp. Ooh, there were guys there from everywhere in the world. And you know what? I ate those guys up. I averaged maybe 17, 18 points a game during rookie camp, so they decided to bring me in with the veterans.

"Let's see. They had Jon McGlocklin, Nate Bowman, some other guys, and I ate those guys up."

Unfortunately for Bob Love, McGlocklin, a six-five, 205 pound rookie out of Indiana — a six-five, 205 pound *white* rookie out of Indiana — made the team.

"Just ate them up. But back in those days, there were just nine teams in the league. Hell, there weren't too many places to go back then. There just weren't enough teams. If there had been more teams back then, I would have been a number one draft pick."

But even though penguins are birds, you'll never see one flying over the South Pole. Bob Love was not a first round draft pick and he was black. If you subscribe to Oscar Robertson's thoughts, a white Bob Love is the twelfth Cincinnati Royal in the fall of 1965. ("I don't know if a coaching change gave him a better chance at making the team the next year. I think Cincinnati had four coaches, which is three too many.") But in the Royals' way of thinking, their fourth round draft choice needed a bit of seasoning before they could dish him out to the hometown guests. He needed time, they believed, to learn about professional basketball before he could survive, not to mention thrive, in the game of professional basketball played at its highest level.

In 1965, the Royals had a working agreement with the Trenton Colonials of the Eastern Basketball League. Just one season earlier, the Colonials were spinning on the brink of bankruptcy and living deep in the Eastern Basketball League's basement. No one knew, in fact, how long the franchise could survive, consistently drawing anemic three-figure crowds for their home games.

As they prepared for the autumn of 1965, the Trenton Colonials scoured the scouts' lists of recent college graduates, scratching and scraping for a franchise player whose marquee value could increase their pathetic gate and add some numbers to the win column. At the top of their wish list was Tony Kimball out of Connecticut. The year before, Kimball led the nation in rebounding. But Kimball chose instead to cross the Atlantic and play basketball in Spain.

Another target in the Colonials cross-hairs was a young fellow just graduated from Princeton, a bright young man by the name of Bill Bradley. But Bradley, who later would star in New York for the Knicks and in Washington for the Democrats, followed Kimball across the ocean, then took a right at Madrid and played his basketball the Appian Way.

At the eleventh hour, the Colonials secured the services of a young forward, six foot eight inch Robert Earl Love. Just as happened in the American Revolution, the Royals' side lost one of its best men to the underdog Colonials. Bob Love would stay on the left side of the ocean.

Chick Craig, then the 39-year-old coach of the Colonials, shares much of the credit for bringing Love to Trenton. And bringing Love to Trenton was, in effect, bringing Love to the threshold of eventual stardom in the National Basketball Association.

"I got to tell you the whole story," says Craig, who at age 67 still scours colleges in search of talent for the NBA. "I knew Pepper Wilson. I followed Cincinnati. Now, Love was scoring a lot of points in college and he went to Cincinnati — he was in their camp — when I was coaching at Trenton. I used to go to the Rutgers tournament all the time, up in Harlem. There they had a guy named Bob McCullough, who had tried out for Cincinnati, too. Cincinnati cut 'em both — McCullough and Love both. I had McCullough at Trenton and I asked him, 'Who looks good in the Royals' camp?' And he told me that Bob Love was tearing it up but that they had cut him, anyway. I got his phone number and I called Bob Love.

"So now I want to bring him to Trenton but he doesn't have any money for the train. We didn't fly 'em in those days. So the owners in Trenton send him a train ticket. And he comes to Trenton and the owners meet him at the train station, they put him up in a nice room, everything. That same week, they took him to the big men's shop and they bought him some sweaters and some pants, and I think it came to something like 400 bucks, which was a lot of money those days. Well, they were going to take so much out of his paycheck — something like 20, 25 bucks a week. And, holy hell, we open the season at Sunbury and Love has 41 — and that's when the Eastern League was tough. It was the only league then — the NBA and the Eastern League. He comes up with 41 points that night, so they didn't take anything out of his pay. From then on, he was by far the best player in the league."

Tom Sargent, then a columnist for the *Trenton Times,* was one of Bob Love's first and staunchest EBL fans. In a column written just a couple of weeks after Love's arrival in New Jersey, Sargent proclaimed:

> ... *Love is probably more valuable to the club now than either Bradley or Kimball (could have been), since the first requirement in the league is strong scoring underneath. In fact, Love turns out to be a combination of Bradley and Kimball, which you may not believe. The fact that Love performs with such ease and power against the pros in his first year is rare for any player, whether he is the best in college play or not.*

During a game in his first week as a Colonial, Love ripped down an incredible 30 rebounds against Allentown. Through his first five games as a professional basketball player — although admittedly one fighting his way through a minor league — Butterbean scored 108 points for a 21.8 average. And, by all accounts, his defense was steel wool tough. Bob Love was off and running on the racetrack of professional basketball.

"The biggest difference, I learned right away, between college and Trenton was that I was playing against older guys," he says. "All the guys were older. They were guys who had a lot of experience and who knew how to bang around."

As Bob Love was emerging within the Eastern league, the EBL itself was emerging as a dependable farm system for the National Basketball Association. It was becoming a revolving gate that was turning players back to the NBA and gladly accepting those who were *this close* to the NBA's caliber of play. The same season Love was sent to Trenton to learn the nuances of the professional game, the Colonials also secured the rights to Walter Dukes, late of the Detroit Pistons, and Elbert Butler, formerly of the New York Knicks. At the same time, Philadelphia's Jerry Costello signed on with Wilkes Barre and the Celtics' John Thompson dropped down to play for Wilmington.

But the elevator also had an *up* button. That fall, Boston dipped into the EBL to acquire Woody Sauldsberry from New Haven and Joe Strawder climbed out of Camden to play for the Pistons. In time, Trenton would provide Bob Love with similar upward mobility. It ... just ... took ... a ... little ... *seasoning*.

"As I recall," Love says, "there were a lot of New York guys playing in the league, a lot of east coast guys who had been around and who knew a lot of tricks. Guys like Walter Dukes and Tom Hoover. One old guy we had on our team was a guy who had played around New York for years, a classic guy by the name of Stacey Arceneaux. (Arceneaux had played for the St. Louis Hawks about four years before Love arrived in Trenton.) Stacey had been around for years, seemed like he'd been around forever. And he was a guy who really knew how to play the game.

"I really learned a lot from guys like Stacey Arceneaux and Walter Dukes during the time I played for Trenton. I learned the inside tricks that we just didn't know about when we were playing in college. I still don't think the Royals should have cut me that year, but there was some consolation knowing that I was able to learn as much as I did while playing for Trenton.

"As I look back on the experience, it seems to me the older guys, the guys from the east coast, were kind of amazed that a guy from Louisiana could play like I played. Back then, those guys used to think that if you were from New York, you could jump higher than anyone else. Guys like Jackie Jackson, man, could he jump. But before I got my back hurt, I could jump higher than anyone else in the world. That's something that no one had to teach me. But I learned the tricks the pros need to survive."

Learn he did, about two days a week with the Colonials. The EBL was a weekend league, its teams playing Saturdays and Sundays. During the week, Love would play as many evening pick-up games as he could just across the state line in Philadelphia. But basketball was not supplying a lonely Bob Love with sufficient contentment, emotionally or financially. Recently married and with an infant son, Butterbean Love found himself separated from Betty and Kevin by 1,100 miles and a lifetime of cultural differences.

Bob had met Betty while they both were enrolled at Southern University in Baton Rouge and they clicked almost immediately. Betty was perhaps the first woman whose presence did not intimidate Love and with whom he felt at ease. When he was around Betty, even when they first met, that awful stutter somehow was suppressed.

Plain and simple, Bob Love found himself to be homesick for the first time in his life. The transition from Wash and Morehouse High School in Bastrop to Dick Mack and Southern University in Bastrop was smooth. It was easy. There were Arthur Hamlin and Robert Smith and Melvin Anderson to make him feel at home. Baton Rouge, though much larger than Bastrop, was still South, and Southern University, like Morehouse High, was still black.

Trenton was none of the above. It was North. It was urban. And Bob Love was living outside his hometown element. Homesickness was getting the best of Trenton's best young player. It is a malady common among young, black rural kids who find themselves in the urban jungles of the north. During the week, Bob had too much time on his hands, too much time to think about whether or not he made the right decision to play in the Eastern Basketball League. Too much time to think about Betty and Kevin. So much time that he thought seriously about quitting, about climbing aboard a Greyhound bus back to Louisiana. He thought seriously about taking his degree in foods and nutrition back home, to a job where he could be with and support his young family. It would not, for sure, be the job he dreamed in his dreams. But it would have been a job, maybe even a career. In Trenton, he felt like he was chasing butterflies with tweezers instead of a net.

"I was by myself. I was all alone and my family was back in Baton Rouge. I guess I was pretty homesick. I couldn't afford a car on the $150 a game they were paying me, and I had a lot of time on my hands between games. I considered packing up and heading home to Baton Rouge."

That's when, with a little help from the Colonials, Love landed a job as an assistant dietician at the New Jersey State Hospital just up the road from Trenton. It was a spiritual boost. It was a financial stimulant, too. Make no mistake, though. Robert Earl Love was not in the penthouse apartment. Not yet, that's for sure.

"I had a lot of time on my hands during the week, too much time. And I wasn't doing too well financially, either. I decided I needed to get a week day job or I was going to be forced to go home. At Trenton, we'd play a game on Saturday and one on Sunday. During the week I'd play in a little pickup league in Philadelphia, just to stay in shape. And I was just about ready to go home when I got an internship working for the state of New Jersey at one of the state hospitals.

"I was living on the hospital grounds during the week, during the time I was working at the state hospital. They had rooms on the hospital grounds, sort of a dormitory situation. On weekends, when we had games in Trenton, I lived at the YMCA.

"Like I said, I didn't have a car, so I got around on the bus. That and there were some guys from New York who would come down and give me a ride when we had to get to a game."

The only time Betty and Kevin saw their husband and dad during that season was during the Christmas holiday.

"Betty came up during the holidays, but that was really the only time I had a chance to see my family. It was the dead of winter. They had me staying in that little dorm room on the hospital grounds. I had to get up every morning at about four o'clock and it was cold. Man, was it cold at four in the morning! And I had to walk about a half mile down the road to the dining hall, where I worked, doing a variety of things throughout the day. It wasn't the most glamorous job I've ever had, but it was a hell of an experience."

Such is the route to the big leagues for some. No no-cut contract for Bob Love. Dirty dishes, yes. No road trips to La La Land. Stirring creamed corn, yes. Autograph seekers at the state hospital? How about wiping off that table instead?

After a few weeks, Love was transfered to the state mental hospital at Woodbridge, a few miles further to the northeast from Trenton.

"That was the New Jersey state hospital for kids. That was a great experience. At Woodbridge, they had this big school for the kids, where I worked, located right across the street from a state prison. They had a lot of prison guys working nearby, out picking vegetables and doing odd jobs right outside the place for the kids. Oh, man, that was the first time I had ever been around guys like that — prisoners. And these were some bad guys, man. We had to go over to the prison every other day to pick up bread. They had a bakery over at the prison and we'd go in and pick up the bread we needed to serve to the kids. Those guys were something, man. Hoo! I'm telling you." Bob Love is big and Bob Love is black. On a dark street corner or in a lonely alley, Bob Love would cut an intimidating figure, the sort of silhouette that causes even brave souls to avoid potential danger. But looks, in the case of Robert Earl Love, are certainly deceiving. Bob Love is a pussy cat — a six foot eight inch pussy cat for sure — but a pussy cat nonetheless.

The arrival in Trenton of Cincinnati's final roster cut was greeted with unprecedented enthusiasm. The struggling Colonials had finally landed themselves a budding superstar, a franchise player who would put fannies in the seats. It was certainly in the club's best interests to assure happiness — emotionally and financially — for their rookie phenom.

Testimony to Love's explosion on the New Jersey scene is contained in a column by Bus Saidt in *The Trentonian* on November 10, 1965. It read, in part:

> *It was the classic case of Love at first sight.*
>
> *There's a new sports celebrity in our town and his name is Bob Love and the Trenton Colonials are mighty happy he plays basketball for them in the Eastern League.*
>
> *Rarely has a newcomer to the demanding Trenton sports scene opened to such rave notices as those which accompanied Love's labors as the Colonials opened the EBL campaign in stunning fashion with the rout of the tough Allentown Jets.*
>
> *Obviously, it's too early to go to the end of the proverbial limb, but every evidence seems to indicate these Colonials finally*

might blend all the ingredients to be a positive pennant contender.

And Bob Love might be the brightest sports star to hit these parts since the Ikeya-Seki comet streaked past our skies.

All he did was come off the bench when Trenton was having a bad case of opening-night jitters, take charge of the ball game with his splendid offense, stop Tom Stith on defense and break the thing wide open. He scored 21 points, took down thirteen rebounds, blocked shots left and right and left the near-capacity Trenton High crowd on its feet screaming his and the Cols' praises.

Love arrived three weeks ago after spending the NBA training period with the Cincinnati Royals, who made him their fourth draft selection on the basis of his brilliant college career at Southern University in Baton Rouge, Louisiana.

He had played in all the Royals' exhibitions, averaging six points a game and rebounding well, but coach Jack McMahon called him in one day and told him he was too light at 210 pounds to take the NBA pounding. It was a bitter disappointment, lightened somewhat when Cincy general manager Pepper Wilson suggested he contact Colonials G.M. Sid Hofing and think about playing ball in the Eastern League.

"Why don't you go over there, play ball and pick up experience so that next time the chance comes you'll be ready," Wilson suggested. Love agreed and the eventual marriage between him and Trenton pro basketball might result in the greatest Love affair since Miss Taylor and Mr. Burton.

Unfortunately for Trenton basketball fans, the marriage would last only about as long as one of Elizabeth Taylor's typical periods of marital bliss — a year, to be exact. Saidt's column also mentioned Love's battle with boredom in the days leading up to landing the job at the mental health facility:

He lives at the YMCA and, as he says, "I'm tired of sleeping all day." Like after the movies change on Tuesday or Wednesday, what is there for a weekend basketball player to do?

... this is Love's first experience in the east. A music lover, he's looking forward to catching some solid sounds in Philly and New York.

If he's going to play regularly the way he played Sunday, the Colonials' biggest worry might be, as one fan put it, "he's too good for this league. He'll be back in the NBA fast."

... Move over, Elizabeth Barrett and Robert Browning. This could develop into one of the great Love stories of all times.

Love's coach at Trenton, Chick Craig, was a man who punched train tickets during the week and pushed the Colonials' buttons on the weekends.

"A real nice guy," Love laughs, recalling Craig's job riding the rails between Trenton and New York City. "The guy loved me and I give him a lot of the credit for helping me learn the professional game. It's funny, but all these years later, a lot of people still remember me in Trenton. I was averaging points in the twenties that year and I was a helluva rebounder, a helluva shot-blocker. I could always jump, at least until I got my back hurt. I guess they still remember some of those things back in Trenton."

Craig still lives in Phillipsburg, New Jersey, where he lived when he coached the Colonials. Though he never set foot on the court as an NBA player or coach, he spent eleven years playing in the EBL and another 21 as a coach. Now an NBA scout and the coach of Hazleton in the Continental Basketball Association, Craig fondly remembers the season the city of Trenton fell in love with Love.

"He was a good kid," reminisces Craig. "I had no trouble with him at all. Boy, he played. He hustled. He'd give you everything. I tell you, one time we went to Hartford. And at Trenton they used to feed all the guys before they left for a game. They made sure they had something to eat before they went away. And we had spare ribs that day. I think Gene Conley was coaching at Hartford at the time. And Love got sick. We had to stop the bus because he got sick as a dog. First half, we're behind and he's sick. Second half, he says, `I can play.' So in the second half he goes out and has 30 and we beat Hartford. That's the kind of guy that kid was."

Craig, whose dialect makes him sound a good deal like legendary Marquette coach Al McGuire, said Love's stutter posed no serious problems between them.

"He stuttered a little bit but I knew how to take him. I never had any problems communicating with him. And his teammates loved him."

A true gentleman, Earl "Chick" Craig enjoys the recollection of a man who may have been his greatest player.

"I'll never forget it. Call me anytime you want."

CHAPTER 16

LOVE: A BULL

With a full year of minor league apprenticeship under his belt, Bob Love made it to the NBA — somewhat inauspiciously but for good — in the 1966-67 season. His rookie year with the Royals, he played in 66 games, averaging 6.7 points per game. His roommate, The Big O, finished second in scoring to San Francisco's Rick Barry with a 30.5 points per game average. But Cincinnati, in what would prove to be coach Jack McMahon's final year, finished third in the Eastern Division at 39-42. The Royals were eliminated by Philadelphia in the first round of the playoffs, winning just once in four games.

The following season, under new head coach Ed Jucker, Love appeared in 72 games and averaged 6.4 points per game. Cincinnati was on a treadmill, despite the coaching change. Under Jucker, the Royals were 39-43 in 1967-68, finishing fourth in the five-team East and winding up as one of just four teams which failed to qualify for post-season play.

Apparently operating in the belief their young forward was destined to be a role player in the National Basketball Association, the Royals left Bob Love available for the expansion draft.

"With the Royals I was being used strictly for defense," explains Love. "And seven points a game for the Royals was pretty good, actually, because they weren't giving me much of a chance to score in those days. Hell, Oscar was averaging 30-something points a game at the time. It was a lot like it was with Michael Jordan and the Bulls. And guys like me had to get the scraps, had to score whenever I had a chance. But I was put in those games to play defense and that's what I concentrated on. I didn't want to go back to Trenton."

But he *was* going elsewhere, specifically to America's Dairyland and the suds capital of the world. Milwaukee, which entered the league in 1968 along with Phoenix, plucked Love off Cincinnati's roster. On the 28th of August, Bob Love and Bobby Weiss, a guard taken in the expansion draft from Seattle, signed contracts with the Bucks. By now, the league had expanded to 14 teams. That's five more franchises and 60 more roster spots than when Love was drafted as a fourth-round question mark out of Southern. It was just the break Bob Love needed. Now 25 years old, Robert Earl Love, Bastrop's very own Butterbean, was ready to blossom. His time was just one more change of venue away. This time, no one would deny him.

Neither Love nor Weiss needed to house-hunt in Wisconsin. On November 7, just a handful of games into their inaugural season, the Bucks packaged the pair and shipped them 90 miles south, to 1800 West Madison Street, Chicago, Illinois. In return, the Bulls sent forward Flynn Robinson, obtained just a year earlier from the Royals, to Milwaukee. The deal was a straight, two-for-one trade, with no cash changing hands. It was the first — and arguably the worst — trade consummated by the Bucks. Ironically, Flynn Robinson was drafted by Cincinnati the same year as Love, taken two rounds earlier.

Dick Motta was preparing for his first full season as head coach of the baby Bulls, just two years removed from expansion themselves. To hear Motta tell the story, the acquisition of Bob Love wasn't as much an addition to the Bulls as it was the subtraction of Flynn Robinson. Motta wanted Robinson gone and he made his wishes crystal clear to general manager Dick Klein.

"I didn't want Flynn playing for us anymore," says Motta matter-of-factly. "When I got there, that first year, Flynn Robinson was supposed to be the Second Coming. I don't want to get into negatives about Flynn, but I didn't want Flynn playing for us anymore.

"I'll never forget the story. It was a Friday night. We had back-to-back games — you don't do that too much anymore — and we had games on Friday and Saturday. Flynn had missed nine shots on Friday night. He was oh-for-nine. We were walking down the stairs to the dressing room after the game and he said, 'I'll never make another shot for (Motta) again.' So what he was saying is that he went oh-for-nine on purpose. That's because I wasn't starting him. I played Clem Haskins ahead of him and he had started the year before. But I was starting a 'slow guard' lineup of Haskins and Sloan and we were pretty good at it.

"Anyway, I called the owner and told him that if Flynn walks into this building tomorrow night, you can look for a new coach. That was Friday night. Saturday afternoon, Klein called me and said, 'I've made the trade.'"

The conversation, as Motta recalls it, continued like this:

"Who did you trade him for?"

"Bob Weiss."

"Who's he?"

"He's a left-handed white guard and he can't play. I want to go on record as saying this is the worst trade in the history of the NBA. (And the Cubs liked Ernie Broglio, remember.) And on top of that, we've got to take this other stiff. We've got to take this other stiff in the throw-in because they're an expansion team and they need to knock their roster down from 15."

"Who's that?"

"Bob Love."

"Good. I don't care. Just get Flynn out of here. I don't care who you bring in."

And in an instant, Flynn was outta there and the Roberts Weiss and Love were part of the Chicago landscape.

Networking is everything in life. Whether it's politics or retailing or professional basketballing, a successful network is what keys the firm's overall success. And so when Earl "Chick" Craig took a scouting position with Dick Klein and the Chicago Bulls, he knew which button to push.

"I'll never forget this," says Bob Love's former coach at Trenton in the EBL. "I was scouting for the Chicago Bulls and Dick Klein was the general manager. Milwaukee comes into the league and Milwaukee took Bob in the expansion. I told Dick Klein — Dick Klein was the first general manager the Bulls had — and I told Dick Klein to make sure he got Love. I'll never forget it."

So a man who punched tickets for a railroad is, in fact, greatly responsible for Bob Love — that stiff from the Milwaukee Bucks — and his ride to glory in the National Basketball Association.

Still, Dick Motta and his Chicago Bulls considered Bob Love an unknown commodity. In fact, the first true scouting tip on Love to Motta was from the other player the Bulls acquired in the trade.

"So about an hour later, Weiss called on the phone," says Motta. "We were playing that night and he asked me when I wanted them. I told him an hour ago, that he should get here if he could. We talked a little bit and he said, `Hey, I think you're going to like Bob Love.'

"That night Bob borrowed someone's car and got in a wreck. His little boy broke his pelvis and Bob bumped his head up and hurt his shoulder. So we didn't get to see him too much that year. He was hurt most of the year."

(In later years, the "bump" on Bob Love's head, combined with the hundreds of miles he would gallop on the hard court, would prove his undoing. The automobile accident would have more to say about his eventual retirement than even his eroding skills.)

Now 62, Motta operates a family-owned gourmet chocolate company in Ogden, Utah. Ask him if he misses life as a National Basketball Association coach and he'll answer tersely, "uh huh, a little bit." Not much more than that.

There's irony to the fact Motta today deals in sweets, because his days in Chicago, particularly in Chicago, were bittersweet. His coaching style was of the firebrand variety and he viewed hard work as the only avenue to success in the NBA. Yet it was Dick Motta, an unlikely source, who was the man to turn a young journeyman basketball player into an NBA all-star.

Ask no higher authority than Pat Williams, who served as Chicago's general manager during Love's glory years. Who was primarily responsible for lighting the fuse on Bob Love's career? He'll readily suggest it was the fiery Motta.

"I arrived early in September of '69," Williams remembers. "I had been in Philly for one year as assistant general manager. Part of the deal that brought me from Philly was the Chet Walker-for-Jimmy Washington deal. Jack Ramsay had been trying in Philly to make the deal all summer to get Jimmy Washington. But the Bulls ownership was in turmoil and everything was on hold.

"Jack finally agreed to let me go, but part of the deal was that the Washington-Walker deal had to be made. And that happened to be an absolute bonanza for us in Chicago. Chet came in and just anchored everything.

"There was another deal pending right after I got there. And that was, we had a chance to acquire Bob Kauffman from Seattle. We would have to give up Bob Boozer, the veteran, but they wanted more. They wanted another player. Kauffman had just finished his first year and Boozer was a good bit older. They insisted that it be Barry Clemens. And Barry Clemens was a player that Dick kind of liked. He did not want to give him up, particularly, but Seattle was insistent. I was dealing with their general manager and we tried to sell them on another player, whose name was Bob Love.

"We said, `Won't you take Bob Love?' And we tried to sell that package with Boozer for Bob Kauffman. But they wouldn't buy it and they insisted on Clemens. So, reluctantly, we threw him into the deal and we made it."

Hindsight being perfect, Motta today insists he would not have dealt away Love, but that he wasn't asked.

"I'd have never traded Love," Motta says emphatically. "There were a couple of times that Pat did things that I didn't find out until later. We could have had Tiny Archibald, but when we traded Jimmy Fox for Norm Van Lier, as I understand now, we had our choice between Van Lier and Archibald and Pat wanted Van Lier. I was never approached on a deal for Love, so there was never that decision."

So Pat Williams, now general manager of the Orlando Magic, was guilty of one of the most disastrous trades never made by the Bulls. He continues:

"So we had Kauffman, with Chet, and we thought our forward rotation was set. Bob Love was a body on the roster. So we go into camp and we start the season and Kauffman is the starter, but he's struggling. By that first weekend, Dick had taken him out of the lineup and replaced him with a heretofore unknown, almost, Bob Love. Bob had been around a little bit but had never really distinguished himself. So Bob is thrown into the lineup. And the rest is history."

Like instant coffee, the freeze-dried granules of Bob Love and Chet Walker dissolved into the best forward combination ever brewed in the franchise's history.

"It's an amazing saga of what he did and he did it immediately. He had a big night the first night and he never stopped. For the next five years, Chet and Bob Love were the Chicago Bulls," argues Williams. "They were the Bulls' forward rotation, maybe the best offensive combine in the league. If it's not your classic set-up with a big forward and a small forward, it's for sure two magnificent offensive players."

To this day, Dick Motta remembers the first game in which he inserted Love into the starting lineup.

"We had projected, on paper, anyway, that Walker and Kauffman would be the starting forwards with (Tom) Boerwinkle at center. The game I finally started Love was against Golden State in San Francisco. Actually, we had been more productive when I would bring Love in as a substitute, but I just made up my mind that I'd start Butter that night. And he started from then on."

Perhaps it is Dick Motta's own ego speaking. Perhaps Dick Motta's system made Love a star, perhaps not. Perhaps a little bit of both system and talent. But Dick Motta isn't sure that Bob Love would have reached the levels of success that he did had it not been for the system in which he played for the Bulls. Right or wrong, the numbers simply don't lie. Love never enjoyed professional success except when he picked up his paycheck on West Madison Street. And Dick Motta, gourmet chocolate fixer, was the only coach in the National Basketball Association who could sweeten Bob Love's game.

"He needed our offense," Motta says. "He'll be the first to tell you that. He was not a free-lance type of player. He needed a set offense, he needed people to bring him the ball inside.

"He was a single-purpose player. He couldn't jump and he couldn't run. He fit in with our group just great. He was a little selfish. He didn't pass. If the players got upset because he shot too much, I used to tell them that if they didn't want him to shoot, then don't pass it to him."

Of course, any conversation about Bob Love, be it about basketball or chopping cotton or marching on the Capitol at Baton Rouge, any and all conversation returns to his problem with speech.

"When you talk about Bob Love," says Pat Williams, "his speech impediment came into play immediately. I remember Bob Love as a very warm, caring kind of a guy. A good guy. I guess my most vivid memory of his speech impediment was the night — I don't remember what season it was. It may have been my first year there. But WGN did an interview. It was absolutely terrifying. You could just picture Bob, at this point, trying to talk. They taped it and it was just," Williams pauses, "absolutely," and he pauses again. "Sad. That would be the only way to describe it. To watch him try and work through that, and then 'GN aired it, anyway. Ooh, boy. Oh, boy. I think that was one of the most difficult moments I can remember in this league."

Williams is not alone in his memory of the incident. Jack Brickhouse, today the retired dean of Chicago sports broadcasting and a pioneer of the trade, was the man who conducted the interview. Present for the agony was Ben Bentley, then the public relations director for the Bulls.

Bentley has since become somewhat of a television cult phenomenon. His most recent career as a talk show host began on Chicago radio station WGN, a powerful, 50,000 watt station which is owned by the Tribune Corporation. For several years now, Bentley has sat in as a Sunday afternoon moderator for a variety of Chicago sports writers who would bitch about this, gush about that and blather about the rest. It's a great show. The success of the radio run gave producers at a Chicago cable affiliate the idea it could be scrubbed up — but not too much — and placed into television syndication. And quick as you can say What's-his-name-the-Bull, Mister Bentley became a television star. As host of the cable syndication *The Sports Writers*, Bentley today entertains a vast national audience of viewers who most assuredly wonder who the hell this guy is. Who this guy is, is a cuddly old gentlemen who has been part of the Chicago sporting scene for generations. On this overcast Chicago day, Ben Bentley holds small court at Eli's Restaurant, itself a Chicago landmark for steaks and gossip among those politically in-the-know. As Bentley spins a tale, Chicago *Sun-Times* political editor Steve Neal and legendary gossip columnist Irv Kupcinet munch and chat a table or two away. On any given day, Mike Sneed of the *Sun-Times* or Tom Hardy of the *Tribune* can be seen lunching with the Illinois secretary of state or the state's attorney general. Eli's, as they advertise, is indeed the place for steaks, but it is also the place for news.

Before he joined the Bulls as public relations director in 1966, a position he would hold through 1973, Ben Bentley served as Chicago's premier prize fight promoter. He was a ring announcer from the golden age of boxing, and he'll readily tell you that the biggest fight he ever hawked was the one in which Rocky Marciano decked Jersey Joe Walcott in fhe first round.

Bentley waxes melancholy as he remembers an old friend, name of Bob Love.

"He undoubtedly is a man that I have admired for a long time," recalls Bentley. His elbows are perched upon the white table cloth and his hands are folded before his chin. His eyes sweep back to the time that he hawked the fledgling Chicago basketball franchise. "What I like about Bob Love is his sincerity, the sincerity that he showed both on the basketball court and off the basketball court. I must admit to you that when I first met him, his family life was bright. I remember Bob and Betty coming into the Stadium, holding hands. To me, they were sweethearts. When I'd see them in the Stadium or at some of the other affairs, he would immediately go to her. Boy, you are bringing back a lot of memories, so many memories."

Ben Bentley is wistful, to be sure. But he is simultaneously as lucid as any man 30 years his junior.

And he remembers the WGN interview as if it were taped yesterday.

"He was afflicted with that stuttering situation and I'd grown used to it after a while. In other words, I didn't wait. I tried to anticipate the questions reporters were going to ask and repeat to him what he was supposed to say. He hated that. If he was trying to talk and you interrupted him and said, `What you really mean to say is ...' He didn't like that. It offended him. He would talk with me, throw his arm around me and wait until he got through.

"I had sportswriters, on occasion, ask me to get this, that, or the other after a game. So I would go to Bob and tell him, `I don't want you talking to the guy. He'll keep you for an hour.' And on many occasions, I would just go back to the writer and give him a quote and attribute it to Bob. I did that on many occasions."

One of the men who Ben Bentley truly loves is the former general manager of the Bulls, Pat Williams. The old man's eyes twinkle and his mellifluous voice drops into bass when he speaks of his former boss.

"Pat Williams was the best general manager they've had," he argues adamantly. "And I don't care about the present-day Bulls. He was the best general manager. Pat was the greatest. He's the one who brought in the (cheerleading) Luv-A-Bulls, you know." Bentley looks straight through your eyes and says, sarcastically, "He was the best they ever had, and I don't care who says otherwise. He was better than the general manager they have now. I don't even know who that is." He could wink, but he doesn't.

"Pat felt that Bob Love was absolutely going to be one of the team's major attractions. Pat Williams once said to me, `Ben, I want you to travel with the team.' And you know, after traveling with the team, I got to realize what those guys went through. After a night game, we'd take the red-eye back to Chicago."

As he speaks, he gestures, and you can almost see Captain John

Carpenter lifting the American Airlines 707 AstroJet charter off the lighted runway at Dallas-Fort Worth. Homeward bound, but wearily so fly the gladiators and their valets.

"Let me tell you, it wasn't pleasant, and I wasn't even a player. But all that travel started to get to me, too, so I got a real good feel for what those kids were going through. There were times when Bob would sit next to me on the plane and he'd say, `I-I-I can't w-w-w-wait to hit the bed.'"

Bentley then shifts to talk about the interview he wishes never would have been aired.

"One time ... we were playing, at that time, the St. Louie Hawks. We traveled to St. Louis and Jack Brickhouse was doing the games on television for WGN at the time. And he said to me, 'You know, I'm going to put him on as a guest.' And I said, 'Jack, with the particular speech impediment that he has, I'd be a little hesitant to put him on in an interview after a game.'

"And Jack said, `But he played a great game.' To which I responded, `Yes, and the fans here know it and the fans in Chicago know it.' And he did put him on.

"The only way I could describe it would be to say that it was tough. I stood on the side and that speech impediment seemed to get the better of him because of the excitement of the game that he had just finished.

"I tried not to get him on. In fact, I saw Brickhouse recently and we recounted the incident. You see, they used to give the players $50 apiece to do an after-game interview. I stood there for the whole five or seven minutes, whatever it was, and I could see the panic grow in him. He came over and he had the towel on him and he came to the microphone. At that point, he was all dried up.

"Suddenly, as the interview commenced and went a little further, sweat — perspiration — began breaking out. And all the while he was talking to Jack, he'd look at me. I tried to use hand signals and body language to give him encouragement. He tried not to be, but he was very self-conscious.

"I remember telling him afterward, `You did all right.' And he kind of shrugged his shoulders to me, as if to tell me that he knew that I was trying to make him feel good."

Ben Bentley wasn't the only one who was trying to put Butterbean Love at ease. Jack Brickhouse has been part of the Chicago broadcast 'scape almost as long as there has been television. Together with Kupcinet, he was for years the radio voice of the Chicago Bears. Long before the National Football League lifted its television blackout of home football games, Jack Brickhouse was the man who brought the Bears into living rooms as well as automobiles. In 1963, if you wanted to know how the Bears were faring against Y.A. Tittle and the dreaded New York Giants in the NFL title game, you had to place your faith in Jack. Believe it or not, the game was not televised in Chicago. So Bears fans clicked on AM 720 and agonized until the final gun gave the Bears a world title.

Brick was a three-sport man — at least. In addition to broadcasting the Bears forever and the Bulls for six years, he was the television play-by-play man for the Cubs for 38 years and the White Sox for 25. Who can forget Jack's call of Ernie Banks' 500th home run as it soared over the ivy-draped walls of Wrigley Field? Or the night of September 22, 1959, when Looie Aparicio stepped on second and fired to first to double up the Indians' Vic Power and seal the first American League pennant on the city's south side in 40 years. Brick called that one, too. Long before "Holy Cow!" creeped into the local vernacular, Brick's trademark "Hey Hey!" punctuated each and every Cubs and Sox home run for the better part of four decades. Yet, after thousands of innings and hundreds of quarters, one interview still stands out in the mind of Jack Brickhouse.

"Well, here's what happened. We used to have that pre-game show where you'd pay the guy. It wasn't a lot of money but it was good pocket money. And, after all, you've got twelve guys on a ball club and if you're gonna interview eleven, you better interview twelve.

"We knew about the problem with Bob. What the hell, we knew it all the time. But I figured, by God, this guy is entitled to not only to be interviewed, but maybe we can do him a little good for his confidence if we play it a certain way. So what I did, I interviewed Bob, but I took it one sentence at a time. Some of it he stuttered on, but when he did it over again, he got it right. And so we videotaped it and then edited the thing so that by the time we had it edited down, we refined it into a decent interview.

"After the first time you try a guy like that, you know better than to put him on the air cold. There's no way he could handle it. And I always had the feeling that Bob appreciated that. Fair play says, *Look, the guy is entitled to his recognition. He's entitled to some television exposure and the right to earn a few bucks with it.* And that's what I tried to do."

You sense that Jack Brickhouse is absolutely sincere as he describes the details of The Interview From Hell. There is no reason to doubt Brick's intent, for he is acclaimed by Chicago news and sports folk as a man of integrity and his word. But the interview, by all other accounts, was rough.

"Oh, man, I'll tell you," says Love, "I didn't say one word. Ahhh! It was awful. Jack tried to help me along. He tried his best, man, but it just couldn't be done. That's all there was to it. I think, finally, he just cut the interview off. It was terrible. I just couldn't say anything. It was just awful."

Not all of Brickhouse's memories center on the speech problems of Butterbean. He tells you how much he admired the skills Bob Love brought to a franchise that was in sore need of a hero, a winner, someone who could carry the Bulls through their infancy and into respectability among the NBA's established franchises.

"You know, if you take Michael Jordan out, those teams Love played on compare very favorably with the recent Bulls teams," argues Brick. "Of course, that's like saying how do you make an animal run if the heart's gone. When he first came, I never saw a guy who could shoot the ball from the corner with such a low trajectory. If you ever take a look at the film on him, you would expect the guy to arch the ball in the air. But he shot a low, line-drive shot and, by God, it went in. That's the way it was with Bob."

Love, himself, recounts the story of yet another incident which caused him profound humiliation. It involved former Cubs catcher Randy Hundley, Love and their two sons, Kevin and Todd, who now catches in the major leagues.

"Randy Hundley and I, our two kids were going to the same elementary school out in Rolling Meadows. The school invited me and Randy out to give a little clinic. Randy would give a clinic on baseball and I was supposed to give a clinic on basketball. So we went over to the school and Randy did his stuff first. You know, he'd show you how to catch with one hand and how to throw and some basic hitting tips.

"Then it came my time to talk about basketball. And it was really, really embarrassing. Even though I did okay, it was really embarrassing. Little kids were laughing and my kid was there and he really didn't know what to say because I don't think he ever thought anything of me talking like that because I was his dad. The other little kids were laughing and it really made me feel bad. But that's not the most embarrassing moment.

"The most embarrassing moment happened to me when I was invited out to Des Plaines. They were having a father-and-son Little League banquet and dinner for this group. This friend of mine asked me to come out. It was a freebie — I never got paid for anything. He said he needed someone to come out, sign some autographs and shake some hands. You know, just say hello to the kids. None of the other guys from the Bulls would go. And I was used to doing everything for free, anyway, so I said I'd go.

"That night they introduced me as the special guest and these kids and their fathers — everybody — stood up and gave me a standing ovation. They were yelling `Bob Love! Bob Love! Speech, speech!' Everybody was looking at me and they made me go up to the podium. I'll tell you. I stood up there for three minutes. Not one single word came out of my mouth. All I could say was `Ah-Ah-Ah.' That was probably the most embarrassing moment of my life. I went back out to my car and I just felt like I was at the bottom of the world. I sat in my car and I cried. I cried and I prayed. I prayed to the Lord to help me, please, help me find a way to talk. I knew I couldn't stop being a basketball player, no matter how bad it was. I had to go back the next day to practices, to games. I couldn't let that get me down."

One of PR maven Bentley's jobs, in the years of Love, was to explain to writers that one of his star players couldn't talk, couldn't say batshit if he had a mouthful.

"I had newspapermen talk to him on stories," remembers Bentley. "I'd tell them, `You must understand. He has a speech impediment. So you might be a little hesitant to take notes. But if you go over the material, he'll give you another answer.' It was very bad, at the time. As a matter of fact, we had somewhat of an understanding that some writers could manufacture quotes for Bob, as long as they were fair. And, I must say, the guys were really very good about it.

"You know, they were trying to do their jobs while, at the same time, trying to comfort him. But, you know, by comforting him, they were doing the wrong thing. In other words, he'd say, `W-w-w-w-hat I really m-m-m-mean is ...' and they'd say, `Yes, I know what you mean.' But there were times they didn't know what he meant, and that got to him.

"He became self-conscious after a while, after he became such a hit with the Chicago Bulls. There were times when I wanted him to meet some of the press and he'd say, `N-n-n-n-ot tonight. I-I-I'm tired.' So I'd go back and tell reporters that he didn't have much to say, that he wants to get back to the hotel, that he's traveled all day, that he's had a tough day and now he wants to go back to sleep."

Over eggs, buttered toast and fried potatoes, Ben Bentley remembers.

"One night, we were at an affair and I was the emcee. And I introduced him. I can remember saying, something to the effect, that Bob Love was there but that he was very, very tired. And because he's a big star, we'll just have him wave to you. Well, he pulls me aside afterward and said, `D-D-D-on't do that sh-sh-shit to me no more.' I'll never forget that. But I meant well. I didn't want him to get up and embarrass himself. But I had to do it in a way that it didn't look like I was the owner of the plantation and he was one of my slaves.

"It was a sad situation. There were times when we were out on the road, and he'd want to tell a story. He would laugh and start to stutter, and everyone would just sit back and wait. He would eventually get to the punch line. First there would be silence, and then everybody would give a little chuckle."

Talk to Dick Motta, the man who *almost* rode the raging Bulls to their first world title, and he'll give you a little chuckle. For seven years Dick Motta and Bob Love carried on Jekyll-and-Hyde relationship. Who was whom is left open for debate.

"You know, he would complain from time to time that he wasn't getting enough money from endorsements. In fact, he even hired a public relations man to help him get endorsements and additional income. And there were times when he had all kinds of requests to go out and promote. None of the Bulls at that time had ever had a basic need for extra engagements because the engagements were always there. They weren't the big-time money engagements that kids are getting now, but we were a good team and we had Chicago pretty much to ourselves. We were having full houses and we were a good basketball team."

To Chicago basketball fans, in fact, they were a *great* basketball team. The Packers couldn't hack it. The Majors died on a sickly vine and the Zephyrs blew away to Baltimore. However, the Bulls stuck in Chicago and the credit belongs to Motta, Love and Company.

"When they would call and ask for Bob Love," Motta recalls, "the PR people would tell them that he would like to come and that he would sign autographs, things like that. But don't ask him to talk because he has a speech impediment. Well, because he couldn't speak before a group, naturally they would shy away from him.

"There were times when I would go with him. They would ask him questions and I would answer the questions for him. Oh, there were quite a few embarrassing moments. Jim Durham was our radio announcer back then and he made the attempt not to slight Bob. He would have one or maybe two interviews a year with him. They would do the interview and tape it, then take it to the studio. Gosh, it was a big job to have an interview where the public could understand him.

"But it was really hopeless because he had basically no social skills. Funny thing is, at the back of the bus, when we were headed to a game or an airport, he hardly ever stuttered. It was only when he got excited. Face it, he had a lot of confidence in his ability to play basketball, but he didn't have much confidence when it came to communicating.

"He got Man of the Year one time, Sports Man of the Year in Chicago, and Johnny Morris was the emcee. We told Johnny ten times if we told him once: Don't have the kid try to talk. They had the awards ceremony in a big amphitheater situation and Bob gets up to accept the award. This thing was held in a big ring, like a boxing ring without the ropes. Well, Johnny Morris reads the accolades about Bob Love and some guy starts yelling for a speech. And, damn, Johnny Morris gives him the microphone.

"And Bob goes `Ah-ah-ah-ah' — I can imitate him perfectly — and he just couldn't get it out. So finally, Johnny took the microphone and told everyone that Bob was so excited, that he was so emotional, that he was unable to speak to them. Which was really bullshit."

Not all of Dick Motta's stories about his stammering star tug at the heart. In fact, perhaps the only way to fully appreciate the humor of some of his stories would to have been there in person. Or to at least hear Motta tell it.

"I remember this one little story," he begins, as he takes you back to a Bulls practice more than 20 years ago. "When the opposing team's screens would come away from the basket, if the forward doesn't warn the guard, then the guard gets his head knocked off. Well, teams were setting a lot of screens against us. And Love's men were setting a lot of back picks on Van Lier and Weiss and Sloan — our guards.

"So one day in practice I said, `You know, Bob, it's too bad that you can't be like Harpo Marx. You know, he had that horn that went *squeak-squeak-squeak*. It's too bad we can't get you one of those horns, Butter.' So after that, he'd make a funny sound, like a squeak, whenever the other team would set the screen. And he did that for seven years. He communicated well that way and he never got any more back picks."

Wait. Motta's stories get better.

"That first year, when we traded for him," remembers Motta, "I had Barry Clemens. Barry's dad was a nuclear scientist at Wright-Patterson Air Force Base. Barry had an IQ of about, oh, hell, you couldn't test him it was so high. But he'd stutter, too. And at one time

I had Flynn Robinson, who stammered. So I had three of them. I used to be able to talk normal until I got around those three guys."

Dick Motta is on a roll.

"Barry Clemens' brain was so far ahead of his voice box that it was incredible. One night we were coming home from Atlanta. We had stayed overnight in Atlanta after playing a game at Auburn. We had won the game and we were coming back on the bus. Barry Clemens was back there trying to teach Butter how to say Peter Piper Picked a Peck of Pickled Peppers.

"Now, Clemens had been to every speech therapist in the world. He could say all the riddles but when he started to talk, he couldn't talk. You couldn't understand *him*, either. And he's back there teaching Butter how to say Peter Piper ...

"I used to talk normal. I get around those guys and, shit, I can't get nothin' out."

Bentley, the former PR guy turned media cult icon, remembers Motta getting the heave-ho on numerous occasions. Not so the forward with the speech problem.

"I don't remember him ever arguing with an official. All he did, when things would go wrong, he would throw his hands in the air and look at the referee in disbelief. And he'd walk away.

"Because of his speech impediment, he'd never get into an argument. I'm not saying he wouldn't disagree, but he'd do it with sign language. (In fact, today Love carries with him a videotape, voiced-over with a rendition of "Good Lovin'" by The Young Rascals, in which he is seen to protest a questionable official's call with only slumped shoulders and palms lifted toward the sky.) There were times when he'd try to come to the aid of one of his teammates, but by the time he was able to get started talking, the situation was over with."

Bentley goes on, "One day there was kind of a rough call that they called on him. He went over to the official and he began stuttering. Finally, he walked over to the audience, pointed over to the referee and then pointed to his own head. Crazy." Ben neglects to recall if "crazy" netted Butterbean a technical foul. (It didn't.) "But I can never remember him being ejected from a game. He always had that big smile. A very, very nice guy."

Oh. One more thing about Ben Bentley. A very important thing, as a matter of fact. So important, in fact, that Ben has been immortalized, to a degree, by the Chicago Bulls, even though he has been out of their employ these last two decades. That happy-go-lucky stuffed mascot, played by a guy who got his diploma from St. Laurence High School in Burbank, Illinois, the red-white-and-black bull who jumps about the home court floor? His name? Benny, of course.

"You know who named it?" beams a smiling Bentley. "Pat Williams. He named it. He's also the guy who named me the public address announcer. One night we did an exhibition game over at Notre Dame. Something went wrong and the announcer never showed up. So Pat looked at me and said, `Look, you're the announcer tonight. Get over there. We're gonna start.'

"And when we got back to Chicago, I was the public address announcer. So the night Bob Love scored 49 points, I announced it at the scorer's table. And they flashed it on the board. When the official scorer told me he had scored 49 points, I said, `Ladies and gentlemen, Bob Love just scored the 49th point of the night, making him the outstanding player of the game.'

"Now, even on the bench, his own teammates started to applaud. One of them — I think it was Van Lier — wanted him to stand up and take a bow. But he wouldn't do it. He was too self-conscious. When I went down to the dressing room that night, I had him sign my scorecard.

"And I never saw anyone as elated as he was that night."

Dick Motta will tell you many things. One thing he will not tell you is that Bob Love was the best forward who ever played under his tutelage, let alone the best player who ever played for him. Maybe that's a part of his stubborn-father and stubborn-son relationship with the man he affectionately calls Butter.

"I had some really good forwards. That set of Love and Walker were a really good set of forwards. Chet Walker, he was our go-to guy more than Butter was. Yet Butter wasn't afraid to go for the big shot, too. But when it came to five seconds to go and we had to get the ball to someone, it was usually Chet. Sloan wanted it that way and I always said Sloan was the one player I enjoyed coaching more than any other. He played.

"But there's no other player that I've been around who could score like Love, but who didn't have the ability. A lot of 'em had a lot more talent than Butter, but he was a man at the moment. He was an over-achiever. The whole team was. We used to get a guy on the all-star team because, back in those days, you had to have one from each team. We wouldn't have had one if there wasn't that rule."

Broadcast pioneer Jack Brickhouse says the only dubious conversation he can remember about Love was uttered by his coach. Part of the love-hate relationship, perhaps?

"The only time I ever heard a really negative expression about Bob Love was from his coach, Dick Motta," says Brickhouse. "We were sitting around in Dallas one time and he said, `Here's a guy who doesn't give it all he can in this game. And yet he's got a contract worth hundreds of thousands of dollars down the road. Yet Dick was only criticizing his talent in a certain branch of the game of basketball. I don't think it had anything to do with his opinion of Bob as a character. But as a coach, he was upset that he didn't have a better defensive effort."

As Dick Motta and Bob Love and Chet Walker and Jerry Sloan and Tom Boerwinkel and all of the rest, as they were scraping and scratching to over-achieve, they did something no one ever could have predicted. They had brought the Chicago Bulls to the brink of glory. They had driven this orphan-of-a-franchise to the precipice of NBA history. They were so close they could taste it, and the people of Chicago began to take notice. This, the paying customers had come to understand, was not the Chicago Packers. It was not the Chicago Majors. This team, this potpourri of players assembled by Dick Klein and now Pat Williams, was not going to be blown away to Baltimore like its most recent predecessor. Perhaps its pedigree was suspect. But this Chicago Bulls team was a true mutt: Beauty is in the eye of the dog-show judge and this dog had no blue ribbons in its bloodline. But it was loyal, courageous and it was ready to run full speed off the porch.

Trouble was, for whatever reason, it always found a way to wet on the rug just when an invader was pilfering the family's jewels.

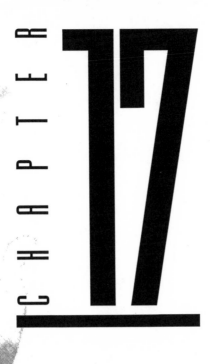

CHAPTER 17

A CONTRACT? JUST a PIECE of PAPER

The love affair between Chicago Bulls fans and their high-scoring star forward is well documented in the sports pages of the Chicago *Tribune*, *The Sun-Times* and two newspapers which now rest in peace: Chicago *Today* and the Chicago *Daily News*. A couple of sportswriting morsels typical of the Years of Love in Chicago:

From Chicago *Today*, March 31, 1971 by Bill Jauss, comes this:

Love's Hot Hand Wilts Lakers

Motta forced the Lakers to isolate Wilt Chamberlain on Love. Love responded with 36 points, giving him 121 through the first four games of this playoff series ... Said Lakers coach Joe Mullaney, "Take Love out of their lineup and we win maybe four straight in this series."

From a column by Robert Markus, April 28, 1975 in the Chicago *Tribune:*

Love's Labor Not Lost in Bay Area

The Chicago press doesn't help much, either. Most of us know better, but the fact remains that when the game is over and Bob Love once again is the high scorer, we gravitate to the volatile Norm Van Lier, or the pugnacious Jerry Sloan or the new miracle man, Tom Boerwinkel.

The members of the electronic media at least have a good excuse. Love has a speech impediment, a nervous stammer, that makes it virtually impossible for him to speak into a microphone.

But when he is relaxed in the locker room, he can articulate well enough, and the truth is, most of us don't realize what Love has accomplished until we go home and look at the box score.

It's becoming a cliche to marvel: Gee, I didn't realize Love had 32 points.

From sports writer Bob Logan, January 5, 1971:

The Court Report

Forward Bob Love of the Bulls should have finished second in all-star balloting (behind Connie Hawkins) instead of third (behind Hawkins and Jerry Lucas), but let's not quibble about that. Love is a bona fide all-star and he should see lots of action for the Western Conference squad against the East stars in the 21st National Basketball Association dream game next Tuesday in San Diego.

It couldn't happen to a nicer guy. Love's emergence from obscurity to stardom since he came to the Bulls in 1968 makes even us allegedly flint-hearted newspapermen feel good.

From *Sun-Times* columnist Bill Gleason, who today shares the microphone with Ben Bentley on the weekly cable television show:

Bulls' Love Deserves Super Star Status

How does one become recognized as a Super Star? Friends

and teammates have offered suggestions.

"What you've got to do is score around 50 points a game."

"All the time?" Love responded.

"No, nobody averages 50 points now that Wilt Chamberlain has become the most active passer since Slingin' Sammy Baugh. Just once in a while. Around 50 points every now and then will draw attention to you and convince the folks in New York and Los Angeles that all the Super Stars aren't in New York and Los Angeles and, even, Milwaukee."

Love tried that. Against the Milwaukee Bucks he flipped the little jumpers like they were coming off an endless belt. He scored 49 points. "That's around 50," he said, beaming.

The next game, while everybody was enchanted by the miniature miracle-maker, Nathan Archibald, Love quietly scored 49 points again.

"That's around 50," he said and modestly withdrew to await a stampede of photographers from the magazines. Nobody came.

... He plays for a coach, Dick Motta, who emphasizes the team rather than the individual. Bob had a serious stammering problem, which is less of a handicap after speech therapy classes at the University of Chicago. And he plays in Chicago, where the Super Star is taken for granted if he wears the uniform of a local team. Love is the Billy Williams of basketball."

Logan, again, in the *Tribune* on April 24, 1975:

Butterbean Getting His Points Across

Love is winning a playoff series in six games.

Love is playing for your team even though you're convinced they gave you a raw deal in contract negotiations — or lack of them.

It sounds like trouble in paradise, as if someone was appreciating a contribution a little less than he should. Or as if someone was expecting a little more of a reward than he should. At any rate, by 1975, it was clear that Robert Earl Love was having technical difficulties with his employers. Unfortunately for everyone involved, including the fans, the newspaper stories about Butterbean Love read more about dollar-sign numbers than they did about points or rebounds or assists. The symptoms actually cropped up a few years earlier. No matter when the ill-will began to spill over the contract negotiations and onto the basketball court, Love today is convinced he was jobbed out of money he had earned as the club's highest-ever scorer until Michael Jordan. And he speaks with bitterness and acrimony.

"I was taken for granted. And I was taken advantage of, immensely. And my speech problems had 100 percent to do with it. I think nowadays your performance would probably overshadow that. They would basically have to pay you for your performance.

"But back then, well, I went through a lot of fines."

Fines, indeed. On more than one occasion, Bulls scoring sensation Bob Love ignored Dick Motta's edicts and held out of training camp. Bob Love believed he was being used and he wasn't about to be used.

"They never really re-negotiated my contract after all those years. When they finally did, I had a guy named Elliott Goodman representing me. The owners of the team were Jon Kovler and Arthur Wirtz. They got (Goodman) to get me to sign a regular three-year deal. In 1975, they gave me $155,000, but I never got into that part of the contract because they waived me."

The flash point of Love's adversarial relationship with the Bulls came in 1971 when the club signed second-round draft pick Howard Porter to a hefty, six-figure contract before he ever stepped foot on an NBA court.

"They had just drafted Howard Porter," Love remembers, "and hell, they were paying him more than $100,000 a year. A rookie guy. This guy wasn't even playing yet and I was one of the top players in the league. You know, by 1973, I had led the team in scoring five straight years and they had me making something like $75,000 a year. They had me on something like $50,000 up-front and another $25,000 deferred. So I held out. The general manager of the Bulls back then was Pat Williams. I had hired a guy from New York — his last name was (Ken) Kaufman, I forget his first name."

Williams vividly remembers his contract hassles with Love and admits the Bulls were somewhat tardy in rewarding their star scorer.

"One of my memories of Bob Love, I guess, would be negotiating contracts with Bob," remembers Williams. "As he got better, you know, he was never paid properly. And I was always in the middle of one problem or another, trying to get his contract worked out.

"He kept improving and he and his agent were never satisfied. And I understand that, because we'd lock him into a long-term deal and within a year he thought he had outdistanced that contract. So my closing years with the Bulls were struggling ones with Bob, just trying to resolve his contractual dissatisfaction. Yeah, I guess dissatisfaction would be the best word."

Even today, Williams, for more than two decades a highly-successful general manager in the National Basketball Association, speaks with an uncommon admiration for his former player.

"Bob has always been one of my favorites. I've admired him and what he has done with his life here in recent years has been a magnificent story."

And Williams readily acknowledges the Porter draft rankled Love to the point of distraction.

"In 1971, we drafted Howard Porter and we gave him a big contract, for that time. And Bob, well, we immediately went into a long-term deal with Bob. We signed him for a five-year period. I think it was the year before we drafted Porter that we signed Bob to that long-term deal, and after we drafted Porter, (Love) was unhappy.

"But our big problem with Bob was trying to get him satisfied with existing contracts. The long-term deal we made with him was with an agent named Ron Grinker, out of Cincinnati. Then came a string of other ones, always trying to re-do the deal."

Love even today remains frustrated over his contention that he was not compensated fairly for the superstar years he gave the Bulls. His frustration reaches a climax when he recalls an incident involving his agent and Pat Williams that probably has no foundation to it:

"Kaufman comes here to Chicago and I was supposed to meet Pat Williams at a hotel that used to be here on Michigan Avenue —

the Sheraton Chicago. (Williams) told us to meet him at two o'clock. Me and my guy got there at about one o'clock. There was a big suite and it had another room off to the side. We were sitting in a big living room and there was a knock at the door at about quarter to. Pat Williams walked through the door. As he was walking through the door ... he was putting an envelope in his breast pocket. He says to Kaufman, `Can I see you in the other room?' They went into the other room. As they were going into the other room, he was taking something out of his pocket — the envelope. They closed the door and stayed in there about 15 minutes.

"My agent came out and said, `Bob, I don't think they're going to renegotiate your contract. I gotta go back to New York. Good luck.'"

After two decades, Love still believes his agent got the envelope and that it was filled with cash.

"To this day, I would swear to hell that (Williams) gave (the agent) the money. The agent left me in there with a shark. I didn't know shit about negotiating with those guys. Williams tells me, `Bob, what I'll do is, maybe add $20,000 on to your contract, maybe $15,000, but you've got to give me another two years on your deal here.' Hell, what I was looking for was more money up-front and they were offering me more money deferred. This guy was taking two years of my contract and he wasn't giving me anything. He really made it confusing fucking for me. I didn't have anybody there advising me. I'm no expert on this shit and the guy I'm dealing with does this shit all the time."

What happened, more than likely, is the agent realized, after talking with general manager Williams, that Love's contract with his employer was iron-clad. But the notion is of no consolation to Love.

Was he renegotiating your contract, Butterbean?

"He was fucking me."

"Much of our troubles with Bob were with contracts," says Williams. "You know, he just was not happy with his contracts. I think he had demands at home with Betty.

"They had bought a home that I don't think they were equipped to live in. They over-bought. I just think he lived beyond his means. At that time, he had a very big contract, but it was never enough. He couldn't keep up."

Ben Bentley thinks Love may have picked up some expensive habits from teammate Chet Walker, who already was a veteran star by the time he and Love joined ranks as a premier forward rotation for the Bulls. Walker, remembers Bentley, enjoyed riding first class. Never park it yourself if you can go with a valet.

"On the road I used to watch those players trying to eat on really small meal money, twelve dollars a day, maybe even less," recalls Bentley. "I saw some of the bigger stars eating in W.T. Grant's, you know, drug stores where they could eat cheap. But Bob went to the better restaurants, and I think he learned that from Chet Walker. Chet never would eat in those little places. Chet always wanted a table cloth, you know? Chet would always say, `It only costs 20 cents more to go first class.'"

And if Bob Love believed that to be true, then it could very well have become the source of his impending financial destruction. If drugs or alcohol or gambling were not the culprits to drain Bob Love's pockets of silver and gold, then a false promise of a bottomless pot of money did. Perhaps he had fooled himself into believing that the spigot had an endless flow of cash in the pipe, that the six-figure contracts would be there for as long as he breathed.

"We tried to help him, but there comes a point where you just can't do any more," Williams says. "He just never could get it under control.

"He had a family. He had children. And he just tried to live up to a standard of living that just wasn't possible. There was never enough income. That was my memory of it. But I don't want to over-dwell. I mean, who cares about the financial end of it? I think the gist of the story is, here's a guy who came from nothing, made a career. He fell to the bottom and now has overcome his impediment. And he's now persevered through it all and has made something of himself. I think that's the story."

Tell Bob Love that Pat Williams speaks in glowing terms of his former star and Love will only sneer.

"Walker and Sloan and Boerwinkel had no problems with their contracts," Love says. "All through my career, I was a nice guy. I got along with the players fabulously. Everybody liked me. But the word around was that this guy can't talk.

"Hell, everybody thought I was dumb. If you can't communicate, people interpret that to mean that you are dumb. And if you talk to any speech pathologist, anyone in that field, they will tell you that people perceive people who can't communicate as really being dumb.

"That's the perception that, hell, I've been fighting all my life. I'm not a dumb person. I've had to work twice as hard, do twice as good, to prove that I'm not a dumb person. Being black, shit, that don't make it any better.

"Motta and the Bulls tried to show me as less than a human being. And I was not going to accept that. They didn't have to do that to me. Whether it was their intent to make me perform at a higher level or not, it probably made me more intense. But, also, it hurts you as a person that they don't respect you. Hey, it was very dehumanizing. You see, that was the reason I probably had a lot of arguments with Motta. It wasn't because I didn't like him as a person. Hell, I loved him as a person. I wasn't going to let him dehumanize me. I wasn't going to let him portray me as less than a human being. I have pride. I have pride in myself and I wanted to be respected, too."

As general manager of the Bulls, Williams shouldered the paperwork side of Love's contract squabbles. It was Motta's lot in life to try and mix a recipe of players into a winner, too often without a key ingredient. And it doesn't take a bell or a whistle or a snooze alarm to awake Dick Motta's memory of his high-scoring forward's repeated contract squawks.

"Big time problems," Motta says today. "He held out about three training camps in a row. I don't know the exact record we had, but I know that he and Van Lier held out about ten games that one year."

(For the record, the year was 1974-75 and the Bulls compiled a 47-35 mark in winning their first divisional title. Van Lier sat out the first eleven games of the season and Love held out for 20.)

"He'd negotiate, then get his contract, then he'd change agents. He was always looking for more money. It wasn't the most pleasant thing in the world to be associated with. He missed training camp and it was important to our team. That year (1974-75) we lost in the seventh game of the semi-finals, to Golden State. We were about 30 percent winners without those two kids. We only won 47 games that year but we were normally a 65 to 70 percent team with the two of them.

"If we'd had the home court (advantage) in that series — it went to seven games, anyway — we might have won the whole thing. I think we finished only one or two games behind Golden State in the overall standings that year. If we could have had our normal winning percentage in the games those two kids missed, we probably would have had the home court advantage."

Any true Bulls fan older than 30 will recall the agony of the seventh game against the Golden State Warriors. In the final two minutes, on the Warriors' home court, the Bulls ran out of gas and lost to Golden State, 83-79.

"I'll never forget that game," regrets Motta. "We had made a big run and had expended a lot of energy. I looked over at the scoreboard and said, `I don't like this. We're playing as hard as we can play and we're not pulling away from them.' We lost, and I always felt that if we'd have had the home court advantage," his voice trails for a moment, "and then they go on and beat Washington four in a row for the world's championship.

"I think if Butter had that to live over, he'd rather have a ring on his finger than that extra little bit of money that he got for holding out. It hurt the team. It hurt us. During the span that they were holding out, we lost two games in a row, back to back, that we never should have lost. The first was in Milwaukee, on a last-minute shot. Then we went down to Omaha, where we were playing Kansas City. We were six points ahead with a minute to go and lost on a last-second shot by Jimmy Walker."

Ah, what if. If the home court advantage rests with the Chicago, Motta and the Bulls win their first NBA title and the 1991 headlines proclaim a return of the championship trophy to Chicago. The headlines would have screamed that Chicago was *again* Number One after 16 years of wait-til-next-years. But ifs don't drive the lane and ifs don't get in-your-face and ifs can't rebound worth snot. With or without a championship ring, Motta still burns from the flames of Bob Love's contract disputes. Sometimes the baby-sitter deserves a raise in pay.

"It was a pain in the butt," he says, mincing no words. "Every year — every year — he'd have tears in his eyes and he'd say, `This is the last time you'll ever see me.' Pat can tell you more about that than I can because Pat renegotiated every year. Every year. I think there was five years in a row where he had five different agents.

"It disappoints me a little bit. I always said that if something else would come along, that he'd turn his back on us in a second."

But if Motta sounds like he wants nothing to do with Love, he's leaving you with a false impression. Both men will tell you today that they share an admiration for each other.

"I will say this," Motta says. "I met him one time up in Seattle when I was broadcasting for Detroit. We went out after the game and he had that gal with him, the speech therapist. We reminisced and he really tried to make up with me. And about three years ago, I was living down in Florida and I got a call from Butter. You know, you get calls from these guys about once a month. You'd be surprised at the people who need money, at the people who are down-and-out. Actually, if you want to write a book, you should write about the calls I get. Some of the people that I've lent money to, who I've tried to help in different ways, it would just shock you. I started coaching in the NBA when there were unscrupulous agents who would do anything and say anything to get a kid (under contract).

"Anyway, I'm sitting in my home in Florida a couple years ago when the phone rings. It's Love. And I'm used to these kinds of calls — like I said before — so I'm just waiting. What does he want? He just keeps talking and he goes along pretty good and he says, `I just wanted to call you.' And I said to myself, `Yeah, but for what? When's it coming?' He said, `Look, I want you to know that the seven years that we spent together with the Bulls were the happiest days of my life.' And he was really sincere. He said, `I want you to know that. I want you to know how much I love you.' And I'm thinking, `What the hell?' That doesn't happen very often. And I really believe that he meant it and that he still does.

"I think that the kid has really grown up a lot. Oh, shit, after Pat left, I fixed Bob's contract the last time. I can't remember the exact details. But without any communicative skills, he was almost considered to be handicapped. I believe in deferred payments. I've got deferred payments coming in right now and they seem pretty damned nice. We had it fixed up — (owner Arthur) Wirtz was pretty good that way — it fixed Bob from the time he retired at age 35 until he could get his retirement pay from the NBA at age 52 — there's about 15 years there. But we had it fixed so that he could get about $50,000 a year until he got his player pension.

"Well, when I left, he got divorced from Betty. A lot of this is second hand, but I know this part is true: He went to Wirtz and said he needed some money. And Wirtz told him that, sure, he's got some money. You don't even need to borrow, you've got some collateral. And he bought him out. I think he bought him out for seventeen cents on the dollar. I think Betty got it all in the divorce. This was before he went to Seattle."

So many years have passed. Dick Motta, former NBA journeyman coach and current chocolate maker, blows hot. Then he blows cold. Like his confection, the memories of Bob Love are sweet. Unlike his confection, the memories of Bob Love are bitter.

"The year we won 57, we were in the 80 percent (winning percentage) range against teams below .500 and less than 50 percent against the teams who were above .500. We won every game we were supposed to win. Very seldom did we stumble against a team we were supposed to beat. We played to our potential. We were what we were. Every night we went out and played. What you saw is what you got every night. We played just as hard against New Orleans two nights before Christmas as we did against the Lakers in the seventh game of the series.

"When I went into the league, they told me, you win some, you lose some, some are rained out. After a season would end, I'd analyze it and maybe there'd be eight games that I'd be disappointed in. That's all. Oh, I'd huff and puff and yell a lot, but, shoot, we played and the people got their money's worth when they were watching us. It was an interesting team."

Interesting it was. But the last couple years in which Bob Love hauled the black Number Ten over his head and pulled it to rest on a field of red over his chest and his back were times of turmoil and stress.

By now he has vented his spleen, this large man with the speech problem. He has purged the demons who have toyed with his soul for more than five decades, the demons who tell him that he was poor, so he never had a chance. The demons who said he is black, so he never had a chance. The demons who poked fun of the way he talked — make that tried to talk — and who said he'd never be like Martin Luther King or John Fitzgerald Kennedy. They could talk, Lord, could they talk. They were eloquent, prodded the demons. You can't talk. You're stupid.

"Heh, heh, heh. I fooled 'em, didn't I?"

CHAPTER 18

BREAKING a STALLION'S SPIRIT ■ There are times
when it's best to keep your mouth shut. There are other times when it pays to speak your piece. And sometimes it doesn't matter if your mouth is closed and silent or open and engaged, particularly if your legs can no longer respond to the gallop of the stallions who are younger and less inhibited by their own inexperience. When a foal becomes a colt, he has no fear of mortality for he knows that his powerful gait will speed him from harm and to whatever peaceful field awaits as his grazing expanse. Death is for others, for the horses and the mares. Life and glory, they are for the youth, for youth is power and speed.

Blessed are they who know when to quit.

By the autumn of 1976, Dick Motta was gone, resigned as coach of the Chicago Bulls. It was a good run for Motta, but he and his team of horses just ... couldn't ... get ... over ... the mountain. And now the best of his stallions were old and could no longer be counted on to pull the wagon up the hill.

The Bulls picked Ed Badger as their new head coach for the upcoming season, and the Chicago Stadium was huddling against the winds of change as they whistled through the big, empty building. On the last day of November, just eight days before his 34th birthday, Robert Earl Love was given a one-day ticket out of Chicago. For seven years the team's leading scorer, the party was over for the man they called Butterbean. On November 30, 1976, the Chicago Bulls traded forward Bob Love to the New York Nets. In return, Chicago received a second-round pick in the 1977 draft (that turned out to be Mike Glenn out of Southern Illinois University) and cash.

In the fourteen games he played that season before the trade, Love averaged just 12.2 points per game, hitting for 22 one night for his season high for the Bulls. The Love story in Chicago was through. Finished. His contract squabbles had done him in and the Bulls were sending him to New York, to a new system, a new coach. And Bob Love, like his coach Chick Craig had seen for so many days of his life, was about to witness the end of the line.

At age 34, his aching back was ready to cash him in. All those games, all those practices, all the banging and the crashing — not to mention the car wreck — had rendered Butterbean a relative cripple. Bob Love was virtually finished as a basketball player.

"My last two years with the Bulls," recalls Love bitterly, "I had a lot of pain. Hell, they told me my knees hurt me. Those motherfuckers — excuse my language — the motherfuckers gave me shots. They gave me cortisone shots in the knees. They gave me muscle relaxers. They gave me all kinds of stuff and they knew all along that it was my back. They knew it was my fucking back."

So Love was shipped to New York and the Nets — the *other* NBA franchise in Gotham, the poor sister to the powerful Knickerbockers. Bob Love lasted just thirteen games in The Big Apple, averaging a paltry ten points a game. It was clear that either Bob Love was too old to contribute, or too hurt to contribute, or too alien to the Nets' system to contribute. The Nets sent him packing cross-country to the Great Northwest and the Seattle Supersonics.

"I didn't really get along with the coach in New York, Kevin Loughery. I never liked Kevin Loughery, even as a player, and it just so happened that he was the damned coach of the team. It turned out to be a bad situation."

He finished up the year with the Sonics and then he, himself, was finished, washed up and washed out.

Bob Love's life, once a rocket firing its after-burners to destinations beyond the Milky Way, was in a tailspin. He was a troubled man whose personal life was coming apart. Bob and Betty divorced. The cause, he admits, was his meanderings outside their marriage.

"I was messing around and Betty, well, she was kind of high-strung."

Bob Love bounced around from job to job, none of which held promise of any permanence or stability. By 1980, Love and Betty had split.

"I scrubbed around, trying to land a decent job and couldn't do it," he says. "I got a lot of fucked-up jobs — excuse my language. I got a little job over at Malcom X. College," a school just a stone's toss from the Chicago Stadium, where Bob Love's glory years had faded away to memory. "What I was doing was going around, trying to recruit students. Just a little bullshit job. It didn't really have any function to it at all. That's when my back started worrying me again. They gave me some insurance, which I needed desperately because I had to have an operation on my back that summer.

"So I filed a lawsuit against the Bulls. I asked for my medical records and, all of a sudden, they had lost them. They wouldn't show me any of my records. They had nothing left. They didn't show where they had given me all those shots, all those muscle relaxers, nothing. They offered to give me an out-of-court settlement. I think they gave me a $30,000 settlement and they gave me the rest of my deferred money — about $40,000 or $50,000, whatever it was. The total was close to $100,000."

By then, Love was living in Seattle with his second wife, and this is where his life gets really complicated. Wash and Dick Mack and John Brown and Chick Craig and Ed Jucker and Dick Motta may have been able to teach Bob Love how to drive the lane, how to try to arch a flattened out shot, how to squeak-squeak his teammates off a back-pick. But all the basketball coaching in the world, all the cotton-chopping, all the wet dish rags across his mouth in Ella Hunter's kitchen, none of that prepared him for the tribulations that faced him following his retirement. Bob Love had entered the real world, the world of post-heroic basketball stardom, armed with a degree in foods and nutrition. But nothing he ever studied, nothing he ever learned, nothing ever prepared him for the challenge that had, by 1982, crept into his life.

"I got married to Denise in 1982," he explains. "It was right about that time that I had to have the back operation and the doctors told me I was going to have trouble walking. Shit, they told me I was going to have trouble *walking* again. They told me I would probably have to use a cane, that I would be on crutches a long time.

"My wife, Denise, she didn't want the burden of being married to a crippled guy, I guess. Or a guy who wasn't going to be able to walk. It was going to be a burden to her.

"So after I got the settlement with the Bulls, they sent the checks to my house. They sent the settlement check to my house. Man, I was so hurt and so down at the time. It got so bad — let me tell you, this woman wouldn't even give me a key to the damned mailbox. We had a mailbox right outside and it was kind of hard for me to get down the stairs after the operation. She was so damned grouchy, hell, this woman would not even give me a key to the damned mailbox. I had to wait until she'd get home in the afternoon to look at the mail.

"So Denise got the checks. She brought them upstairs and I looked at them, then I laid them on the counter. I just said, 'I'll hold them for a day or so, then I'll try to get downtown and deposit them in the bank.' I got up the next morning and Denise got up and put the checks in her purse. She took them. I knew they were missing. I called her at work and asked where my checks were. She said, 'Oh, I got them. Don't worry about it. I'm just going to hold them so they won't get lost.'

"Well, this went on for a few days. I'd tell her to give me my checks and she'd tell me she left them at work. About a week passed and I got real upset. Then she said she didn't have the checks. that she had deposited them.

"I said, `You deposited them? How did they cash my checks?' I called the Bulls and they had gotten back the checks. Apparently, she put them in (the bank) the first day she got them. I went down to the bank.

"Man, I was so upset. I was so nervous, I didn't know what to do. That was all the damned money I had in the world. I went down there and I asked the bank manager — it was a bank called Old National. And I asked the lady at the bank if Denise had cashed some checks that had belonged to me. She said that, yeah, `Denise brought them in and Denise told us that you signed them and that you gave her permission to cash them. Denise wouldn't lie. She came in and showed us her badge' — see, she was a police officer.

"I was so fucking upset, man. Hell, I couldn't even see straight. I was scared. I was stammering and stuttering. The lady said, `Mister Love, if you don't get out of here we'll call the police on you. We're going to have you arrested.'

"I walked out of that bank and I was crying. I had tears running down my eyes. I went to see a friend of mine and he told me to go to the police department and file a report. They asked if I wanted to file forgery charges against her. I filed forgery charges against her. They sent me to their internal investigations unit. A guy said, `Well, we'll call you back in a day or so.' They didn't call me for a few days and I was getting scared. I was scared of the police."

The last time Bob Love was scared of the police was when he was being pelted with tear gas, when he was scampering back to Southern University's campus after he and the rest of the students had marched on the Capitol in protest for the right to eat at a lunch counter. Now, he was scared again.

"I finally called a detective and he said, `Well, this is Denise's handwriting. But we're not going to do anything about it. It's your word against her word. She told us that you told her to do it.'

"I mean, the fucking cops ..."

As he speaks, Bob Love's eyelids are flickering vigorously. He is stuttering. It is clear he is under a good deal of stress as he recounts the incident.

"Man, when they told me that, it looked like my whole world —

my whole fucking world — just tumbled. I didn't have one fucking cent, not one damned penny, man. This woman had stopped buying groceries. I'd heard that she was messing around with another guy, a married man.

"This was a Friday night, and I had noticed that every Friday night, Denise wasn't coming home. She was out on the fucking streets and dancing. She was a very pretty girl. All these guys were falling all over her. I left home that afternoon to look for her. Man, I was so fucking hurt, it's a wonder I didn't kill her. I left home that afternoon and I had my cane. I rode the bus downtown and I went to this black night club, where a lot of black people would hang out. I got there kind of early and I hung around and hung around.

"About two o'clock in the morning, Denise and this guy came in there. At that split moment — I can see what they mean by crimes of passion. When you see somebody you love come in with another guy, and you know that they're sleeping together, I mean, that hurts. That was probably the biggest hurt I've ever had in my life. He had her on his arm and they walked by me on the (dance) floor. I had to compose myself. They walked out onto the floor and they were dancing. They were all hugged up. All of a sudden, it felt like all the blood was rushing to my head."

This was five seconds left in the game. This was when Dick Motta tried to get the ball in low to Bob Love or Chet Walker. This was crunch time and Bob Love was engaged in an unfamiliar game. This five-second drill didn't call for a screen or a low-arched jump shot from the corner. This was a situation in which Bob Love didn't really know what to do.

"I grabbed my fucking cane. Man, I hopped out on that floor and I grabbed her by the fucking neck. I grabbed her by the motherfucking neck. This guy she was dancing with, he was kind of a short guy. Man, he ran out of that place!

"And she yelled, `Oh, don't start no fight!' The people on the dance floor started scattering and I had my fucking cane and I wanted to hit her so fucking bad, but I didn't touch her. I didn't fucking touch her with my cane."

The outside of Bob Love's head was being flashed by strobes and bombarded by the rhythmic beat of percussion. Lights swirled about the dance floor at a dizzying pace. His eyes were wide open. He was a buck — a crippled, helpless buck — caught in the headlights. His gaze was wide and aimed at nowhere. The inside of Bob Love's head throbbed at the same drumbeat, the same deep bass rhythms, as the hot lights of passion exploded within. He was unable to think rationally, unable to put this event in any calm perspective. He was this-close to being totally, completely, out of control. It seemed as if a thousand eyes focused on the large, black mass as it stood alone on the dance floor. Except for the pulsations of the music, there was silence in the club. Everyone was waiting for the big man's next move. His next move, uncharacteristic for an animal whose existence is threatened, whose back is against the wall, was simple. He limped, cane in hand, off the dance floor, his head bowed, a tear squeezing from each eye. He passed through the door of the night club and the air became cooler, calmer, quieter. In the cold drizzle of the early Seattle morning, Bob Love, a six-foot-eight crippled giant who leaned on a this piece of wood for support, slowly limped out of the club and into the darkness. Empty of pocket and even emptier of soul, Bob Love walked into the darkness, wondering what was happening to his world. What once was his oyster was becoming a septic tank. Bob Love was confused. He was broke and he was broken. He didn't know what to do.

"I walked outside and the guy she had been with was walking down the street there. And all of a sudden, I realized, hey, fuck it. I just told the guy, `Hey man, Denise is my wife. I would appreciate it if you wouldn't mess with her until we got our divorce. I am asking you to respect me as a man.'

"This fucking asshole guy, he says, `It ain't up to me. It's up to her.'"

Here is a general rule — one which should be abided by virtuously: Small people should understand and respect big people's abilities to pummel them. This is experience — common sense, mind you — talking here. And if the big people are carrying a walking stick, more important is the reason to show respect. Or fleet feet.

"But he knew I was crippled. I could hardly walk. I was hurting."

No punches were thrown. The cane was not driven across the little man's brow. The only thing broken in the encounter was Bob Love's spirit. And it was in splinters.

"I had to walk about a mile to pick up the bus. Here it is, two-thirty in the morning and I'm trying to catch the last bus home. Man, that was the longest fucking walk of my life.

"My whole life, everything flashed back ..."

Spit it out, Robert Earl ... JD's Grocery Store ... Bob Love, the singing quarterback, he fades back to pass ... Ghosts, all those ghosts ... I used to have a little radio ...

"... how people had fucked me all my life. All through my sports career ..."

A white Bob Love would have made that final cut ... I went through a lot of fines ... A hundred thousand for a rookie guy ...

"... how hard I had to work for my money. Then, in the end, I have a woman take it from me, just like that. For no fucking reason. I got home that night and I got on my knees and, hell, I prayed to the Lord. I prayed to the Lord to give me strength. I prayed to the Lord not to let me do anything wrong. I could have easily hit her in the head with that cane. I could have hurt her."

Most assuredly. The big black man could have certainly delivered an impressive blow to the petite lady's skull. Could have done some real damage. But he spared the rod and she got the spoils.

Life in the NBA was nothing like this.

CHAPTER 19

SOMETIMES THERE'S a RAINBOW ■

Seattle, Washington is one of the beautiful cities in America. A visitor to this northwest outpost is greeted in a January visit by potted floral arrangements in the misty afternoon as he leaves the Sea-Tac Airport by cab. While most of the rest of the continent is enduring snow and bitter frost, the residents of Puget Sound are faced only with seemingly endless clouds and relentless drizzle. Mount Rainier is dusted with snow at its peak, but most often Seattle gets by without the white stuff.

As he turned to face his life at its most critical juncture, Bob Love needed to make a choice: Wallow or fight. It's a choice a 42-year-old man never wants to make. This was the morning after, and the hangover wasn't likely to be washed away by a greasy Midwestern breakfast of biscuits and gravy or a pot of hot, black coffee. No, this hangover needed therapy. Lots of therapy, both physical and psychological. This was a test, perhaps the crucible of his life.

"The next morning, I just got up, man, and I just started walking," remembers Love. "We lived up on a little hill. I walked down to the end of the road that morning and then I walked back. I was really weak, man. That afternoon, I walked a little further.

"The next morning, I walked about a mile and a half. And I came back in the afternoon and did the same thing. After about a week — you talk about hard, man, hell. I'd just lost the woman I loved. I lost every fucking cent I had. I didn't know how I was going to fucking survive.

"I was on disability with Social Security. That was the only income I had. One day, I left that damn cane at home and I walked down that hill, three, four miles maybe. Man, I was sweating."

That evening, the cold winter drizzle was like pin pricks on his dark brown face as he walked down the streets, dodging puddles, his hands plunged deep into the pockets of his beige trench coat. This was it. Somewhere, some how, some way, Bob Love needed to find a job. He needed help.

"That was the day I finally got strong enough to walk back down to Nordstrom's. It was around Christmas time. And I asked them for a job."

All the other times, Bob Love could get interviews, he could easily get his foot in the door because of his celebrity. There was always someone around who would be more than happy to try to suck up to a big-time star from the National Basketball Association and get him a job interview. Love was good at getting interviews. Like the smoker who can't quit, he was good at it because he'd done it a million times. With the same results, of course.

"I could always get into the personnel office," he says today. "They'd say, 'Bob Love? Oh, come here. Have a seat.' Then the guy would go over my history. 'Against New York you scored 30 points. Man, you killed them. Against Detroit you shot 37. I remember that night you passed Bob Lanier and he didn't even see you.' All about basketball.

"But when I started to try selling myself to get those jobs, nothing would come out of my mouth, man. Then, all of a sudden, these guys would start looking at their watch. They'd start writing stuff or they'd get on the phone — 'Bob, excuse me a second. I have a phone call to make.' And they'd call their secretary and tell her to put all their calls through. It was fucking embarrassing, man. And you knew there and then you weren't going to get the job.

"I'd go through with it. I endured all of the embarrassment. And every time I'd leave a place after the interview, I felt like I was the smallest person in the world. But I knew I had to keep going. I couldn't stop. I continued to have my dreams and I continued to keep my hopes up. I guess I did that all my life, all through those years."

But that night at Nordstrom's, something different was happening. No one was looking at his wristwatch. No one was telling a secretary to put calls through. No one was doodling without paying attention to what was being said. Here he was, just his big black self and the rotund, mustachioed, smiling Eugene Snodgrass, cafe manager at Nordstrom's. Snodgrass did not seem profoundly bothered by the big man's stammering, nor was he startled enough by Bob Love's trench coat, khaki pants and sweatshirt to turn him back into the darkness without a chance. After all, Eugene Snodgrass was not interviewing a prospective executive here. No branch manager's position had been posted on the cardboard affixed to the rain splattered door, the red lettering running beneath the plastic wrap. He was looking for someone to scrape dirt and grease off plates and forks and spoons. He needed someone to run a wet wash rag across a table, sweep a floor here and there. Eugene Snodgrass took his time and he listened. And, glory of glories, Eugene Snodgrass offered Bob Love a job. The offer was made simply and directly, almost in a whisper. But to Robert Earl Love, former NBA All-Star and Singing Quarterback, to Butterbean, on this cold and wet December night, glory was just a whisper.

"They said, 'We'll give you a job, but you've got to start out at the bottom.'

"I said, 'Hey, I don't care. Just give me a job.' They started me off busing tables and washing dishes. I did that shit for about six months. Hell, I didn't take a day off. I started on December 28. I'll never forget that day. It was my first fucking day of work and I didn't even have a decent pair of shoes.

"I started out at the minimum wage, just $3.35 an hour. I worked six fucking straight months and didn't take a day off.

"I was trying to forget Denise, I was trying to forget the hurt. I was trying to forget all the fucking money I lost. Everyfuckingbody in town, they were talking about me. They'd come into the restaurant and they'd say, `Hey, that's Bob Love. The guy lost all his money. He used to be an athlete. What happened to him?'

"The hurting thing was that Denise had heard that I was working there and she and this guy would come down to the Nordstrom Restaurant. With the money Denise had stolen from me — hell, she always liked to dress. She had bought herself a fucking fur coat, man. Had bought herself one of those things you wrap around your neck, one of those long stoles with fox heads all over it.

"Her and this guy would look over and start whispering this shit. I could see them. They'd smile, she'd laugh. It was fucking embarrassing, man."

Perhaps the only consolation to Bob Love was that he wasn't busing tables in the town that he once owned, a little village named by Indians for an onion field, hard by a big lake back in the Midwest. Had Bob Love been assigned a towel and an apron at a restaurant on Taylor Street or Rush Street or in Lincoln Park back in Chicago, virtually everyone who walked in the door would have known who the big black man was. In Seattle, at least, he had played just a fraction of a season — just 32 games — and the Sonics were not exactly a juggernaut that year, finishing at 40-42 and thirteen games behind the division-winning Lakers. But, nonetheless, he was recognized, and even if he wasn't, he most certainly stuck out like a giant ebony thumb.

"A lot of people would bring their kids in there and say, `That's Bob Love. He used to play for the Chicago Bulls and the Sonics. He used to be a great athlete. I wonder what happened to him. Now he's busing tables and washing dishes. What a shame.'

"A few NBA players would come in from time to time and have lunch. And I'd have to go and wash their tables off. Oh, man, that was the pits. Obviously, I had to just smile and say, `Hey, how you guys doing?' I could imagine the thoughts running through their minds, like, `Man, what the fuck happened to this guy?'"

But slowly, the tedious work Bob Love was performing was beginning to gain the attention of the people at Nordstrom's, the people who mattered, the people who made decisions and promotions. Starting at the bottom is difficult, especially at age 40-something. But his efforts were getting some notice at the corporate level, believe it or not.

"One day, finally, the owner of the company came in and told me that I had been doing a great job. But he also told me that they couldn't give me a promotion until I did something about my speech. If I was willing to take the time to do it, they'd pay for the therapy. They would back me up. The day they told me that, it was like the weight of the world fell off my shoulders."

John N. Nordstrom, now 57 years old, is co-chairman of the Nordstrom chain of department stores and cafes. If you shop at a Nordstrom store, you understand the quality of service that the company provides. It is not uncommon for a Nordstrom store employee to drive out of his way after hours to a customer's home to deliver a commodity that needed additional alterations or attention. The Nordstrom family opened its first stores in 1901 and for 63 years, it specialized solely in shoe sales. It has been owned and operated by family members for each of the last 93 years and promises to operate in that manner for some time to come.

"I'm part of the third generation," explains John Nordstrom, whose grandfather John W. Nordstrom founded the chain. "And we already have six of the fourth generation in responsible positions in the company. So the third generation's about through."

Fairly or not, Nordstrom's has been plagued by a reputation that it does not exactly embrace the employment of minorities. John Nordstrom is quick to defend that label and has a ready explanation for the tag:

"I'll tell you where that came from," he says. "We had what started out as a Teamsters Union here in Seattle. But way back in the 'teens there was a group called the Wobblies. They were communists that were organizing the waterfront here in Seattle. So we ended up calling in what was a non-communist union — which was the Teamsters — to organize the store so the Wobblies wouldn't get us.

"It was a real nightmare around here. It was a long time before I was born but my dad tells me about it. We had that union in here for 70 years. Well, our employees finally got fed up with paying the dues. The dues kept going up and up and up and they were just taking the employees' money. So they wanted to get rid of that union.

"We had a big fight about three or four years ago where they wouldn't let our employees vote on representation. It went on for some time. Part of that fight is that they said we were tough on minorities. That was nonsense. But when you're fighting for your life, you'll throw anything out there. And, of course, the press loves that sort of stuff so they wrote some stories about that. It was nonsense. Since our employees threw the union out, it's all gone now, anyway."

What is not gone now is the recollection by Bob Love that John N. Nordstrom is largely responsible for a new career, new speech and a new lease on life. Nordstrom doesn't deny a role, nor does he lunge at the opportunity to take credit.

"As I've told Bob, I'm a little fuzzy on the fact that maybe I was the guy, because it was the person who ran all of our restaurants and myself who were noticing that he was in the cafe, clearing tables on his very first days. And Bob mentioned to me that he was very reluctant to speak because he had a very serious speech impediment."

As an extra touch of class, Nordstrom's offers its shoppers the opportunity to quality dining while they shop. The co-chairman and grandson of the founder speaks with pride as he describes the cafe operation.

"A customer can get high-quality food in our stores very quickly and at very reasonable prices," he beams. "Just to give you an example, when we serve turkey, it's all fresh turkey breast that we buy and cook ourselves. We don't buy the prepared turkey, which would be easy for a store like ours to do."

So when the Nordstrom chain hired Bob Love, it was not out of pity, but rather with an eye to the future. The chain saw some potential in his background of food preparation and nutrition, and he was going to be given a chance to prove his worth.

"He had been there, at the cafe, for some time, and he was at the point where he could have been working in the restaurant, taking money from customers, making change, that sort of thing," explains Nordstrom. "But he was reluctant to do it because of the way he was having difficulty communicating with customers. So I wondered, Gee, has anyone ever tried to help him?'

"Well, we talked about it within and one of the fellows who helped run our restaurants — his name was Jim Dickinson — he went to Bob and asked him if he had any help before. And he said that, yes, he had, but that he couldn't afford any help at that time. So I thought about it for a while and figured, gee, if he'd go out and get some help, why wouldn't it be in our interests to go ahead and pick up the cost?

"He obviously was someone who has the qualities that we were looking for. And to my surprise, he accepted our offer. Because my first thought was that he'd tell us that he had help from a dozen people and none of it worked. So, frankly, it was a surprise to me that he accepted our offer to pay for some help."

Dick Motta, too, remembers the Bulls trying to find some help for their star forward. And although the man who had more success on the court than any other remembers no difficulty in communicating with his player, he does remember the club trying to help.

"We knew from the first day, when we traded for him, that he had a problem," Motta says today. "He says now that no one ever did anything for him. But we had him, probably, to every speech therapist in Chicago. We even did things like hypnosis. Whenever there's a problem like Bob had, every Tom, Dick and Harry — every kook in the world — wants to come around and solve it.

"But he never had any luck with them. By the time he was up in Seattle, he had hit rock-bottom and was almost desperate for something positive to happen to him. Basically, until he hit rock-bottom, he didn't fully realize that he needed something to turn his life around."

And by the time he came knocking on the restaurant door at Nordstrom's, he was more in need of being turned around than at any time in his 42 years.

"He couldn't say anything," John Nordstrom says about Love's speech pattern. "After the first syllable, he would lock up and I don't know how long we would sit there, but we would sit there two or three minutes before anything came out."

If you talk with John N. Nordstrom, you come away with the impression that his company was not in search of a celebrity to hawk his stores' wares. The merchandise and service sells itself, he'll tell you. No. Nordstrom was simply performing a management technique he believed would improve his product and its delivery.

"If you know our company at all, you know we don't like figureheads," he says emphatically. "So that, actually, was working against him. We used to own the Seahawks, so we had plenty of jocks around. We weren't looking for famous jocks, by any means. We had Steve Largent and Jim Zorn and Jacob Green — all those guys — all those guys who would have been happy to serve as figureheads for us. If anything, his fame as a basketball player worked against him.

"And I'll take it one step further and say that what we do not tolerate is jobs where we do not produce anything. If you're a department manager and your department doesn't have increases in productivity, you're not going to stay in that department very long. What we demand is the `Big R' — results."

So Nordstrom told Robert Earl Butterbean Love that the company would foot the bill if its emerging star pupil would take the time to find a therapist who could turn him around. Teach him how to talk. Today, Bob Love shakes his head and smiles.

"All those years that I had been living in Seattle, I had been passing by this speech clinic. I would see it, but I wouldn't pay any attention to it. I knew exactly where it was. So when the people at Nordstrom's told me they would pay for the therapy but that I would have to find my own therapist, this place flashed in my head. All of a sudden, it flashed. And I thought to myself, `Hey, I know of a speech and hearing center.' I called that place and a lady named Susan Hamilton answered the telephone."

This was a telephone call that would literally again open the universe to Bob Love. After all, in some of his dreams, he dreamed about playing against those ghosts who kept floating out of the old

Motorola radio in Ella Hunter's tool shed. And in the backyard of Ella Hunter's shotgun house, he beat those ghosts on dirt. Later in life, he beat them on wood. But the ghost which had haunted his soul for 42 years was still in his face, the demon which convinced him that he could not speak, that he was unable to communicate in the simplest of degrees. The dream that he would deliver a sermon about life, that he could articulate the feelings that stirred within his heart and within his soul, that dream was lost. Lost was the dream that he would stand alone, like Martin Luther King, Jr., or John Fitzgerald Kennedy, and with eloquence and confidence deliver an address to a mass of humanity.

What had been lost was about to be found.

"She had just got through with another client," Love recalls, "so I was lucky that she answered the damned phone. My timing was perfect. She said she had to look at her schedule. I waited for what seemed like an eternity. Then she said, `You can come in on this day and I'll give you an evaluation.'

"Well, I went in there and this girl had to take me like I was a little kid. I had to learn how to talk all over again, just like a little fucking kid. I didn't know anything. The only thing I knew was stuttering and stammering.

"Hell, I would always imagine myself being a Dr. Martin Luther King or being a John Kennedy on a platform, a podium, talking to all these people. And they would be listening to what I said and the words would just flow out. I kept that dream alive for all of those years.

"No matter how fucking hard the times got, even during those embarrassing moments while I was playing, I never lost that dream. Playing over 700 games with the Chicago Bulls and never once being voted star of the game. Missing out on thousands of dollars in speaking engagements, in endorsements. Hell, I got nothing. I got none of that stuff while I was playing. Still, I maintained my pride, I maintained my dignity. But most of all, I maintained my hope that one day I would stand before a crowd and be able to make a speech.

"You see, nobody really knows what causes stuttering. It's important to treat the speech pathology field correctly, to portray a person who stutters not as a dummy, but as a human being with a handicap. This is basically what it is. When I was playing, management acknowledged that I had a problem. I had some speech therapy a couple of times. I would go to these people and they would have me reading a book, or they would want me to go out on the street, stop a perfect stranger on the street, and tell them I stuttered. That was really embarrassing for me to do that.

"That's scary to do that stuff. And these people wanted me to do that stuff. I didn't want to do that. I thought I needed some techniques to learn how to talk, but I was never given any techniques.

"But all of that changed when I started working with her. After, well, I could start telling the difference after three months. I could feel my confidence really, really coming up. Despite all of those years, here I am a 42-year-old man going to a speech therapist, understand, but all of those years, hell, I kept that dream alive."

Susan Hamilton earned her undergraduate degree at Miami University in Oxford, Ohio. She did graduate work at Washington State University and Case Western University in Cleveland, Ohio. Her business card tells you she is a speech and language pathologist at University Way Speech Services in Seattle, Washington. In addition to helping stutterers, Hamilton works with people who are trying to lose their accents, foreign or regional.

In her second floor office overlooking a quaint shopping district of brownstones on University Way, Susan Hamilton explains her trade and how it helped change the life of Robert Earl Love.

"I get mainly people with foreign accents and a lot of people with southern accents," she explains.

The conversation darts quickly to stuttering and what she does to walk her clients down the arduous path of confidence and clear, audible and understandable speech patterns.

"There are 3,000,000 stutterers in the United States, about one percent of the population," she continues. "Oddly enough, a greater percentage of them are males.

"The causes of stuttering are really unknown. But most of the recent research indicates that there is something physiologically different with people who stutter. Sure, there are old wives' tales that tell us that people who stutter, that they're emotionally weaker than the rest of us, that they have psychological hangups. But those are old wives' tales and there is absolutely no truth at all to them. There is more evidence today that stutterers are physiologically different. Unfortunately, we haven't yet pinpointed what that physiological difference is. We're still working on that."

It is mentioned to Hamilton that Bob Love exhibits rapid blinking spells when he stutters, even today. She is asked if that is a common symptom among the clients she takes for therapy.

"All stutterers are different," she says. "All stutterers have different behavior. In Bob's case, he didn't have any eye contact with me at all when he first came to therapy. He had absolutely no eye contact at all. In fact, you might still see a little of that when you talk with him now. But when he first came to therapy, he had no eye contact at all.

"Now, the lack of eye contact isn't necessarily due to shyness. It's just something that happens to be common that you find with people who stutter. I want to show you something. This will give you an idea of how far Bob has come since he started therapy."

Susan Hamilton reaches for a videotape with Bob Love's name on the jacket and pops it into a VCR. Simultaneously, she clicks on the television and video casette recorder to the play mode.

"When I first saw him, I would classify him as a moderate-to-severe stutterer. Now, what I want you to see is the tape I did of him during his first visit and a tape we did a few months later, after we had an opportunity to work through a few sessions."

The monitor flashes momentarily, then the colors begin to co-agulate into a picture. Sound soon begins to hiss from the speaker. So, soon, does Robert Earl Love. He stammers, he stutters. He valiantly attempts to tell the camera his name and what the hell he's trying to do, but the result is pathetic. The guy can't talk, plain and simple.

"Now, take a look at this."

She repeats the procedure. This time, however, the only hiss comes from the heavy treble level of the amplifier. This time, the man with the short-cropped, kinky hair is speaking clearly, calmly and slowly. But there is virtually no evidence of hesitation, of stutter.

It's like two different guys went before camera, both dressed in the same costume, both wearing the same mask.

"If you watch this," Hamilton offers, "I think you'll see that he was actually further advanced than he is right now. He hasn't had therapy recently and he probably should do that or he'll begin to regress."

Susan Hamilton explains that stutterers experience a physiological punch in the nose every time they undergo stress, each time they get panicky. It's not a unique phenomenon, by any means. Some people get nervous and their faces flush. Others experience the embarrassment of sweaty, clammy palms. Still others feel a pain in the pit of their stomachs. In Bob Love's case, stress accelerates his ability not to speak.

"What happens with stutterers, which is what happens with any other person who has any sort of a problem, is that when their stress level goes up, then the problem is intensified. And that's just one reason people may have thought that stuttering was an emotional problem, that when stutterers stood in front of an audience, they wouldn't be able to speak because they were afraid to speak. In that regard, their stress levels are at an increased level. It sounds simple, perhaps, but it's true.

"It's just like anything else. If you have difficulty with anything, the more anxious you feel, the more difficulty you're going to have with whatever problem you have. At this point, people start to develop avoidance behaviors. Some people develop more avoidance behavior than others."

What irony. Bob Love never, ever made an attempt to avoid Rick Barry during one of their classic, nose-to-nose confrontations. No way. Get in his face, show him who's the best defensive forward in the NBA, that's what Bob Love said whenever he squared off against Rick Barry. But stand before a group and say good morning? No way.

"You can imagine that if you stutter, if you have trouble speaking with people, if you have trouble speaking with crowds of people in front of you, you will start to develop a behavior that will cause you to avoid those kinds of stressful situations."

A puzzled acquaintance wonders aloud to Hamilton why Bob

Love, the Singing Quarterback of Morehouse High in Bastrop, Louisiana, never had a hitch when he was barking signals on the gridiron. How could a kid who couldn't even ask his grandmother for a drink of water on the hottest day of a bayou summer manage to get off a play before the referee could reach into his back trousers pocket to throw a yellow handkerchief?

"What happens with some people is this. Most people who stutter have certain things they can say without stuttering. It's called automatic speech. His ability to play quarterback in football, without stuttering, was probably automatic and that's most likely the reason he had little or no problem in situations like that."

It is obvious that Susan Hamilton, speech-language pathologist, has impressed upon her star pupil one lesson. She — and Bob Love repeats her words — is emphatic when she tells you that emotional strength or weakness has nothing to do with the speech pattern of a person who stutters. Nothing at all.

"It is important to know — the key is, people who stutter are not emotionally weak. They are not emotionally weaker than the rest of us. One of the problems with society is that people have the misconception that stutterers are emotionally weaker than the rest of us. That is simply not a fact. It's a misconception that I dearly wish we could eliminate from society."

So Bob Love, cotton-picker-turned-NBA-superstar-turned-dishwasher, finally found the help he needed. It was the therapy he craved, the therapy he needed to wish you a good morning or to speed you to a good night. After, in the words of Dick Motta, "Bob had hit rock-bottom," Bob had found and utilized the therapy of a speech pathologist, the world once again began to open its arms to his future. Sometimes a frigid spring blizzard will blanket a bed of daffodils, giving us the dreadful impression that winter has snuffed out spring. But the next day the warmth of a March sun will dab the ice crystals from the green, spiked leaves and clear the way for warmth and spring. So, too, did Susan Hamilton dab away the peril of life's winter from the soul of Robert Earl Love and make him viable again, this time as a former jock who was beginning to emerge from within the corporate board rooms of a national chain.

"I was like a kid," he says. "Here was a 42-year-old man, and I was like a little kid starting out at school, learning my ABCs and learning how to count. That's just how it was, too. It was really, really hard. But I had a person who I consider to be the best speech therapist in the world. This young lady's good. She gave me a lot of confidence. She stuck with me in a lot of hard times. I started to see the results in three months. After about a half year of therapy, it just so happened they were having the NBA All-Star Game up in Seattle, and there was a guy who wanted to interview me. He did the interview with me and he was really impressed with how my speech had improved. All of a sudden, I started to get requests from people to come around and speak."

And John N. Nordstrom is pleased as punch to have played a role in Love's emergence.

"He's an interesting guy, because he's not the least bit shy about the problem that he had speaking," says Nordstrom. "It doesn't seem to bother him at all. He's very proud that he fought his way through it. More power to him. It's great.

"You know, after he got through the therapy — you asked if he was given preferential treatment because he played ball — he began to rise through the chain. Like I said, we serve only fresh products, like the turkey breast. So that leaves us open to problems with health departments, because we're dealing with very fresh food. So we have to be careful with how we handle that food. Therefore, we needed someone to make sure that our procedures were correct. And he had a lot of training in that area. He really knew what he was talking about. And that's interesting in itself because it had been so long since he'd really been involved in the industry. So it was a really natural fit for us all.

"When his speech started to come up, when he was able to converse with people, he just fit into a spot where we needed someone of his caliber. So he traveled to all the stores all around the country and made sure that our procedures were above reproach. As it turned out, after he got on the job, I don't think we had one problem with any health department around the country. I don't recall one problem at all. So he obviously did a good job."

You'd be remiss if you failed to ask John Nordstrom if he didn't go out of his way to help Bob Love because he knew Bob Love would become an ambassador for the chain, a quick and dirty 30-second commercial for a department store. So you don't fail. You ask.

"It's amazing. We have a couple of guys who started in our shoe shine stand who are managers with us today. I can't say we would or wouldn't have done the same had we not known he was, at one time, a basketball star. That's a good question. But if someone had a speech impediment and he appeared to be the right kind of person, we probably would do the same thing.

"You know, if you appeared to have the spirit and the desire to do it, then I think we'd be there for you. Bob, I don't think, gives himself enough credit, even when he had the speech impediment. He was a tall, clean-cut, smart-looking guy. He was not just some guy off the streets. So he cut an imposing figure, even when he was clearing tables."

Too bad nobody does videos of guys clearing tables. The sight of a six-eight busboy, palms turned skyward and a look of disbelief after a glass of water tumbled into a customer's lap would be worth a slow-mo replay.

Love today speaks reverently of John Nordstrom and readily sends credit his way for his new-found ability to communicate.

"You know, nobody knew it was going to be this big. John Nordstrom played a major role in getting me out there where I can give a speech. They were helping out one of their employees and I am grateful to them for their interest and help. They were looking to help someone improve his life and help him move on.

"But it really turned out to be bigger than they hoped — and I hoped — it would be."

So big, in fact, that John Nordstrom accomplished something that even Captain John Carpenter couldn't do today, even though the American Airlines 707 AstroJets have been replaced by bigger and faster aircraft. In effect, John Nordstrom did the same thing the Milwaukee Bucks did in November of 1968. He sent Bob Love flying back to Chicago and to the Bulls.

Only he didn't have to take Flynn Robinson in the deal. It's nice that sometimes a rainbow follows a downpour.

CHAPTER 20

MAYBE NOT PERFECT, but a '10' NONETHELESS ■

Has anyone ever gotten inside — truly gotten inside — Bob Love's head? Maybe. Probably not. If anyone has, the most likely suspects are Smitty — Doctor Robert Smith, chancellor of Southern University at Shreveport, Louisiana. Or maybe Susan Hamilton, M.A., CCC-Sp, speech-language pathologist in Seattle, Washington. Or maybe Ella Hunter, his grandmother who built the foundation for his life. At one time, maybe even Betty Love, former wife, mother of his children. Certainly not Denise. Not Ben Bentley. Maybe William Washington, high school coach, maybe for just a little while. Arthur Hamlin didn't. When they were together, the only things in their heads were dreams and hopes, the things that young people think about. Not Pat Williams, certainly not him, not when he was trying to renegotiate contracts to keep his star forward happy and his team intact. Certainly not Dick Motta.

The only person who can tell you if anyone has peeked inside his head, has penetrated his soul, is Robert Earl Love himself.

"He's a very, very complicated young man," offers Motta.

So complicated, in fact, that his birth-mother, Lula Cleveland, still lives in the heart of Watts, one of the most miserable neighborhoods in Los Angeles, in California, in the United States. Maybe in the world. Despite the fact that in his prime, Bob Love earned healthy, six-figure incomes, Lula Cleveland lives in a small house in America's premier war zone.

When you visit Lula Cleveland's home, there is fried chicken sizzling in the kitchen. Greens are in a serving bowl on the kitchen table. Lula Cleveland is a very shy woman, perhaps intimidated by the presence of her guests, who are strangers to Lula and stranger yet to Watts. Outside, a helicopter hovers overhead, its chop-chop clatter accented only by the piercing column of white as it spills from the spotlight aboard the rotary-winged aircraft. Aboard, Los Angeles police scour the schoolyards in the black of a January night, looking for gang activity, drug activity, any activity which would intrude on the life of Lula Cleveland, her guests, her neighbors. Steel bars decorate living room windows at virtually every house. This place is one goddamned tough neighborhood.

Today, 51 years after Lula Hunter brought her baby into the world, Bob Love is back in Chicago. Today, January 14, 1994, a dream is about to come true for The Singing Quarterback from Morehouse High in Bastrop, Louisiana. Yes, today is a very special day. But today is a result of a little jockeying here, a little jostling there. Some poking, some prodding, some not-so-subtle hinting. But before today happened, yesterday did, and much of yesterday gives birth to today.

On September 1, 1992, Bob Love started a new job. On that day, crisp and fresh from his successful metamorphosis in Seattle with the Nordstrom chain, Robert Earl Love — Butterbean — began work in the most unlikely circumstances, unlikely if you had heard him speak — try to speak — a decade earlier. On that first September day of 1992, Bob Love took his position as director of community relations for the two-time world champion Chicago Bulls.

Ultimately, John N. Nordstrom probably had as much responsibility as anyone in the equation — albeit indirectly — for seeing to it that Love was given an opportunity to move back to Chicago. After all, it was the department store co-chairman who made it possible for Love to receive the speech therapy necessary to allow him to stand before an audience and tell his life's story of poverty, riches, failure and rebirth. And Love's departure from the great northwest and Nordstrom was bittersweet for Nordstrom himself.

"Obviously, we were sorry to see him leave, but it was an incredible offer for him," Nordstrom says. "A nice increase in pay, a tremendous increase in prestige in going back to an organization where he was once revered. In a lot of regards, he was in the right place at the right time. In fact, I was surprised that he was almost reluctant to take that job. You can't pass that up. That's a dream job."

John Nordstrom may not realize, but the dream of which he speaks is as literal as it is figurative. All those nights in Bastrop and in Baton Rouge, when Bob Love would dream about being a great orator like King or Kennedy, those dreams were being fulfilled. The lion's share of Love's responsibilities is to give public addresses to assemblies of school children and civic and charitable organizations. Dubious as it would have seemed a few years ago, Robert Earl Love had become a spokesman for the basketball franchise with which he couldn't even talk back in the 1970s.

I used to dream that I could speak like Martin Luther King or John Kennedy ...

The principal owner of the Chicago Bulls also happens to be the man who also calls the shots for the Chicago White Sox. Jerry Reinsdorf, a native of Brooklyn, New York, accumulated his wealth in real estate developments before he first helped purchase the White Sox from Bill Veeck. Then he did the same with the NBA Bulls. In Chicago, he is held responsible by many old-time White Sox fans as the man who dismantled a baseball cathedral, the venerable Comiskey Park. Yet just a couple years after his association with the American League charter franchise, the team won its first Western Division Championship. He is a businessman who owns huge toys, and he treats his toys like businesses. Today, Bob Love works for Jerry Reinsdorf. One wonders if Reinsdorf would have tolerated the protracted contract hassles, of if he would have jettisoned Bob Love when he was bitching about not making as much money as he deserved, much more money than Howard Porter.

Reinsdorf denies all responsibility for Love's hiring. Not because he suspects Bob Love's work habits or doubts Bob Love's worth to the franchise. On the contrary, Jerry Reinsdorf will tell you that Robert Earl Love is an employee with exemplary work habits and organization loyalty. He just doesn't take the credit for bringing him into the Chicago Bulls corporate family.

"I'm a very small part of this story," says Reinsdorf. "I didn't know Bob before and I didn't discover him and he didn't call me. I really didn't have anything to do with him being hired."

Reinsdorf lays all credit for Love's Second Coming to Chicago at the feet of Steve Schanwald, vice president of marketing and broadcasting for the Bulls.

"Steve came to me and told me about Bob and his availability and how he'd worked out his problem, and how he'd like to hire him. I told him that it was great. I thought Bob would make a great representative for us. But I had really very little to do with it."

Reinsdorf was already an established, if transplanted, Chicagoan by the time Bob Love was helping to bring the fledgling Bulls into national prominence.

"It was pretty easy to get tickets in those days," he says.

This is the guy who sat a few feet from Michael Jordan on October 6, 1993, the day Air Jordan told the world that he was no longer a professional basketball player. This is the guy who held the living chess pieces in his hand and watched as they delivered to him and his partners three consecutive world professional basketball championships. So this is a guy, who after watching Dick Motta's Bulls from the outside, can today make a cerebral comparison while living on the inside.

"It's very difficult to compare players of different eras," offers Reinsdorf. "I think that, in most sports, athletes are better today. You know, conditioning techniques are better, nutrition is better. So the athletes of today, I think, are better than the athletes of yesterday. I'm not sure what all that means, though. If Bob Love were to play today, and have all the benefits of modern conditioning and modern techniques and nutrition, he'd be an all-star player."

How much would he be worth?

"Millions, obviously. Certainly, if he could score the points today that he scored then, he'd be worth a multi-million dollar contract. I don't know exactly how much, but it would certainly be a heckuva lot more in one year than he made in his entire career."

(Or, as Jack Brickhouse so bluntly says it: "Those owners in any sport will hire Adolph Hitler if he can do the job for them. Christ, the name of the game is: *Can he score points?*")

Reinsdorf, in Chicagoland, has a reputation for being practical. No argument about it, he sure as hell knows how to make money. His detractors interpret practical as being cheap. But he also has earned himself a reputation as being a leader in the field of civil rights in sports. In any case, he takes exception to Oscar Robertson's contention that Bob Love failed to make the final cut as a rookie in the Royals' camp in 1965.

"I don't know why anybody, other than an out-and-out racist, wouldn't want to pick the twelve best players he could get. You don't have to like them, as people. If I were a racist, I'd still want the best players I could get.

"I don't even believe that was the case then, that race would have entered into it at all. Everybody is so dedicated to winning, I can't believe anybody would not take the twelve best players, or at least what he thought were the twelve best players. At any rate, I haven't seen any racism in my years here."

Ask Jerry Reinsdorf if the Bulls, today, would see to it that a stutterer would receive therapy — successful therapy — and he doesn't dodge the question. But he does suggest that an owner might not necessarily be the source of help.

"You'd like to think that working with his agent, if he had a good agent, that you could find therapy. But why didn't they do it then? Why didn't the ownership try to do something? I don't want to sound critical because I don't know what efforts they went to back then.

"Maybe he had to hit rock-bottom before he was prepared to make the commitment. I don't think that just showing up for therapy was gonna do it. My understanding was that he had to work pretty hard for what he was being taught."

Reinsdorf gives high marks to his community relations director's performance for the club.

"Hardly a week goes by that I don't get at least two or three letters complimenting him and saying what an inspirational story he has and how much the kids that he spoke to have enjoyed his presentation. He's doing a fine job. I did not know him until he came back to work for us. I didn't know what to expect. He's certainly been everything I could have hoped for. In fact, I didn't even know the whole story about Bob Love until he came back to work for us. I knew he had a speech problem, but I didn't know how bad it was. It's just a delight to have him with us and he's a real credit to the organization."

Jack Brickhouse shares Reinsdorf's delight in the successful comeback of the man whose glory Brickhouse broadcast two decades ago.

"After he left and all those years passed, finally he comes back to Chicago and it's the culmination of a truly inspirational story," says Brickhouse. "To see the difference in this man, from the man who left, is to me one of the most remarkable turn-abouts I've ever seen in my life.

"He's a helluva guy, he really is. He's motivational. He's an inspiration to a lot of kids now. He's helping society battle the drug culture and trying to keep kids away from that stuff. He's just an all-around good guy. I'm very proud of him."

You can add old Ben Bentley to the list of those who admire Love's triumphant return to the Windy City.

"He's really fought his way back," Bentley remarks. "I was at an affair recently with my grandson. And Bob came in and he spotted me. I jumped out of my chair and he came over and gave me a big hug and he kissed me. He absolutely kissed me. I said, `Bob, you and I go back a few years.' And his answer was straightforward: `A lot of water under the bridge, Ben.' And I said, `Isn't this wonderful? I can talk with you now. That speech impediment you had — you beat it.

You've come such a long way since then.'"

And former coach Dick Motta cannot help but gush just a little about his former star, although he feels the need to punctuate his remarks with a slap at the Bulls.

"You're right," offers Motta, "he's a real Horatio Alger story. An impossible dream. But are the Bulls paying him anything at all, or is this just a bone that they've thrown out of guilt? You know, the Bulls don't do anything for anybody. They try to forget us as much as they can. How could they not have retired the numbers of Bob Love and Tom Boerwinkel and Norm Van Lier along with Jerry Sloan? Those numbers should have been retired years ago. I look up there to the rafters of the Stadium — you know, there would be no basketball in Chicago if we hadn't saved it. It was dead and there was nothing to it. That was a really good team."

So Motta begs the question: Why is there a solitary red Number Four — the jersey number of Jerry Sloan, pugnacious guard, hanging above the court in the Chicago Stadium? Owner Reinsdorf, himself no stranger to retiring uniform numbers (he retired former White Sox' Harold Baines' Number Three after the club traded him to Texas and he was still an active major leaguer) defends the lack of numerals displayed from the rafters.

"The Bulls haven't had very many great players until the present collection," explains Reinsdorf. "I don't know what went on before me, but the last thing that was on my mind when I came here was retiring numbers. Quite frankly, for a long time, when the question came up about retiring Bob's number, my thought was that since the Bulls had established a history of so few retirements — in fact, one — that we ought to keep it that way. That maybe we ought not retire another number until Michael (you remember, Jordan) retired.

"You go to Milwaukee, you go to Portland, you see numbers of players retired who weren't even that good. You know, I think that cheapens retirement. My original intent was to wait until after Michael retired. But then, I got to know Bob and realized how important it is to him. I realized how it would sort of complete the circle of his resurrection, of his coming all the way back. Of leaving the Bulls, hitting rock-bottom, coming back, becoming a valuable part of the

Bulls organization in another capacity. I realized that it was something that he was really hoping for and wanted. I decided to go ahead and do it."

In fact, Bulls general manager Jerry Krause had said, only months earlier, that no other numbers would float among the steel beams of the Stadium until Jordan's Number 23 was hoisted toward the heavens.

"Krause doesn't decide what numbers to retire," Reinsdorf corrects. "It was my decision. Krause picks the talent. I spoke to Steve (Schanwald) about it. I spoke to Krause about it. The only concern was really B.J., because B.J. is wearing Bob's number."

B.J., as in B.J. Armstrong, a diminutive guard whose own Ten sometimes gets tucked into his shorts.

"But he's wearing it with Bob's consent. Nobody else will wear it again."

Okay, it's only a little bit retired for now. But remember, Harold Baines could always come back and then ...

So on this cold January night, as the Chicago Stadium faithful shuffle into the old building which sits on death row while a shiny new replacement looms across the street, another dream is about to come true. The banner is fresh and clean, white and red and black. Square in the middle it is stitched, the Number Ten.

As the lights go down, tears begin to fill the big, brown butterbean eyes of Robert Earl Love. He reaches into his trousers pocket and clutches the silver dollar — the one minted in the year of his grandfather's birth — and he remembers Ella Hunter.

Robert Earl, you take this silver dollar. This silver dollar was born the same year as your grandfather. It was his lucky silver piece. You carry this with you for the rest of your life and you will never be arrested for vagrancy ...

The ceremony is a blur. There are words of testimony for Bob Love. Words praising his athletic abilities. Words singing the praises of his struggles, the fight to survive as a youth and the fight to overcome desperation and despair. They are words of Love, indeed, and they echo off the brick walls of the building and bounce back and forth among the rafters as the white and red and black banner ascends toward the heavens. The roar of the crowd is deafening in what is arguably the loudest sporting venue in America. It is Bob Love's night, the night his uniform number is being retired, the night of his dreams for some 51 years. On this night, the Bulls are poised to play the Utah Jazz, coached by Jerry Sloan himself, the man whose Number Four is getting a long-awaited buddy on this cold winter night.

Sloan and Love, two old buddies themselves, join in an embrace courtside. The Bulls purposely scheduled the ceremony to coincide with tonight's visit by the Jazz. The crowd is deafening. Bob Love's big, brown butterbean eyes aren't the only ones splashed with tears tonight.

As he turns to return to his seat on the mezzanine, Bob Love spots Joey Burgin. Joey is a resident of the Little City Foundation in Palatine, Illinois, a home for people with mental retardation. Bob has met Joey at the foundation, where he has helped out in recent years. As he wraps an arm around the boy, he reaches with his free hand into his trousers pocket and grasps the silver piece for the last time. He holds out his big, brown hand to Joey. In his palm rests the dollar coin, more gray than silver after more than a century of wear.

"Here you go, Joey. I won't be needing this anymore."

INDEX of NAMES